THE CRIMINALISATION OF SOCIAL POLICY IN NEOLIBERAL SOCIETIES

Elizabeth Kiely and Katharina Swirak

BRISTOL
UNIVERSITY
PRESS

First published in Great Britain in 2022 by

Bristol University Press
University of Bristol
1–9 Old Park Hill
Bristol
BS2 8BB
UK
t: +44 (0)117 954 5940
e: bup-info@bristol.ac.uk

Details of international sales and distribution partners are available at bristoluniversitypress.co.uk

© Bristol University Press 2022

British Library Cataloguing in Publication Data
A catalogue record for this book is available from the British Library

ISBN 978-1-5292-0296-0 hardcover
ISBN 978-1-5292-0297-7 ePub
ISBN 978-1-5292-0299-1 ePdf

The right of Elizabeth Kiely and Katharina Swirak to be identified as authors of this work has been asserted by them in accordance with the Copyright, Designs and Patents Act 1988.

Cover design: Nicky Borowiec
Front cover image: Adobe Stock #270048783: Song_about_summer
Bristol University Press uses environmentally responsible print partners.
Printed by TJ Books, Padstow

Contents

Acknowledgements

Thanks are extended to colleagues, who gave their time voluntarily to read chapters in this book and to provide very valuable comment; Aoife Dorney, Fiona Dukelow, Louise Forde, Máire Leane, Denis Linehan, Rosie Meade, Caitríona Ní Laoire, Kevin Warner, Samantha Williams and Joe Whelan. Thanks to the anonymous reviewers, who also gave of their time generously; your insight and feedback were very helpful. Thanks to Rebecca, Freya, Millie and all at Bristol University Press, whose assistance and support have been unwavering. The support provided by the National University of Ireland's publication grant is gratefully acknowledged. Finally, thanks to our families, whose constant support in all our endeavours is much appreciated.

1

Introduction

The motivations to write a book titled *The Criminalisation of Social Policy in Neoliberal Societies* came from a variety of sources, but from one in particular. Over the years, in our roles as university teachers in social policy and criminology, we have observed growing numbers of students pursuing studies in subjects such as psychology and criminal justice as distinct from sociology and social policy, a trend already noted by Jock Young in his 2011 book *The Criminological Imagination*. This trend is probably a consequence of the increasingly dominant perception in wider society that the 'solutions' to crime and poverty are more likely to reside in 'fixing individuals' through criminal justice and other social interventions, and not in the redistribution of wealth and income, sound policy-making, good working conditions or comprehensive welfare provision for all. After graduation, criminology and social policy students enter into professions (as social workers, probation officers, youth workers, community workers and so on) where they are, in turn, increasingly expected to service the public at large by fixing and moulding individuals enough to assume productive roles in an unequal social and economic order. In response to, and in order to counter such practices, this book seeks to contribute to the rich body of academic work, across the academic disciplines of social policy and criminology and their related professions, which challenges these dominant perspectives and approaches (Ferguson, 2008; Young, 2011; Levitas, 2012; Featherstone et al, 2014a; Williams, 2016; Gupta, 2018). It calls for greater intellectual commitment to the integration of critical strands within criminology and social policy in the interests of better serving those at the margins of society, while at the same time working towards more radical societal transformation that can result in more just and equal societies, that are respectful of individual human rights for everyone. In writing the book and in each individual chapter, we have maintained our sights on the reality of the lived experience of policy subjects, individuals and families who are in receipt of welfare or who are caught in the interstices of welfare and criminal justice policy. This has been done throughout by showing, with the help of policy case studies, how abstract policy decisions are about ultimately 'governing the soul[s]' (Rose, 1990, 2016: 431) of persons and families impacted, while having significant material effects on their lives and wellbeing, sometimes in unanticipated ways but at other times entirely intentional.

Some of the early chapters of this book were crafted as the climate crisis intensified, Brexit loomed large, nationalism and the political right across the globe gained momentum and many European governments were showing their hostility, rather than hospitability, towards refugees and migrants. The post-2007 economic crisis was followed by a period of state-imposed austerity in many countries, the consequences of which are still being felt. The latter chapters of this book were written while the COVID-19 pandemic became a new normal and we were working from home rather than in our university offices. Whatever frustrations and challenges we as individuals were confronting, they were dwarfed by those being faced by those persons and families who are this book's focus; those whose homes are immigration detention centres, refugee camps and centres, prisons, care homes, refuges from domestic violence, homeless hostels and the streets. Like many others, COVID-19 forced us to reassess whose work was more vital to helping us through the pandemic, and to meeting our needs during repeated lockdowns. It required overdue consideration to be given to the most under-paid, unrecognised and underappreciated workers in our societies; those most precarious, providing our much-needed public health and essential services and care for our most vulnerable citizens. Responses to COVID-19 focused our attention, in a new way, to the inequalities in our societies. We were told 'we are all in this together', but knew we were not, given that the pandemic was being experienced in so many different and highly unequal ways. The consequences of sustained neoliberal neglect of our health and social services, our community provision and our welfare safety nets were made apparent. Governments were turning to civil society organisations and groups to address their neglect by marshalling quick and flexible responses to those most in need. Investment in public services and positive policy innovations, that we were told could never happen, were ushered in quickly (Dukelow et al, 2020; ILO, 2020; McGann et al, 2020). In the UK, while Boris Johnson's government struggled to implement measures to contain the outbreak of the virus, it did act quickly to provide the required financial supports to lessen the impact of unemployment, business failure and local hardship (Mitha, 2020). Responses to the pandemic however also brought active policing of our welfare and our movement, new laws, modes of surveillance and state regulation assisted by artificial intelligence and new sanctions including the criminalisation of virus transmission in some contexts (Staunton et al, 2020) in the name of public health.

Audience

Our book is written for a few different audiences. Because of its key focus on the interconnections between crime and social policy, it has direct relevance for students and university teachers in criminology, social policy, sociology and their related professional disciplinary fields of practice. Beyond this, the book identifies important interconnections and overlaps between both the conceptual as well as applied dimensions of social policy and criminology. Given that it is concerned with relations between the state, market and civil society in the sphere of welfare, it also has relevance for scholars, students and researchers in the fields of government and public policy. It is intended that this book will provide the impetus for researchers to conceptualise or trace different elements of the criminalisation of social policy in their own jurisdictions and thematic research areas. Because it can also be viewed as a critical review of recent legislation, policies and practices in fields of social policy and criminal justice that illustrates how criminalisation works, its subject matter should also appeal to practitioners across public, private and voluntary sectors in both the social and justice domains. It is hoped that the book can serve as a resource for change makers and activists intent on bringing about much-needed political and social improvements and transformations in our societies and communities.

'Criminalisation of social policy': what does it mean?

In this introduction, we dwell on the concept of criminalisation of social policy before moving on to subsequent chapters. The term criminalisation of social policy is polysemous in that it has been construed somewhat differently on different occasions of use and its meaning is not always clear. There is also variation in its use and in the emphasis when it is used. It is categorical in that it comments on culture and society and gives recognised identity to something happening in society. It is also contested as seen in Chapter 2 and it is part of a cluster of interrelated words that have an affinity with it (for example, governing through crime, cultures of control, punishment of the poor, criminalised/criminalisation of poverty, penal welfarism, disciplinary/regulatory welfare state, securitisation of social policy), some of which also commonly occur together in texts.

The criminalisation of social policy brings together two words from two spheres often viewed as separate: social policy and crime/criminology. It is our view that it is important to conceptualise criminalisation in broad terms, as a process that starts before and includes but also goes beyond the actual legal codification/criminalisation of any particular social action. For us, Kaaryn Gustafson conveyed its meaning aptly when she wrote that the criminalisation of poverty 'includes state policies and practices that involve the stigmatization, surveillance and regulation of the poor; that assume a latent criminality among the poor; and that reflect the creep of criminal law and the logics of crime control into other areas of law including the welfare and immigration systems' (Gustafson, 2009: 646–7). Following Bach, the criminalisation of social policy should not lose sight of the 'regulatory intersections' (Bach, 2019: 819), which emerge out of inter-agency working practices and the shared information systems of social and criminal justice agencies. Criminalisation of social policy directs the critical spotlight at the creation of a crime or the use of custody to provide care or treatment or the embedding of welfare services and supports in the domain of criminal justice, if such services and supports are not available or are under-resourced in communities (Bach, 2019). It is important to highlight that throughout this book we view the criminalisation of social policy as states' determination to criminalise, rather than to conceive of criminalisation solely in the narrow legalistic sense. In other words, criminalisation of social policy, as defined by us, considers the confluence of strategies of government that create suspect populations, stigmatise, exclude and penalise, which sometimes are closely intertwined with and weaponised through formal or legal criminalisation, but not necessarily at all times.

The criminalisation of social policy as a concept is ideological. It deliberately takes us in the direction of critically assessing the negative policy developments, which provide us with the clear view of the conditions, the persons and the behaviours targeted by states for double and triple modes of suspicion, regulation, discipline and punishment. Here again, the term encompasses an analytical field that combines the interests of both critical social policy analysis and critical criminology. Although both are not in themselves unitary fields, certain key commonalities can be highlighted, which include the focus on social harms and injustices initiated, sanctioned or tolerated by states, socio-economic and other inequalities and asymmetries in power relations. Another important caveat to draw attention to is that the term criminalisation suggests that the process impacting social policy (its criminalisation) has already happened and is complete. In contrast, social policy is perceived to be a complex field always in process and open to power struggles and alternative logics taking hold. When the criminalisation of social policy is used, it is not the intention to give the incorrect impression that criminalisation has swallowed up social policy so that social policy is no more its own domain with its own logic. Rather use of the concept is designed to help us to attend to pertinent developments in social policy that merit our attention, our critique and resistance due to their criminalising intent or their criminalising attributes. Here, inspiration is drawn from the work of social scientists who call for a shift from the study of state-defined crimes to wider social harms (Hillyard et al, 2004; Dorling et al, 2008), the reclaiming of the 'criminological imagination' (Young, 2011) to consider issues of redistribution and social justice, and who call for the disarticulation of crime from punishment (Ruggiero, 2018).

In the field of criminology, this resonates with a longstanding strand of work that has called for the pursuit of criminology without the concept of crime and instead challenges us to shift our focus from criminal justice to social justice (Muncie, 2000; Knepper, 2007) and towards the analysis of social harms (Hillyard and Tombs, 2017; Canning and Tombs, 2021). As one of many of its claims, social harm perspectives redirect the focus of responsibility for harms beyond the individual, towards collective social responsibility (Dorling et al, 2008). The social harms perspective also converges with penal abolitionist claims, in seeking to abolish and de-centre criminal justice in favour of social policy. A disarticulation of crime from punishment (Ruggiero, 2018: 95) holds radical potential for rethinking social policy as well as in terms of moving away from conditionalities, that always include punitive elements (McNeill, 2020).

The reason for choosing to write about the criminalisation of social policy stems from the perspective held, that this concept and thesis has significant relevance for the times in which we are living, and it is hoped that this is shown throughout this book. We assert that many of the developments we discuss throughout the book are not new. As shown in Chapter 2, regulation and control of the poor has been a longstanding feature of our societies and of both welfare provision and criminal justice intervention, well before, during and after the establishment of welfare states. It is our contention that we are seeing criminalisation attach itself to specific fields of welfare discourse, policy and practice in new ways, some of which are more intensive than they were in the past and some of which are being helped along by the potential offered by new technologies. These more intensifying regulatory and conditioning aspects of social policy are also mirrored across criminal justice policy (McNeill, 2020) as the two fields of policy and practice overlap. We also claim that we are seeing a reassertion of the regulatory dimension of the welfare state, accentuated after the financial crisis as combinations of responsibility for and delivery of welfare among states, civil society, markets and individuals have become more diverse, complicated and as a result more amorphous. In the book we have sought to attend to the criminalisation of social policy thesis in a manner which is sensitive to the social categories (gender, social class, ethnicity, migrant status, disability and so on) that make up persons' identities. In this context, the focus has been put on policy case studies (for example, adoption of looked-after children, activation of lone parents) which show how intersectional positioning central to persons' identities and everyday lives has a bearing on how they may experience cumulatively the impact of criminalising and punitive policies and practices. In the chapters that follow, the ways in which states propagate criminalisation and responsibilisation through the continuous use of 'dividing practices' (Foucault, 1982: 208) and 'liberal othering' (Young, 2011: 64) are identified. Poor people are 'stereotyped as the unemployed and the unemployable, outside of the economic circuits … they are the other half of the binary of the responsible, honest, law-abiding citizen' (Young, 2011: 64), attracting policy-making attention and intrusive intervention. The book responds to the call by critical scholars, who admonish us to shift our gaze up from dissecting the poor towards teasing out how powerful state actors create conditions that make it impossible for many amongst us to be part of the economic and virtuous community of inclusion (Rose, 1999: 335).

It is also acknowledged, while not the focus of the book, that in the various policy fields discussed in the chapters, processes of resistance and innovation are pursued by some policy, civil society actors and organisations, who actively contest dominant paradigms of organising welfare and criminal justice and who offer genuine alternatives. In order not to lose sight of social policy's potential and that of the welfare state to improve all our lives in significant ways, we have sought to stay hopeful. We have made an effort to nurture a utopian imaginary in each chapter, to conceive of better social policy, a more caring society and an alternative future, and it is this imaginary that is re-engaged with, in the concluding chapter.

Periodisation

If the emergence of the concept and scholarship of the criminalisation of social policy is traced, its antecedents are seen in the 1970s, its proliferation in the 1990s to the 2000s and its renewed relevance post-2007 (economic crisis followed by austerity, the climate crisis and the COVID-19 global health crisis). In this book, the significance of events and policies pursued in the 1970s, the 1990s and the early 2000s, which inspired scholars to develop or enrich the criminalisation of social policy thesis, are acknowledged. We deliberately concentrate on the period after 2007 because, as is seen in Chapter 2, the criminalisation of social policy prior to this period has been addressed in significant ways in the work of others, but also because we observe a continuation and sometimes intensification of punitive policy approaches, even after they are shown to be unsuccessful, as for example in the fields of welfare activation (Hansen, 2019) and anti-social behaviour (ASB) (Johnstone, 2016; Brown, 2020; Demetriou, 2020).

Therefore, our book focuses mainly on the period after the economic recession (2007) followed by neoliberal austerity, which extended from 2008 onwards in many countries. Welfare states, under both ideological and fiscal pressure for some decades, came under increasing attack after 2008 (Ocampo and Stiglitz, 2018). The austerity policies which followed the crisis brought assaults on wages, social services and public ownership across Europe in different country contexts (Stetter, 2018). Wage reductions, selective tax increases, emigration driven by unemployment, significant reductions in public spending and cuts to welfare and services were all part of the austerity landscape. While the privations that marked austerity were undoubtedly social and material, austerity was not purely economic. In a skein of literature (Bramall, 2013; Jensen, 2013; Allen et al, 2015) it was usefully conceived of as a discursive and disciplinary field, bound up with the future (Bramall, 2016) as it so comfortably aligned with neoliberalism in diverse country contexts. Social and cultural austerity was visible in our rural and urban landscapes with the proliferation of half-finished housing estates, charity shops, food banks and so on (Murphy, 2017). Fiscal austerity was unevenly experienced and the poor suffered most (Lynch et al, 2017).

As argued by others, since 2008 we have witnessed the more powerful production of a greater number of newer, finer and precise sites of regulation and an intensification of surveillant, exploitative and disciplinary practices being applied to poor people (Jordan and Drakeford, 2012; O'Neill and Loftus, 2013; McGimpsey, 2017; Povey, 2017). The new depths being plumbed in the negative construction and representation of groups of welfare claimants by state and media actors has been receiving attention in the UK (Hancock and Mooney, 2012; Tyler, 2013; Jensen and Tyler, 2015; De Benedictis et al, 2017; Barton and Davis, 2018; Shildrick, 2018); in Ireland (Devereux and Power, 2019; Gaffney and Millar, 2020; Meade and Kiely, 2020) and in Scandinavian countries (Hirdman, 2015). Stigma, disgust, resentment and mockery have all been identified in the affective class distinction work directed at poor working-class people (Skeggs, 2004; Lawler, 2005; Raisborough and Adams, 2008; Tyler, 2013, 2020). A unifying concern in this literature is on showing how such 'distinction work' advances the interests of the upper and middle classes to the detriment of the working classes through the policy choices that are selected, legitimated and enacted in these societies. This has also coincided with the active non-targeting of the criminal behaviour of the most powerful in our societies (Mooney, 2009; O'Flynn et al, 2014). Welfare services and public services showed themselves to be among states' most crucial institutions when confronted with the COVID-19 pandemic, but the aftermath of the pandemic is likely to put further pressure on states' public finances. How this plays out in the long term, and with what implications for the criminalisation of social policy, remains to be seen.

Geographical context and limitations

Covering comprehensively the interconnections between crime and social policy on a global scale would not have been possible. In a book of this size, a high degree of selection was necessary in relation to thematic areas covered, the policy examples from selected jurisdictions discussed, as well as in the specific trends that received attention. The approach taken to social policy, as the chapters indicate, is broader than a straightforward discussion of social security policy and activation, yet it is far from complete. For example, some notable omissions, which have received attention by others, include the criminalisation of nuisance/ASB (Phoenix, 2008; Rodger, 2008; Squires, 2008a, 2008b; Jamieson, 2012), of poor pregnant women and mothers (Gustafson, 2013; Cammett, 2016; Amnesty International, 2017; Goodwin, 2017; Bach, 2019; Hughes Miller, 2020), of environmental activism (Mireanu, 2014), of black culture and music (Fatsis, 2019), of HIV and sex work (Jeffreys et al, 2010; Vanwesenbeeck, 2017; Minichiello et al, 2018) and of dissent and protest (Giroux, 2012; Sabir, 2017; González-Sánchez and Maroto-Calatayud 2018; Gilmore, 2019).

In the book, we have made a choice not to enter into protracted, nonetheless important, discussions relating to whether there is more or less criminalisation of social policy now than in the past; regarding how far back the history of the criminalisation of social policy stretches beyond its contemporary expression and the extent to which it should be attributed to neoliberalism. We agree with others (Soss et al, 2011; McFadden, 2014) that welfare, as much as modern penal logics, have always been concerned with disciplining the poor and altering their conduct so that they fit into an unequal economic and social order. However, the usefulness of the criminalisation of social policy thesis lies in the potential it offers at this moment in time to interrogate the various intersections between the social and the penal and between welfare and punishment. It is also accepted that the criminalisation of social policy is not the subtotal of social policy, but our approach is deliberately singularly focused to show that criminalisation serves as a technique to obscure social problems, to gloss over structural causation and to reframe social problems in a way that makes conduct its most logical target.

Furthermore, the inclusion of a number of policy areas enriches our understanding through its illustration of the diverse forms the criminalisation of social policy takes, while also revealing new and complicated ways by which welfare spreads it tentacles of control into poor people's lives. The authors recognise that they are not in a position to understand all national contexts' social, economic and political structures, penal and welfare traditions, cultural histories and fiscal circumstances and that these would all merit more attention than our book permits. Yet our intention was to move beyond a tendency to focus exclusively on the contexts of the USA and the UK and elsewhere too (Knepper, 2013: 18) by deliberately including some of the most concerning or promising policy developments from a number of countries. It is recognised that the book is focused on the Global North, as we could not claim sufficient understanding of its relevance for other regions, as important and interesting as this would be. Nevertheless, our hope is that the book provides further impetus for more work to be done, so that a higher level of granularity is brought to bear on the criminalisation of social policy as it continues to be critically assessed in the penal welfare apparatuses of different local, national, inter-state and international contexts. Strong in a shared belief that good social policy and universal welfare states make a positive difference in societies, we include models in each chapter that make the case for policy and welfare redesign; to move away from criminalisation and conditionality, towards solidarity, social justice and enhanced human wellbeing.

Structure of the book

What follows in the remainder of this book are substantive chapters and a concluding chapter. Chapter 2 builds on this introduction by elaborating on the concept of the criminalisation of social policy with reference to those who have developed it, given it shape, shown its significance over time or indeed contested it or aspects of it. This chapter provides the foundation for the subsequent six chapters on different thematic policy areas. Chapter 3 focuses on the recent projects of welfare reform, which have gained momentum over the last few decades in a number of country contexts. Extensive reforms to social security and the labour market activation of groups of welfare claimants have been characteristic of diverse European countries with significant negative implications for the groups impacted. This chapter shows how unemployment and poverty are primarily constructed as 'lifestyle' problems, to be addressed through employment incentives and the disciplinary turn in activation. At the same time as projects of welfare reform have gained momentum, governments have concentrated their attention on what they claim to be hidden economy activity and benefit fraud as crimes which are supposedly rampant, costing states millions and in need of serious clampdown. While there is a longstanding history of criminalising the poor, which is acknowledged in the chapter, the particular shape this has taken since the mid 2000s across different social and cultural spheres is given significant consideration. With a focus on recent positive developments in Scotland, the case for a new welfare imaginary is asserted.

Chapter 4 draws attention to the interrelated processes of the criminalisation of immigration, as well as the growing imbrication of immigration control with social policy, that arise in a world where national sovereignty, citizenship and the corresponding attribution of rights are inextricably linked. It is shown how this not only includes the overtly violent and punitive practices of border policing, detention and deportation, but extends to the exclusion and penalisation of migrants through the operation of the welfare state and what at the surface appear to be liberal policies, affecting poor migrants disproportionately. Consideration is also given to how criminalisation of migration is discursively and materially weaponised through ethno-racial othering strategies. Throughout this chapter, it is apparent that the exclusionary processes in operation for those who are deemed to be outsiders of our 'imagined nations' (Anderson, 1983), are similar to the dividing practices deployed by neoliberal welfare states to determine deservingness amongst its citizenry, yet they are experienced much more harshly by those excluded from the citizenry. The chapter concludes by suggesting that a world without borders must be kept on the horizon, if also not immediately achievable.

Chapter 5 is concerned with how the management and criminalisation of perceived 'problem populations' has intensified across contemporary cities and is achieved through an increasing array of different exclusionary legal mechanisms, interventions and technologies of urban policy. The consequences are that spatial and urban policies become imbued, transformed and subsumed by priorities of crime control and disorder prevention. Attention is given to how strategies of gentrification and privatisation and regulation of public spaces have sweeping impacts for poorer urban and homeless populations. It is also shown how crime prevention through environmental design (CPTED) and the deployment of hostile architecture signify the securitisation of urban policy agendas. The chapter points to the problematic relationship between homelessness and softer policing practices, which results in distinctively new forms of surveillance and coercive care of homeless populations. It is argued that urban renewal strategies and public investments, particularly targeted at territorially stigmatised areas, can be interpreted as governance strategies that do little to address structural problems which manifest in unequal societies. It is proposed that housing models based on rights-based frameworks and cooperative principles can offer viable alternatives to conditional models of housing.

In Chapter 6, with the help of conceptual tools provided by the criminalisation of social policy, the policing of families (Donzelot, 1979) and parenting cultures studies, what has been dubbed the 'new politics of parenting' (Gillies, 2008) is given attention. It explores the void between the social and economic realities of working-class parenting and family life and the unrealities of what working-class parents and families are expected to achieve. Forays into Adverse Childhood Experiences (ACEs) research and programmatic interventions into working-class families demonstrates show how the responsibilisation of parents, who are being identified as deficient, is increasingly constructed as the solution to addressing the reproduction of crime and poverty in legislation, policy and practice. As is argued in the chapter, the pursuit of adoption-driven child protection practice sends a clear message that poverty-informed policies and unconditional, relational family support are approaches to working with families, which are required more than ever.

In Chapter 7, attention is directed to the separate processes and contexts at play that shape how rehabilitation and reintegration of justice-involved persons play out in contemporary times. The chapter shows how the class-based assumptions behind or underpinning reintegration and rehabilitation policies often remain hidden. It is argued that the failure to live up to expressively middle-class norms can systematically exclude those in need of reintegration supports from successful access to much-needed supports and, therefore, directly contribute to criminalisation. Attention is given to how the provision of reintegration and rehabilitation services for justice-involved persons is strongly determined by the broader political economies in which they are situated. In particular, how neoliberal political economies and penal regimes interlink with the shape of reintegration policies and services are highlighted. It is also proffered that the neoliberal forces universally at play have shaped and permutated the ideal subject of rehabilitation and reintegration at a deeper level. Demands of self-activation and entrepreneurship of the self unduly responsibilise justice-involved persons *as if* they were entirely in charge of their rehabilitative journeys, potentially criminalising them further along the way. This chapter is concluded by making the case for a more extensive reimagining of punishment, crime, subjectivity and, as a consequence, reintegration.

Chapter 8, the concluding chapter, revisits key themes arising from the earlier chapters and considers the alternative trajectories for social policy and criminology that could be pursued. This chapter explores the potential for both these fields of study, criminology and social policy and the practices they inspire to conjoin in ways that are not about disciplining populations and/or are not in line with late neoliberal goals, but instead about generating fairer, more just societies in the twenty-first century.

2

Introducing the Criminalisation of Social Policy and an Overview of Relevant Scholarship

Introduction

This chapter sets the scene for subsequent chapters by reviewing the scholarship relevant to the conceptual and empirical development of the criminalisation of social policy. It maps three distinctive moments; its emergence in the 1980s and 1990s; its further consolidation and proliferation in the early 2000s and the attention it received in the period after the economic crisis and during austerity (2007 onwards). The literature reviewed is broad in focus, in that it includes literature considered relevant for understanding the depth and breadth of the criminalisation of social policy, even if this particular concept was not explicitly used or an alternative conceptualisation was chosen for the exploration of similar concerns. Much of the literature discussed is concerned with the contexts of the UK and the USA, where the criminalisation of social policy has been given much attention, but it is also supplemented with the literature from other European countries.

First, the chapter sets out general introductions to the fields of social policy and crime policy before exploring some of the commonsensical ways in which the two fields meet or intersect. It then uses the different timelines described above to elaborate three key periods in the development scholarship on the criminalisation of social policy. A specific focus is placed on the body of work relevant to understanding the criminalisation of social policy inspired by the contributions of Donzelot (1979) and Foucault (1977). Prior to concluding the chapter, contributions which challenge the utility of the criminalisation of social policy thesis or call for its conceptual and empirical refinement are elaborated.

Introducing social policy

Social policy is both an academic discipline and a field of government policy concerned with a wide variety of social issues. Welfare or social policy functions to construct and support the welfare state by guaranteeing economic protection and addressing the social risks associated with old age, illness, disability, unemployment and so on and by introducing measures to support human wellbeing (Gallo and Kim, 2016). For example, the Beveridge Report in 1940s Britain established social security, education, housing, health and employment as the five pillars of the British welfare state (Knepper, 2007). These pillars have over time changed and increased in number to reflect changing societies (Grover, 2010) and for example, personal social services (local authority provided services for vulnerable groups) were also incorporated (Knepper, 2007).

There is a long tradition in scholarship that has problematised state power and has contended that social welfare provision is designed predominantly to fulfil the needs of capitalism and to discipline the working classes rather than to address poverty and inequality (Fox Piven and Cloward, 1971; Gough, 1979; Offe, 1984; Hillyard and Percy-Smith, 1988; Squires, 1990; Jones and Novak, 1999). Fox Piven and Cloward's (1971) influential work on US welfare showed how welfare sustained the capitalist economic system by protecting persons from the worst excesses of inevitable economic downturns and by disciplining working-class people, who were compelled to see paid work as the only way of avoiding the penury associated with unemployment. Different regimes of welfare capitalism have their own distinct features and interact in diverse ways with capitalist political economies (Esping-Andersen, 1990, 1996; Hicks and Kenworthy, 2003; Schröder, 2009; Hemerijck, 2013) and the analysis of developments and permutations across these different regimes forms part of the core social policy canon. There are those that draw attention to the aspects of welfare that continue to receive a high level of public support in Europe that have endured over time (Roosma and Van Oorschot, 2017). At the same time it is accepted that provisions supporting particular groups in the population (for example, migrants, single parents, long-term unemployed, young unemployed) do not necessarily command the same level of public support and may be at risk of erosion (Van Oorschot, 2006; Van der Waal et al, 2013; Deeming, 2018; Taylor-Gooby et al, 2019).

Despite significant variations in welfare state regimes, increasing convergence towards more conditional welfare states and welfare state retrenchment are two factors uniting different regimes. Among European countries, political economies are increasingly shaped by supranational bodies of influence (the European Union (EU), IMF, OECD) (Camack, 2010; Greener, 2018: 30) and there is evidence of policy transfer (Obinger et al,

2013) and 'transnationalizing fast' policy (Peck and Theodore, 2010: 195) across states. This is particularly apparent with respect to labour market activation and welfare conditionality, both of which are given greater attention in Chapter 3.

Introducing criminal justice policy

Criminal justice policy is usually associated with the designation, prevention and regulation of crime through the institutions of policing, prosecution, criminal courts, prisons, probation and increasingly a wide range of community-based organisations (Knepper, 2007; Gallo and Kim, 2016).

Traditionally, the analysis of criminal justice policy has been dominated by state-centric approaches, often oriented towards assisting governments, criminal justice organisations and increasingly also international organisations in developing their approaches to crime control, crime prevention and the implementation of the rule of law across legal systems and institutions. Narrowly defined, socio-legal approaches to criminal justice policy analysis and formulation have focused on understanding processes of criminalisation through criminal justice systems with a view to identifying what works across various themes relevant for criminal justice (West and Farrington, 1973; Clarke and Mayhew, 1980; Clarke and Hough, 1984; Farrington et al, 1986; Hirschi, 1993).

Depending on the particular sociocultural and political contexts, different ideologies ranging from various tough-on-crime to welfarist- and rehabilitation- focused approaches have influenced criminal justice as a policy and practice field, as well as an academic field of study and research (Newburn, 2007; Tonry, 2013). Over time, new social phenomena, such as cybercrime or environmental crimes, facilitated by different effects of globalisation and technological developments, have broadened the scope of criminal justice policy, both in terms of geographical focus as well as new forms of criminalisation.

Criminal justice policy, both as a governmental field and as an academic discipline, has, particularly from the 1960s onwards, been critiqued from various left-leaning and critical strands of criminology. Different perspectives including cultural, radical, (post)-Marxist, feminist, post-structuralist, abolitionist and postcolonial criminology have highlighted why and how criminal justice policy analysis must locate its analysis in wider socio-political, historical and cultural contexts. Importantly, contemporary criminal justice policy analysis informed by these different critical perspectives, also acknowledges and investigates how criminal justice policy and institutions differentially affect and criminalise along the lines of race, class and gender (Smart, 1976; Davis, 2003; Gilmore, 2007; Alexander, 2010; Vitale, 2017).

Often posited as a response to the pressures of running effective and affordable public administrations, criminal justice policy research that seeks to create an evidence base for various types of criminal justice processes, interventions and processes, has become a predominant concern of research, institutions and academics across different jurisdictions (Dodge et al, 2012; Ugwudike et al, 2018). Critical scholars have critiqued the development of what has been dubbed 'administrative criminology' (Young, 1996), for its apolitical nature and its neglect of the harms created or tolerated by states and their various criminal justice institutions (Muncie, 2000; Hillyard et al, 2004; Dorling et al, 2008; Ruggiero, 2018; Canning and Tombs, 2021).

Criminal justice policy analysis has also widened its scope by acknowledging that it is exercised beyond the state and is also shaped by criminal justice professionals. The widening of criminal justice policy analysis has also included an acknowledgement that punishment is 'pervasive' beyond the institution of the prison (McNeill, 2018b) and that the post-9/11 anti-terrorism agenda has resulted in an increasing securitisation of criminal justice policy that has, amongst other things, also led to the increasing criminalisation of new population groups such as refugees, asylum seekers and migrants (Chacón, 2009; Barker, 2013; Bosworth, 2019; Franko 2019).

Criminal justice and social policy intersections

In the study of social policy and criminology, broadly similar groups of people are often the de facto focus of discussion (Grover, 2010). These are usually the poor and more specifically, unemployed persons, single-parent families, drug users, migrants or ethnic minorities, the homeless, young offenders and so on. These groups of people are more likely to have interactions with penal and welfare agents because their conduct is more publicly visible, at greater risk of being defined as illegal and more likely to be punished than that of other groups in society. This also means that agents of criminal justice are more likely to have them in their sights, to interact with them and to sanction them (as, for example, with young people deemed to be engaging in ASB). Poor material circumstances, arising from social and economic inequality, while not the direct cause of crime, are recognised as important contextual factors bound up with offending and overall rates of violence and crime (Currie, 2010; Wilkinson and Pickett, 2010, 2019). Poor people are at greater risk of being targets for state intervention, in terms of both the welfare and criminal justice systems (Rabuy and Kopf, 2015; Morris et al, 2018). Victims of crime are also predominantly drawn from the same groups of people (Grover, 2010) and victim–offender overlap is also getting increasing recognition (Heber, 2014; Bailey et al, 2020). Therefore, it is often argued that the task of reducing crime or responding to its aftermath cannot be left solely to criminal justice intervention. As many have observed, among the measures called for to reduce societal offending, are more equal wealth redistribution, better social service provision or specific social interventions to rehabilitate offenders and to respond to crime victims (Grover, 2010; Currie, 2013).

Poverty and social policy, as well as crime and criminal justice policy, have tended to be conventionally located in different spaces, distinct from each other institutionally, to be studied and analysed separately (Knepper, 2007; Rodger, 2008). Strong arguments have been made to keep them separate as policy, practice and academic fields, particularly when the progressive values of welfarism risk being lost (Gilling and Barton, 1997; Dixon, 2006), but the case for bringing them together into one single frame for the purpose of critical analysis has also been made (Wacquant, 2009a).

In the social policy literature, matters of penal policy, crime control, policing and criminal justice generally have at times been hived off from social policy's more central fields of concern (Wincup, 2013). Yet there are intersections between the two fields and disciplines of social policy and criminology. For example, Garland (2001) used the term 'penal welfarism' to capture the ways in which crime policy moved closer to social policy in the twentieth century. This refers to how crime's social structural causation was accepted rhetorically and how there was some acceptance that redistribution in the direction of the poor was an effective crime reduction policy, especially if supported by correctional rehabilitation for those who committed crime (Gilling and Barton, 1997). What became known as the punitive or the disciplinary turn in social policy prompted new understandings of the relationship between crime and welfare, as welfarism was perceived to be on a much more penal trajectory at the same time as an emerging new penology was shifting criminal justice policy towards greater punitiveness (Feeley and Simon, 1992; Garland, 2001). Furthermore, as discussed later in this chapter, trends since the 1970s generated analyses that saw welfare and penality as being increasingly integrated into one single policy regime designed to punish the poor (Beckett and Western, 2001).

Scholars have also sought to locate countries on a penal welfare continuum (Pratt and McLean, 2015). The Nordic countries are often placed at the progressive end of the scale with the USA located at the other end. While both of these geographical regions have been labelled exceptional for different reasons (Pratt, 2008), the degree of exceptionalism of each since 2012 is also contested (Dullum and Ugekvik, 2012; Scharff Smith, 2012; Barker, 2013, 2017; Ugelvik and Scharff Smith, 2017). Ugelvik and Scharff Smith (2017) presented the case that the embrace of a powerful welfare state such as in Sweden can be more suffocating than liberating, while Barker (2018) highlighted that the generous welfare state in Sweden was being preserved but only for nationals. The state's response to the Roma in Sweden illustrated its capacity to practice 'benevolent violence' (that is, to be both ameliorative and coercive at the same time) (Barker, 2018: 120). Other European countries are usually located in between the two 'exceptions'.

The study of the relationship between crime and social policy can be categorised as taking different forms but two trajectories are fairly distinctive (Gallo and Kim, 2016). One of these involves assessing countries' relative generosity in terms of their welfare and social policy provision and the degree of punitiveness of their crime control policy (Melossi, 1998; Beckett and Western, 2001; Cavadino and Dignan, 2006; Downes and Hansen, 2006; Lappi-Seppälä, 2008). The second trajectory focuses on what has been happening in the aftermath of the reversal of penal welfarism since the 1970s, as manifest in welfare state reform, the rise of neoliberalism in advanced capitalist economies and penal trends in the direction of retributivism and a culture of control (Feeley and Simon, 1992; Garland, 2001; Wacquant, 2009a). This latter form of enquiry is credited with better elucidating those aims that are common to both social policy and crime policy interventions and with highlighting their material and disciplinary implications for the poorest, most marginal groups in countries' populations (Gallo and Kim, 2006). Furthermore, social policy scholars have highlighted that despite evidence of welfare retrenchment, welfare states are not being dismantled entirely (Taylor-Gooby, 2016); rather they are reconfigured and realigned with market principles and used to enforce capitalist standards of conduct and compliance on those constructed as being non-compliant (Soss et al, 2011). The degree to which there is a convergence or divergence between European countries and the US model is also considered by Wacquant (2001, 2009a), who pointed to a particular form of convergence in his work, as welfare policies in European countries enhanced their carceral capabilities but did not pursue the kind of punitiveness evident in the mass imprisonment of poor people, which is such a recognisable feature of the USA.

Emerging concern with the criminalisation of social policy

Throughout the 1980s and 1990s, a number of scholars (Cohen, 1985; Gilling and Barton, 1997; Crawford, 1998; Jones and Novak, 1999) increasingly raised concerns about the buttressing of a more disciplinary state or the co-option of social policy for the fulfilment of crime prevention, reduction and management agendas in the UK. Cohen (1985) warned that social programmes seeking to do good also needed to advance social justice. Gilling and Barton (1997) claimed that in a UK ideological climate that was growing ever more hostile to welfare in public policy, criminal justice policy was also tending towards the incorporation of a depleted welfarism into its crime prevention and community safety policy agenda. As they saw it, this was a process carefully managed by agents of the state, who perceived that welfarism could be co-opted to provide the required velvet glove for the iron fist of penal policy. Gilling and Barton (1997) were pessimistic about this development, perceiving it to be detrimental to a genuine welfarism. Jones and Novak (1999) also provided a sustained critique of the 'retooling' of the welfare state, which they asserted was evident in the relentless pursuit of disciplinary social policies from the 1970s onwards. Crawford (1994, 1998) studied the formalisation of top-down corporatist, multi-agency partnership structures in the UK context, which emerged in the 1980s and became customary practice by the early 1990s to address crime prevention and community safety purposes. He found that they represented 'the administration of selectively defined "problems" in so far as these problems had criminal and disorderly consequences' (Crawford, 1994: 514). Resources were only being leveraged by the multi-agency partnerships because of concern about crime but not because good policy-making and public provision in what were very deprived communities were seen as important in their own right. He highlighted the potential the partnership structures held to become 'highly disciplinary and authoritarian forms of administration' (Crawford, 1994: 514). The proliferation of state-directed local partnership working reflected a new form of governance, whereby welfare-oriented agencies and criminal justice ones increasingly worked together in relationships that were viewed (Crawford 1994, 1998; Rodger, 2008) as preparing the way for the goals of welfare to be superseded by those of criminal justice.

Consolidation and proliferation of the criminalisation of social policy in the 2000s

The UK New Labour governments from 1997 to 2010 rooted criminalisation in social policy processes in a multitude of ways and this was reflected in growing attention given to it in the literature in that particular context (Cook, 2006; Knepper, 2007; Rodger, 2008; Grover, 2010). Cook (2006), for instance, showed the significant intertwining that was happening in both social policies and criminal justice policies under New Labour in Britain and in the objectives of these policies. She problematised the fusing together in a disciplinary continuum conduct labelled unacceptable, anti-social and criminal. She identified how at that point in time, policy responses to ASB were some of the most concerning examples of the criminalisation of the social (Cook, 2006). Other writers shared Cook's (2006) concern with the enforcement activity tackling ASB in Britain, viewing it as a prototype of the process of the criminalisation of social policy/poverty (Squires, 2006; Jamieson, 2012) and the working classes (Goldson and Jamieson, 2002; Gillies, 2005; McCarthy, 2011). ASB sanctions were seen to provide the supreme exemplar of the curious 'admixture of civil and criminal law' (Larkin, 2007: 298) that was becoming more common from the 1990s onwards (Larkin, 2007; Squires, 2008a). Others also wrote about the displacement of social policy through crime control (Reiner, 2007; O'Neill and Loftus, 2013), the criminalisation of protest (Welch, 2000), of incivility (Hillyard, Sim, Tombs and White, 2004) and of nuisance (Squires, 2008a).

Resonating with the concerns that had gained ground in the 1980s and 1990s, Paul Knepper queried if by making the welfare state into a solution for crime, it was diminishing its capacity for improving social welfare. Knepper (2007) dedicated a chapter in his book to the criminalisation of social policy, which he identified as having occurred when social welfare issues were redefined as crime problems and when the goals of social welfare became secondary to crime reduction in social policy. He presented social crime prevention in particular as paving the way for social policy to be used in criminal sanctions. He noted key indicators of the criminalisation of social policy. One of these was the changing approaches in the 1990s and 2000s adopted by leading welfare states of Europe (the Netherlands, Sweden and Denmark), which saw them becoming more enthusiastic for crime control policies, as their faith in welfare as a crime reduction measure declined. Others were provided by the increasing evidence that the logic of social services increasingly revolved around risk management and that there was an enhanced disciplinary orientation in the social professions. The emergence of joined-up service provision merging social service and criminal justice agents in partnerships facilitated information-sharing beneficial for social regulation. To fashion an alternative policy response to the criminalisation of social policy, Knepper (2007) proffered social justice as providing the appropriate moral framework.

In Rodger's (2008) view, criminal justice and social policy were never detached but they had grown closer together, so that at the time of writing in 2008, he perceived the process of criminalising social policy to be well underway. For Rodger, the shift from the welfare state to the workfare state, as elaborated by Jessop (2002), merited specific attention in terms of bringing the discourse of coercion into the sphere of welfare, thus ensuring that 'needy persons' would be supported in a way that was contingent on their conduct. Rodger (2008) highlighted the centrality of the politics of behaviour and particularly the policy preoccupation in Britain with the elimination of ASB. The use of civil law or civil procedures (for example, housing legislation) and social/therapeutic interventions to address anti-social or 'problem' behaviour was of particular interest to Rodger, as he drew out their very significant and distinctive contribution to the criminalisation agenda. He interpreted the *Respect Agenda* (a top-down, joined-up approach initiative designed to tackle ASB in communities more effectively) pursued by New Labour in Britain from 2005 until 2007 as a discernible political project, which involved a commingling of the universes of criminal justice and social policy. Criminal justice was, as he saw it, spreading its tentacles into societal spaces where it had had no significant presence in the past. Services and programmes targeting poor people and their families seemed to be taking on an increasingly penal hue (Rodger, 2008).

Rodger (2008) argued that governments and media were actively engaging in steering public opinion away from supporting the welfare state and wealth redistribution. They did this by presenting the welfare state and economic redistribution downwards as the main contributors to the creation of pathological, crimogenic sub-populations of persons, whose lifestyles and behaviours are not like the 'rest of us'. The structural causes of social need, poverty, unemployment, homelessness and poor parenting were denied as they are attributed to particular kinds of problematic cultural subjectivities. As Rodger (2008) saw it, the rise in governmental forms of power required the cultivation of particular kinds of subjectivities. This then gave impetus to the disciplining of persons and groups so that they engaged with services that would enable them to 'turn their lives around' and make the positive choices that would enhance their prospects in unequal societies. Welfare was conceptualised as the lever of behaviour change with sanctioning or withdrawal of benefits and so on, becoming part of an arsenal of measures to foster compliance or, in the event of non-compliance, to dish out punishment (Rodger, 2008).

Grover (2010), acknowledging the growing scholarly interest in the relationship between crime/criminology and social policy at that time, set himself the task of critically examining the empirical evidence in support of the criminalisation of social policy thesis. He chose to examine the interconnections between crime and social policy with reference to two substantive policy areas: income maintenance and housing/ASB. Each of these areas of policy, when examined in a British context, showed considerable evidence of a conjoining of crime and social policy. By way of illustration, he identified the legislative provisions enabling the deduction of fines imposed by a criminal court from a social security payment and the withdrawal of housing benefit from tenants evicted for ASB. Nonetheless, Grover (2010) had misgivings about whether the criminalisation of social policy thesis was something new, because, as he claimed, the aims of social policy had always been ambiguous, while states' concern with the character and morality of working class or poor people was not a novel phenomenon.

As he put it: ' Since collective responses to various needs emerged, there has been concern with how policies may affect the character and behaviour of recipients' (Grover, 2010: 447).

However, Grover (2010) left it open to debate, that what may have always been a general feature of social policy in times past – fixing the character and behaviour of individuals and families – was seemingly becoming a more concentrated strategy. In this context, he argued that Rodger's contribution to our understanding of the criminalisation of social policy had value and called for a shift in focus in social welfare away from behaviourism towards the reduction of economic inequality and to non-conditional social support.

Wincup (2013: 4) focused on the period between 1979 and 2012 in the UK and especially England and Wales to explore the 'increasing interconnections between crime and social policy'. She noted the rapid increase in the number of acts that were made criminal in the 15 years prior to writing her book. She acknowledged the part played by the Labour governments in Britain between 1997 and 2010 in deepening and widening a criminalisation project. She characterised this as constituting Rodger's (2008) criminalisation of social policy, which took two forms. One was the blurred boundaries between welfare and punishment as evidenced in partnership modes of working between agencies in both fields. The other involved crime control becoming a goal of social policy interventions as social policy shifted from remedying the social conditions causing crime and instead becomes the instrument of criminal justice. By way of illustration, Wincup (2013) highlighted the legislative measures introduced to tackle school truancy, from 1998 with the introduction of the Crime and Disorder Act, which moved truancy from welfare into the criminal justice arena. She also drew attention to acts (for example, possession by an under-18-year-old of an adult firework) that were defined as criminal for the first time under the Criminal Justice and Police Act 2001 and to the criminalisation of rough sleeping that happened in tandem with policy measures designed to address street homelessness. Wincup (2013) characterised British New Labour's *Respect Agenda*. Some years later, O'Neill and Loftus's (2013) claimed that the threat of the surveillance power of the private sector in the UK was far outstripped by the potential for state police surveillance afforded by the Crime and Disorder Act in 1998, followed by the Regulation of Investigatory Powers Act 2000. Their ethnographic research on covert policing and policing partnerships, revealed a high level of data gathering and sharing between police and their public sector partners. This data sharing was focused on the poorest individuals engaged in very petty crime and the data being gathered was being used for social control purposes. Data gathering and sharing was done in mundane, unseen ways and it was not problematised by those involved, even though it involved highly personal material about people's everyday lives, movements, behaviours and habits (O'Neill and Loftus, 2013).

From the late 1990s onwards, situational crime-prevention researchers (Felson and Clarke, 1997; Wiles and Pease, 2000) were also increasingly voicing their opposition to social programmes being used for crime prevention, arguing that only situational crime prevention (that is, reducing crime by limiting the opportunity for crime to occur) should be designed to achieve this purpose. Dixon (2006) highlighted, at the time he was writing, the growing consensus from different sides converging on the view that crime reduction could be a spin-off of social policies or interventions but that it was not ethical that such policies and interventions should only be pursued to achieve a crime reduction result.

Criminalisation, the penalisation of poverty and governing through crime

In the US context also, a burgeoning body of scholarship that raised concerns about issues at the heart of the criminalisation of social policy could be noted. In this regard, scholarship that drew attention to the culture of control (Garland, 2001), the criminalisation or the penalisation of poverty (Wacquant, 2001; Gustafson, 2009, 2011), as well as the practice of governing through crime (Simon, 2007) were critical. Garland's (2001) work, which proved hugely influential, pointed to the emergence of 'a culture of control'. His contention was that crime came to be viewed as an everyday feature of life that needed to be understood as a societal risk and managed accordingly. Therefore, rehabilitation was no longer viewed as a welfare end in itself but as a means of managing the offender population and their risk of committing further crime, the end goal being public safety. He observed that the respective discourses of welfare and criminal justice institutions were no longer so distinct and that this was in turn reflecting a reworking of class interests in a way that favoured those in the middle classes; middle classes who increasingly conceived of the welfare state as an unnecessary, costly provision, unfairly redistributing from them to those below them (Garland, 2001).

Drawing attention to the generalised increase in prison populations in advanced capitalist economies, Wacquant (2001) argued that it was a consequence of the penalisation of poverty, which took a noteworthy form in the US context. Wacquant (2009a: xviii) wrote that the 'postindustrial proletariat' were subjected to 'double regulation' and this was made possible 'through the joint agency of the assistantial (workfare) and penitential sectors (prisonfare) of the state.' The *centaur state* was Wacquant's (2009a: 43) chosen term to describe a new type of neoliberal political regime characterised by 'a liberal head mounted on an authoritarian body'. According to Wacquant

(2009a) the centaur state employs strategies of consent and compliance with corporations and ruling classes, while it is much more coercive and controlling in its approach to the lower social classes, including the poor. Prisonfare and workfare are both emblematic of this regime, as they commingle and intensify the discipline and punishment of the poor. However, he also pointed to the penalisation of poverty's diffusion to Europe, where there was intensification of conjoined social and penal responses to poverty and a mobilisation of the policing functions of welfare, creating what he called a form of social panopticism (Wacquant, 2001: 401). Welfare and criminal justice were, according to Wacquant (2013: 249), 'two modalities of public policy towards the poor' and thus needed integrated analysis and a project of reform.

Also, in relation to the US context, Gustafson (2009: 646–7) used the term criminalisation to describe the web of state policies and practices related to welfare, which were historically embedded in the USA and which monitored, stigmatised and regulated the poor. This web also encapsulated reforms implemented in the latter half of the twentieth century, which as she saw it, brought the criminalisation of welfare to a new level from the 1990s onwards. She argued that what policies had in common was an underlying assumption of the poor as criminal. Furthermore, she drew attention to the growing intersection between criminal justice and welfare as exemplified by shared goals and attitudes, collaborative practices and shared information systems. Finally, she pointed to the policy preoccupation with punishment of welfare fraud as a felony crime. She called for a disentangling of the welfare and the criminal justice systems in the USA 'from root to tip' (Gustafson, 2009: 716).

Another strand of literature in the US context drew attention to how schools started to resemble criminal justice institutions from the 1990s onwards via 'the criminalisation of school discipline' (Hirschfield, 2008; Kupchik, 2009, 2010; Brent, 2016). These studies showed how criminalisation of discipline in schools proliferated with the greater use of procedural rather than discretionary punishment, introduction of zero-tolerance practices and the greater use of criminal justice technologies (video cameras), methodologies (bag searches, use of metal detecting, drug sweeps, referral to court) and personnel (employment of security staff and police) (Hirschfield, 2008). Such work explored the confluence of factors, economic and otherwise, which have given rise to this phenomenon (Brent, 2016). It also revealed that while the criminalisation of school discipline was widespread in the US context, it was not an equal opportunities phenomenon as its associated practices tended to be more intense in urban disadvantaged schools where there were higher concentrations of students of colour (Hirschfield, 2008).

Criminalisation of social policy after 2010

Logics rationalised by the economic crisis, migration and terrorism prevention (Carvalho et al, 2020) have punctuated the criminalisation of social policy for the past ten years. Each of these logics is associated with an expansion and diffusion of criminal justice and wider punitive social interventions and these are addressed in subsequent chapters of this book. The economic crisis followed by austerity provided the context for extensive projects of welfare reform in many countries, combined with a cultural project of rendering the status of welfare claimant akin to that of being a criminal. In relation to anti-immigration and terrorism prevention, increasing research attention has been given to the criminalisation of borders (Barker 2018; Aliverti et al, 2019), pervasive 'everyday bordering' practices (Yuval-Davis et al, 2018), the hyper-criminalisation of migrants and migration (Stumpf, 2006; Chacón, 2009; De Giorgi, 2010; Bowling, 2013) and the securitisation of social policy (Patel, 2017; Nguyen, 2019; Galantino, 2020).

Taking Wacquant's *Urban Outcasts* (2008) and *Punishing the Poor* (2009) as their key focus, Squires and Lea (2013) produced an edited book that emerged from a conference on Wacquant's work at the University of Brighton in the UK. Wacquant's neoliberal penality thesis provided the starting points for contributions and each chapter in the book highlighted various ways in which that thesis was highly relevant and merited attention, while still needing to be refined, modified, critiqued and challenged. The significance of national specificities was a recurring theme as contributors welcomed Wacquant's thesis and called for its close and critical examination in contexts outside of the USA (Müller, 2013). There were warnings against oversimplifying policy transfer. This is on the basis that the penal agenda was showing itself to be manifesting differently in individual European countries and also different when comparing Europe with the US context, notwithstanding the variation also evident within the American context. For instance, Pitts (2013) queried whether the ascendance of neoliberalism could adequately explain the punitive exceptionalism of the United States, noting empirical evidence that showed its longer history. He also questioned the truism that the neoliberalisation of the economy should automatically bring about an intensification of the penal, on the basis that a penal state is neither ideologically necessary nor economically viable (Pitts, 2013: 79). Resistance from below, which required a view of the poor as not simply victims but also agents, was perceived by some commentators to be more promising and possible than Wacquant's contribution acknowledged (Measor, 2013; Ruggiero, 2013; Stenson, 2013). There were also calls not to neglect the wider security state, its significant technological capacities and its middle-class targets by focusing all the attention on the penal state and the poorer classes (Lea and Hallsworth, 2013).

Particularly salient for the purposes of our book were those chapters that directed critical attention to the roles of benign welfare agencies in the social control of marginal populations, including poor women (Hancock and Mooney, 2013; Martin and Wilcox, 2013), or those Measor (2013) referred to, as the 'urban outcasts with prams'. Hancock and Mooney connected Wacquant's concept of penal pornography with that of poverty porn in the UK to explore the part played by the media in constructing how poor people were coming to be known and disliked. Overall, the volume was presented as contributing to an analysis of 'disciplinary welfare and the penalisation of insecurity' (Squires and Lea, 2013: 14), an analysis which became even more urgent as austerity became more entrenched.

Austerity and the criminalisation of social policy

Austerity provided the economic and moral logic for significant and far-reaching criminal justice and social reform projects in diverse country contexts (Wong et al, 2014; Pavolini et al, 2015; Joy and Shields, 2018; Nygård et al, 2019). The economic crisis was widely reframed as being caused by flagrant public spending and an out-of-control culture of welfare dependency. Indeed after 2008, criminal justice was only one dimension of a more general intensification of resentment directed at the poor and 'underserving' in our societies (Jensen and Tyler, 2015; De Benedictis et al, 2017; Monahan, 2017). Such was the hostility and punishment directed at people and families on benefits, that it was viewed as having the potential to match that directed at the subjects of the criminal justice system (Grover, 2010; Adler, 2016; Carvalho et al, 2020). The emphasis on responsibilisation, compliance with conditions, monitoring, surveillance and sanctioning associated with the experience of being on welfare were stepped up (Monahan, 2017; Carvalho et al, 2020). In the UK, Wincup (2013) argued that the state had become increasingly concerned with not just governing through crime as such but through unemployment; a status not transgressive but being constructed as criminogenic and anti-social and requiring responsibilisation.

Drawing on Wacquant's concept of the 'carceral–assistential net' (retrenched welfare support conjoined with penal expansion), Povey (2017) described a paradoxical 'archipelago' of interventions, jointly assistential and carceral, reflecting the different faces of the neoliberal state and concomitantly experienced as supportive, repressive, punitive and protective. Furthermore, she argued that her research on women at the intersection of systems of welfare and penal reform in the UK added to the growing body of evidence indicating that austerity policies resulted in an intensification of disciplinary welfare practices. Chiming with the theme of welfare punitiveness targeting women was Smith et al's (2017) study of how social welfare policy actively contradicted and undermined Michigan State's programming intent to reduce female incarceration. They found that women's loss of monetary assistance (due to cuts in social assistance) and unmet need for housing assistance were related to their risk of reoffending while on community-based orders (Smith et al, 2017). Interestingly criminal justice policy in this instance was found to be subordinate to welfare policy in its harsh and punitive effects on the women researched (Smith et al, 2017). A burgeoning body of research has drawn attention to the use of chemical endangerment and foetal assault laws in the USA against women (Amnesty, 2017). These laws, in addition to the legal requirement on medical practitioners and hospital staff to report women using drugs and alcohol during pregnancy, provide additional evidence of the criminalisation of poor, predominantly African American women, their public shaming (Gustafson, 2013), and their punishment by detention and loss of custody of their babies (Gustafson, 2013; Amnesty 2017; Goodwin, 2017;). These provide clear illustrations of how social problems become redefined as crime problems and how social policy can be made even more criminalising and punitive in its impact than criminal justice policy, for the people caught in the 'carceral–assistential' interstices.

Marketisation, penal/mission drift and the criminalisation of social policy

Wincup documented the shift away from 'Big Government' as exemplified in the UK coalition government's 'Big Society' agenda, which gained momentum after 2010. As a concept, the 'Big Society' referred to a society with higher levels of personal professional, civic and corporate responsibility for activities traditionally undertaken by government (Wincup, 2013). The Conservative/Liberal Democrat coalition built on key reforms made by the preceding New Labour governments. The austerity agenda was used to justify the case for fiscal reductions and to orchestrate an increasing transfer of service provision from state providers to civil society but also to private sector organisations through mechanisms including commissioning and payment-by-results models, such as social investment bonds (SIBs) (Dowling, 2016; Joy and Shields, 2018, 2020). The shift from welfare pluralism to mixed markets is now well underway (Corcoran et al, 2018) and it has implications for the criminalisation of social policy (Koch, 2018; Maguire et al, 2019). Maguire et al (2019:430), for instance, identified the process they called 'penal drift' or 'mission drift' as one manifestation of the criminalisation of social policy. This involved the diffusion of criminal justice values, practices and dispositions into and within voluntary sector organisations' (VSOs') practices in the UK, as such organisations became more closely implicated in the delivery of punishment and its goals via commissioning and contract arrangements. As they noted, VSOs had become much more directly involved in the delivery of punishment than in the past and had traversed into reporting non-compliance and non-attendance by service users (Maguire et al, 2019). In the context of a mixed economy of penal welfarism, Monahan (2017) also warned that while forms of decriminalisation or community correction of minor offences or petty crimes at first glance seem more progressive than incarceration, they also risked ensnaring poor people in punitive debtscapes, surveillance and monitoring, all features of what she called exploitative poverty capitalism in the United States. For instance, when placed on probation for minor infractions in the USA, people are required to wear electronic monitors for which they pay fees to the private companies providing the surveillance service.

Securitisation of social policy

Fox O'Mahony et al (2015: 39) used the concept of criminalisation to refer to a governmental agenda that extends the use of the criminal law to respond to individuals who are viewed as problematic or as displaying social problems. Their elaboration of the concept captures the reconfiguring of social harms as crimes and other kinds of social conduct, not previously categorised as criminal, to be defined as such. Pointing to the introduction of legislation in the UK in 2012 to criminalise squatting, they highlighted a shift from a social state to penal state (Fox O'Mahony et al, 2015). They argued that the criminalisation of social policy is not simply about a declining welfare state and an expanding penal state, or indeed a predominantly US phenomenon. They underlined its relevance for other contexts where the conduct of the poor is targeted in new ways or where social problems are subjected to such moralisation that sanctions or punitive measures come to be perceived as acceptable and just responses (Fox O'Mahony et al, 2015). Increasingly, the phenomenon elaborated by Fox O'Mahony et al (2015) is manifest in the securitisation of social policy and its associated professional practices.

Increased attention has been given to the securitisation of social policy and social work in diverse country contexts in the wake of the 9/11 attacks (Manjikian, 2013; van der Woude et al, 2014; Mythen et al, 2017; McKendrick and Finch, 2017; Ragazzi, 2017; Ericson, 2018; Ahmed, 2020). Increasingly, securitisation is the term being given to the process by which an issue 'comes to be seen as a matter of national security and becomes removed from the realm of politics as usual to instead be treated as extraordinary politics' (Manjikian, 2013: 5). The language or lens of securitisation is thus used to construct a problem as one of security when prior to this it was understood as a different kind of social problem. The invocation of security enables governments to bypass the usual modes of debate and deliberation, to consult with security experts or to appoint committees to report on the problem and then claim justification to act secretly and hastily on the experts'/committee's proposals (Aradau and van Munster, 2007). Migration and housing are identified as policy issues that have been subjected to increased securitisation in the early twenty-first century (Manjikian, 2013; Ericson, 2018; Ahmed, 2020). Securitisation often involves the creation or identification of an enemy or threat to garner support for what would otherwise be seen as unpopular or excessive legislative measures or policies. The identification of the enemy permits lower standards to be applied to those labelled as such, as they are constructed as other than us and thus perceived as less entitled to the usual human rights and privileges afforded to persons in society. The value of understanding securitisation as something that can be operationalised by a wide variety of actors at different levels (for example, international, national and local) and along a spectrum (for example, more or less securitised) has been recognised (McInnes and Rushton, 2004; Manjikian, 2013). Counterterrorism measures that seek to prevent the emergence of a security threat via profiling practices, surveillance and campaigns, that responsibilise people to report suspicious activities or that call on communities to defend themselves against outsiders, are just some of the ways in which securitisation comes to be embedded from the top down (Manjikian, 2013). Studying urban property squatting in France, the Netherlands, Britain and Denmark, Manjikian (2013) showed four trends common to each country. Increased penalties were employed against squatters; in the media and in the political sphere there was an intensified use of racist and exclusionary language to define and differentiate the squatter; there were more violent clashes between law enforcement agencies and squatters and squatting was located within a crime frame rather than viewed as a housing need.

Securitisation of social policy also means that social policy becomes displaced through the overarching goal of crime control. A very problematic effect of the displacement of social policy through crime control can be that those who actually need services find it more difficult to access them. This is particularly the case in contexts where welfare provision is not universal and rights-based but is built around programmes that have to demonstrate their success. Working with less entrenched poor or risky persons, for example, who will make visible progress during short interventions, is clearly more in the self-interest of supports services and programmes across a whole variety of social policy fields. The implications of this are that for some people 'the *only* way to access much-needed services is through the criminal justice system' (Vitale, 2017: 213).

'Policing the family', governmentality, discipline and the criminalisation of social policy

Donzelot's (1979) and Foucault's (1977, 1984) work have made possible fruitful reassessments of relations and operations in the family, the state, among professionals, non-governmental organizations (NGOs) and civil society groups – reassessments that prove salient for excavating the criminalisation of social policy. Donzelot (1979) produced an influential Foucauldian analysis of the twentieth-century family. In this, he appreciated how the family, over time, became a site for the government of conduct. As such a site, it could be accorded privilege if it successfully took care of its members and if not, it could be placed under tutelage and subjected to disciplinary power (that is, blame, surveillance, sanction) for failing to comply with the normative standards promulgated by the agents of state: the health and social professions. For Foucault (1977), charitable, philanthropic activity and 'social' work provided by organisations or professions made possible the discipline of poor people. For, in his view (Foucault, 1984: 428), government did not only refer to 'political structures or to the management of states; rather it designated the way in which the conduct of individuals or of groups might be directed'. The usage of the term 'government' allowed Foucault (1984) to show how through various, procedures, practices and techniques, the state and its agents could govern populations and subjects. However, government is not solely the occupation of the government (or its proxy the state apparatus): across society and the economy a range of actors, operating at different levels and sometimes in competition with each other, address themselves to the problems of government (Kiely and Meade, 2018). Government can be best achieved through the exercise of productive rather than repressive power, as subjects have to be free to be governed and to govern their own conduct. It involves the state providing the conditions for subjects to do that which is expected of them.

Following Foucault, welfare projects are frequently and productively viewed as technologies of governance (O'Brien and Penna, 1998; Penna, 2005; Rose and Miller, 2010; Schram et al, 2010). According to Rose and Miller (2010: 289) welfarism involved the 'assembling of diverse mechanisms and arguments through which political forces seek to secure social and economic objectives by linking up a plethora of networks with aspirations to know, programme and transform the social field'. It is through welfarism that persons as individuals responsibilise and enterprise their lives and look less to the state to create the conditions that can optimise their endeavours (Rose, 2000). It explains why the unemployed become job seekers and refugees become asylum seekers as the expectation is that people in general, are required to become seekers of something (Rose, 2017).

Inspired by the work of Donzelot and Foucault, Squires (1990) focused on the 'anti-social' aspects of social policy and used this as his lens to re-read British welfare discourses from the nineteenth and twentieth centuries and up until the late 1980s. Squires' (1990) approach proved innovative for bringing to the fore the disciplinary relations at the heart of social policy and particularly social security policy. His argument that social policy was over time becoming increasingly anti-social was somewhat prophetic in the context of further developments in the field in the 1990s. While he did not clearly spell out what an alternative genuine or positive social policy should look like, his contribution undoubtedly set the scene for the further crystallisation of the criminalisation of social policy.

Concepts of ruling by kindness or caring power (Svensson, 2003, 2010) inspired by Foucault's analysis, captured how irrespective or how empathetic they may be as individuals, social workers' and probation officers' work and relationships with poor people are embedded in 'a fixed structure of categorical inequality' (Svensson, 2003: 98). For instance, McDonald and Marston (2006) noted social workers' (in Centrelink – Australia's welfare-to-work service provider) increasing capture by workfare in their practice. Research studies (McCarthy, 2011; Birk and Fallov, 2020) have also provided evidence of new surveillant, more punitive and controlling dimensions of crime-prevention work finding their way into practice, even if at times they are ameliorated by the actions of professionals. For example, there are study findings showing that community workers in Denmark occupy the middle ground engaging in social control while making life at the margins more liveable (Birk and Fallov, 2020). Similarly, in Britain, despite their good intentions, professionals' judgements and actions were found to reproduce inequality and engage in activities to correct working-class conduct in the field of early intervention with families (McCarthy, 2011). Research on probation supervision also showed how supposedly more progressive and welfarist forms of punishment carry with them 'significant yet poorly understood pains of supervisory punishment' (McNeill, 2019b: 207).

Scholars have proffered the concept of governmentality or realist governmentality as helpful to analysing the multiplicity of inter-state and intra-state relations that intersect in the processes of discipline and regulation (Rose, 1990; Stenson, 2013; Gray and Smith, 2019). Considering that governmentality studies appreciate 'the historical variability and situational contingency of the *problems* that have seemed appropriate to be governed' (Rose, 2000: 322, emphasis in original), there is potential to explore what new knowledge, expertise or governmental rationalities and technologies emerge at different times. It is also recognised that as states devise new powers and new sites of governance assisted by new technologies (that is, security states), the most marginal groups are not the only ones within their sights; rather much wider sections of society including the middle classes are also a target (Lea and Hallsworth, 2013; Vaughan, 2015).

The criminalisation of social policy corrected and contested

The criminalisation of social policy thesis has its critics. Shiner (2009, 2013) has argued that it lacks nuance, tends to overstate policy changes, neglects the continuities and rests on mythical versions of a past that never were. With reference to British drug policy, he pointed out that the demise of penal welfarism led to more punitive and coercive drug control policy, but that it was because criminal justice became increasingly harsh, not because it colonised other policy fields (Shiner, 2013). Challenging as possibly exaggerated a depiction of the British social security system as a 'quasi-adjunct' of the criminal justice system due to its punitive turn in the 1990s, Larkin (2007: 319) provided a detailed analysis of legislative reforms in social security introduced from the 1990s. He argued that the reforms had to be viewed in the context of the history of British welfare state provision, which demonstrated that a right to welfare was a relatively novel concept that had never taken hold. He did, however, recognise that any excessive emphasis on welfare conditionality could potentially have quasi-punitive effects on those impacted.

Fletcher (2019), with reference to his research with people engaging with Jobcentre Plus (working age support service) in Britain, took issue with Rodger's (2013) conceptualisation of welfare reform at the heart of his criminalisation of social policy thesis. Rather than viewing it as a 'civilising offensive' seeking to inculcate good habits in the working classes via disciplinary activation, Fletcher (2019: 408) argued, that it could be best understood as a de-civilising offensive as it drove persons into poverty, deprivation and survival crime.

Lacey (2010) did not contest that there had been a rise in unjust punishment, particularly in the USA, and she endorsed the attention given by Wacquant and others to the use of policing and punishment in the governance of the socially marginal. Focusing on what she viewed as a renaissance in criminalisation scholarship, Lacey (2009) argued that there were significant obstacles that had to be overcome to validate any claims of contemporary over-criminalisation. She pointed out that there is neither a clearly delineated concept of criminalisation or a set of normative criteria to help distinguish between levels of criminalisation as appropriate or not, nor indeed sufficient empirical knowledge of practices of criminalisation to facilitate assessment even if a normative benchmark was established. More recently, Lacey (2018) welcomed the approach developed and piloted by McNamara et al (2018) in Australia for providing an important step forward in enabling systematic and careful tracking of patterns of criminalisation over time.

There are also research findings which challenge the dominant representations of professionals and their implication in the criminalisation of social policy. For instance, empirical research in Australian and British contexts reported that diverse front-line workers in criminal justice or community agencies did not perceive themselves to be agents of state and that penal welfarism still informed their views, relationships and day-to-day practices (Coleman and McCahill, 2011; Hodgkinson and Tilley, 2011; Clancey, 2015). Such studies cautioned against dystopian accounts of crime prevention and other practices and argued that the day-to-day crime-prevention work observed or reported was not in accordance with what would be expected if the criminalisation of social policy had taken hold.

Conclusion

In this chapter, three key shifts in the 'criminalisation of social policy' literature have been traced; its emergence in the 1980s and 1990s, its proliferation in the 2000s and the attention it received after the financial crisis in 2007–8. The criminalisation of social policy is evident in the ongoing definition or redefinition of social problems as crimes (Wincup, 2013) and the use of criminal justice as the tool of choice of governments to show their power and capacity as they shift from welfarist to penal modes of governance of poor people and marginal groups (Rodger, 2008). It is also evident in the myriad ways in which a wider number of private interests, social actors and organisations work with government in the management of crime and in the moral regulation of behaviour (Wincup, 2013; Maguire et al, 2019). It also finds expression in the identification and targeting of those perceived to be undeserving, for discipline and responsibilisation and in the creation of the socio-economic conditions that exacerbate their exclusion and increase their risk of formal criminalisation (Fletcher, 2019). Most worrisome, as highlighted, is evidence of social policy's capacity to exert even greater punitiveness than criminal justice policy (Smith et al, 2017). Governments, via funding requirements, policy and practice innovations and modes of accountability, many of which are new, require professionals to see the persons they work with through a moralising lens of personal inadequacy and to monitor and change their behaviours accordingly under the threat of punishment (Rodger, 2008). Even if professionals actually think or do differently, it merits attention that they have at their disposal significant powers of monitoring, surveillance, enforcement and punishment to effect compliance and to sanction non-compliance with projects of government. The discussion of the development of the literature on the criminalisation of social policy provides a foundation for what now follows in the different thematic chapters of our book, as a more careful exploration is undertaken as to how social policy and criminal justice continue to intersect and often operate through more intensified, modified and fine-tuned mechanisms.

3

Disciplining the Poor: Welfare Conditionality, Labour Market Activation and Welfare 'Fraud'

Introduction

Throughout the period of austerity, projects of welfare reform already underway in many different countries gained momentum (Muehlebach, 2016; Cummins, 2018; Koch and James, 2020). Such was the scale of the reforms and cutbacks in some states that it became increasingly difficult to know what elements of welfare states remained and if their objectives had anything to do with reducing poverty and with offsetting the worst effects of inequality. At the same time as social safety nets were being disassembled, states pursued new modes of governance and regulation, which bore down on the poorest, most vulnerable sections of society (Koch and James, 2020). In the UK, the Welfare Reform Act 2012 introduced an under-occupancy penalty (the bedroom tax), which reduced the benefit paid to claimants in social housing if they were deemed to have too much living space (Gibb, 2015). It also introduced universal credit, a welfare benefit which replaced six means-tested welfare benefits and tax credits and was accompanied by increased conditionality and harsher sanctioning (WelCond Project Team, 2018; Carvalho et al, 2020; Williams, 2021).

It has been consistent in history to blame and criminalise the poor for their poverty, though the intensity with which this happens can vary (Jones and Novak, 1999; Macnicol, 2017; Pantazis, 2016). American neoliberal paternalists (Mead, 1989; Murray, 1990) and communitarians (Selbourne, 1994; Etzioni, 1997) advocated for the withdrawal of state supports for the purpose of disincentivising a culture of welfare 'dependency' as exemplified by the existence of the 'underclass' (Whelan, 2020a: 6). Yet the underclass analysis has been traced back to the writings of social commentators in the nineteenth century and to the 1834 Poor Law (Macnicol, 2017). Therefore, much of what is reported in this chapter is not necessarily new to our time but the shape the underclass logic is now taking merits attention, particularly at a time when economic inequality is so pronounced. Unemployment in many country contexts is being overwhelmingly constructed as a lifestyle problem to be addressed through a disciplinary turn in the form of activation and welfare conditionality (Wacquant, 2009a; Tyler, 2013). This coincides with politicians and media sources decrying hidden economy activity and benefit fraud as crimes which are rampant, costing states millions and in need of serious clampdown (Gantchev, 2019; Headworth, 2019). With a focus on the disciplinary turn, which is evident in contemporary labour market and welfare policies, the construction of persons in receipt of welfare payments as a suspect criminal population is a key theme in this chapter.

In the first part of the chapter, the focus is on labour market activation and welfare conditionality and the 'corporate welfare' (Farnsworth, 2013: 1) which scaffolds these policies. Narrowing the focus to lone parents in Ireland, it is shown how these policies play out in real terms and in ways which are comparable with other country contexts. In the latter part of the chapter, attention is turned to the implications arising from the intensifying political interest in the detection of welfare fraud and in the emergence of the digital welfare state. Consideration is given to the stigmatising representations of poverty and welfare that have proliferated over the course of austerity, reproducing the culture of poverty in new ways and legitimating particular policy choices. Before concluding the chapter, the scope for resisting dominant welfare discourses and for propagating a new welfare imaginary is explored.

Labour market activation policy

Activation as a concept is not new. It has been traced back to developments in Swedish employment policy in the 1940s and '50s (Weishaupt, 2011) but its more recent advancement is explained by the proliferation of new public management ideas about the role of employment services that happened in the 1980s in the UK (Weishaupt, 2011). Indeed, activation policy has been characterised as the most consistent and expanding labour market policy reform process in Europe since 2000 (Turrini et al, 2015: 11). Influential agents, for example the OECD and the EU were to embrace activation early, in their bid for more inclusive labour markets (Weishaupt, 2011) and the appetite for it since, as described by Hansen (2019), is insatiable. The OECD, for instance, assesses individual countries' activation strategies' effectiveness and advises them on what actions to take to make them more effective (Martin, 2015). The activation paradigm became so pervasive from the 1990s onwards that key distinctions between EU welfare states became blurred (Weishaupt, 2011). The financial crisis in 2008 did not derail activation policy as many countries strengthened their activation infrastructure and strategies, including Ireland, which moved more definitively in the direction of a 'work first' approach (as distinct from an education/train first approach) (Collins and Murphy, 2016: 88). The 'active turn' (Hansen, 2019: 3) seeks to make people active and closer to the labour market and to welfare conditionality (Murphy, 2020). It provides the means for what Dean (2012: 353) has referred to as 'pimping the precariat' or for remoulding passive welfare recipients into active subjects for capitalism's insecure labour markets (Boland and Griffin, 2015; Wiggan, 2015). Activation, if understood as compulsory compliance with states' labour market policies, is distinguishable from workfare (compulsory participation in paid work). However, both have in common their impulse to bring persons closer to employment with the assistance of focused, results-oriented public employment services. Activation, for instance, can require of welfare claimants their attendance at job fairs, evidence of their job search activity and participation in mandated training or unpaid work experience. It can oblige them to engage in psychological interventions dressed up as incentives designed to change the attitudes, feelings and behaviours perceived injurious to willingness or capacity to engage in paid work (Mehta et al, 2020). While activation acquires different emphases in different welfare regimes and involves diverse modes of translation and mediation (Newman and Clarke, 2009) due to diverse factors such as levels of expenditure (Weishaupt, 2011), regulatory and punitive aspects are common to all (Brodkin and Larsen, 2013). In this context, the usefulness of the binary distinctions often made being made between careful/carefree, good/bad, carrot/stick activation has also been questioned (Hansen, 2019).

Welfare conditionality policy

Welfare or behavioural conditionality is not new. The UK's 1834 Poor Law set out to influence behaviour and to promote self-reliance as much as to address social need and alleviate poverty (Watts and Fitzpatrick, 2018). Having to meet conditions to access welfare provision was a feature of the workhouse and work-related conditionality has been integral to welfare states since their beginnings (Powell, 1992; Garrett, 2015; Dukelow and Considine, 2017; Gray, 2019; McNeill, 2019a). However, welfare conditionality intensified during austerity so that it has come to be identified as a form of social control (Watts et al, 2017) and one aspect of the wider trend towards the criminalisation of social policy (Knepper, 2007; Rodger, 2008; Fletcher and Wright, 2018). It is defined by Watts and

Fitzpatrick (2008: 1) as 'a form of support more focused on promoting pro-social behaviour than on protecting people against classic social risks like unemployment.' It involves the linking of welfare benefits and services to obligations and behaviour and has been dubbed 'authoritarian therapeutism' (Wacquant, 2013: 249). Other key components include the monitoring of behaviour and sanctioning of non-compliance. Welfare conditionality is now a key feature of democratic welfare capitalist countries, though it tends to have a more punitive orientation in the Global North than in the Global South and it is perceived as ranging from relatively recent, modest and paternalistic in some country contexts (for example, Ireland) (Cousins, 2019) to more punitive in others (USA, UK, Australia, New Zealand) (Fletcher and Wright, 2018). In the 1990s conditionality started to be increasingly applied to working-age welfare claimants in many different country contexts and these were strengthened and expanded with the passing of time. For example, a more punitive approach to welfare recipients was instigated in the 1990s in the UK and was further strengthened in 2002 when it was helped along by the establishment of Jobcentre Plus, which was formed from the amalgamation of the employment service and the social security benefits agency (Fletcher and Wright, 2018). Welfare reform after 2010 in the UK strengthened compulsion and sanctioning to the extent that it was conceptualised as 'a criminalising strategy' (Wright et al, 2020: 281). For instance, from 2008 in the UK, in a move to activate cohorts of lone parents, they were directed from income support to jobseeker's allowance based on the age of their youngest child (Fletcher and Wright, 2018). Welfare claimants with illness and disability were recategorised following assessment into two different groups depending on capacity and suitability for work. For those in the Work Relative Activity Group (WRAG), failure to engage in work-related activity results in payment cuts or sanctions, which can extend as far as a 100 per cent payment cut (Mehta et al, 2020).

Aside from the UK, there are also key moments in Australia's welfare conditionality trajectory. These include its introduction of work-for-the-dole in 1997, Income Management in 2007, which reported no sustained benefits (Bray, 2016) and, since 2014, the introduction of the Cashless Debit Card (CDC). The CDC policy designed by government is a key iteration of income management. The Howard government first introduced Income Management with Australia's Indigenous communities in the Northern Territory in 2007. Over time, it was extended to more regions, specific geographical communities and deployed also as a child protection initiative (Parliament of Australia, 2015). In Australia, Indigenous people comprise the majority of persons who experience Income Management. Among its listed objectives as set out by the Australian Parliament are to 'reduce the amount of discretionary income available for alcohol, gambling, tobacco and pornography' as well as to 'encourage socially responsible behaviour particularly in the care and education of children' (Parliament of Australia, 2015: n.p.). The CDC, a cashless welfare card administered by a private company, ensures that only 20 per cent of a welfare payment can be used as cash and the remaining 80 per cent cannot be withdrawn as cash from an automatic teller machine (ATM) or bank; neither can it be spent in retail outlets associated with gambling or alcohol sales (Henriques-Gomes, 2020).

Welfare conditionality is also not simply restricted to income support policy. Internationally, as for example in France, Sweden, the UK, Austria, Australia and Ireland, housing policy and practice is recognised as a key site for welfare conditionality (Watts and Fitzpatrick, 2018; Clarke et al, 2020). In Australia, welfare payments and subsidies have been denied to parents who do not have their children immunised (Churchin, 2019). Unemployed parents whose children do not attend school can also have their welfare benefits reduced as a result of the School Enrolment and Attendance Through Welfare Reform Measure (SEAM) (Parsell et al, 2020). Such measures construct unemployed persons or categories of them, as persons failing to live responsibly and that they deny them agency to exercise self-determination and the rights afforded to other citizens.

Though Ireland came late to recent iterations of welfare conditionality, with the economic crisis in 2008, concerted activation and welfare conditionality intensified. The state actively rolled out new forms of regulation in the Irish context and became more actively involved in the regulation of private and non-governmental actors in the welfare landscape. In 2010, guided by the OECD and monitored by the Troika, the Irish government willingly adopted an activation regime and set about integrating its welfare benefit system and its employment services in a new one-stop shop 'INTREO' in 2012 (Hick, 2018; Whelan, 2020a). The government *Pathways to Work* (Department of Social Protection, 2016) strategy strengthened Ireland's pursuit of activation policy by setting out conditionalities attached to new labour schemes and allowing it to catch up with other countries (McCashin, 2019; Whelan, 2020a). Private welfare-to-work providers (for example, Seetec and Turas Nua) became part of the Irish welfare landscape in 2014 (Boland and Griffin, 2015). They were contracted to deliver activation for long-term unemployed persons in a process of payment for results, which constitutes a form of 'double activation' (Considine et al, 2015: 30). In the past few years, there is increasing consensus that it is a work first mode of practice that increasingly permeates the Irish welfare state (Collins and Murphy, 2016; Millar and Crosse, 2018).

The impact of welfare conditionality and disciplinary administrative sanctioning

Social security/welfare sanctioning denotes a punitive turn in welfare policy considered analogous to David Garland's elaboration of the punitive turn in penal policy (Adler, 2016), as elaborated in the introduction to this book. Since 2006 there has been a dramatic rise in sanctions and disqualifications imposed by the Department for Work and Pensions in the UK and in 2013, the 1,000,000 sanctions overtook the number of fines imposed in the criminal courts in the same year (Adler, 2016). The complexity and severity of the sanctioning system in the UK have been ratcheted up via legislative measures, particularly since 2012, so that more people are impacted, in more severe ways and with more situations covered than ever before (Adler, 2016). In the Irish context, non-compliance with job-seeking efforts and conditions also results in more intensive surveillance and support as well as benefit penalties (25 per cent of benefit payment) (Murphy, 2020). There have been significant increases in the number of social welfare payment penalties applied since they were first introduced in 2011, from 359 that year to 13,503 in 2017 and 12,380 in 2018 (Minister for Employment Affairs and Social Protection, 2019, 10 July). A total of 66,628 penalties were applied from 2011 up until 2 June 2019, which impacted on 46,300 persons (Minister for Employment Affairs and Social Protection, 2019). Furthermore, there is a complete dearth of transparency, information and accountability pertaining to the application of social security penalties in Ireland (Collins and Murphy, 2016). Indeed, lack of proportionality and transparency, overtly complicated appeals systems, high success rates of sanction reviews frustrated by long waiting periods for outcomes leaving persons destitute, are just some of the reasons why social security sanctioning has come in for critique in diverse country contexts.

The experience of stigma and shame induced by the ongoing monitoring and surveillance experienced by diverse welfare recipients has been documented in research conducted in the Irish and UK contexts (Redman, 2020 Whelan, 2020a). Punitive conditionality has also been found to cause symbolic and material suffering and to have life-threatening effects (Wright et al, 2020). There is also evidence that persons are pushed into what Ruggiero (2013: 173) termed the 'carceral social zones' or the economy of the outcasts, increasing their risk of having to engage in perilous, sometimes criminal behaviours. Researchers have found a relationship between welfare sanctioning and food bank use in Britain (Loopstra et al, 2018; Wright et al, 2020). Using longitudinal qualitative data between 2014 and 2019, Wright et al (2020) reported that sanctioned welfare recipients who lost much-needed income used food banks for the first time, resorted to survival sex and crime and contemplated suicide. An increase in self-reported anxiety and depression attributable to job seeker's allowance sanctions has also been found (Williams, 2021). The evidence shows that welfare conditionality and sanctions do little to effect sustained change in the employment status of individuals or to alter their motivations and behaviours to prepare for, seek or enter paid work (WelCond Team, 2018). For a minority who access work, the dominant picture is short-term insecure work interspersed with periods of unemployment (WelCond Team, 2018). However, the punishing conditions they induce for the health and wellbeing of persons with disability in the UK have been documented in a growing body of evidence (Geiger, 2017; Dwyer et al, 2018; WelCond Project Team, 2018; Mehta et al, 2020). Furthermore, there is a lack of evidence internationally that the imposition of welfare conditionality on lone parents and children generates positive outcomes for them (Butterworth et al, 2006; Campbell et al, 2016; Podesta, 2017; Millar and Crosse, 2018). Homeless persons, lone parents, ethnic minorities and persons with learning disabilities are identified as being at greater risk of sanctioning than others in the UK, indicating that those who are most vulnerable are being particularly impacted by sanctioning and their social exclusion is further compounded (Loopstra et al, 2015; Reeves and Loopstra, 2017; Redman, 2020).

In-work poverty and 'corporate' welfare

To reinforce and scaffold activation and welfare conditionality are state-provided 'In-Work Benefits' (IWBs) and employers' subsidies as more people find themselves activated or pushed into low-paid, insecure employment. These measures provide the means by which states seek to make work pay by compensating workers or by incentivising employers. Initiated in the 1970s in different country contexts, they have expanded rapidly in recent years, but lack transparency (Collins and Murphy, 2016; Greener, 2018; McGann et al, 2020). They comprise a form of 'corporate welfare' (Farnsworth, 2013: 1) that in the Irish context adds up to a total of €1 billion state investment to make low-paid employment sustainable (Collins and Murphy, 2016). These benefits and subsidies prompt questions as to whether or not it is correct for states to take on the burden of low-paid employment and if they do, to what extent and with what level of democratic accountability (Collins and Murphy, 2016; Clegg, 2017; Greener, 2018). The influence the existence of such provisions exert on employer practices and on the structure of the labour market, also merits consideration in the context of a growing percentage of workers in Ireland and other countries experiencing low pay, underemployment and temporary and precarious work conditions. Some 23 per cent of workers in Ireland are in the low-paid category in comparison to

19 per cent in the UK and an OECD total of 15.4 per cent (Social Justice Ireland, 2020). Meanwhile, 16.1 per cent of Irish workers experience poverty (Social Justice Ireland, 2020). With reference to political economy perspectives, it shows how states are thus complicit with the interests of capital in the reproduction of a precariat by securing for employers a more consistent labour supply for insecure work at the low end of the labour market (Standing, 2011). In this context, it is unsurprising that we see such trends as a growing gig economy (Standing, 2016), rising involuntary part-time and temporary jobs, increases in low-paid work and greater in-work poverty, all trends experienced disproportionally by poor young adults and women (Shildrick, 2012; Nugent et al, 2019). Indeed, Eurofound (2020a) reported on nine new forms of non-standard employment (for example, voucher-based work, casual work, platform work and so on), which now exist in most EU member states, even if on a minor scale. It was acknowledged that in a number of these new forms of employment, the employment and working conditions are less favourable than in standard employment and worker protections more limited (Eurofound, 2020a). In the next section, the part played by activation directed at lone parents in Ireland is explored.

The activation of lone parents: case study

The gendered character of social welfare and the challenges for women caught in a penal welfare nexus have been identified by others (Haney, 2004; Povey, 2017; Roberts, 2017), as discussed in the introduction to this book. As considered in more detail in Chapter 6, parenting alone, which is significantly gendered, has never been put beyond scrutiny by states in many country contexts. Policy responses continue to categorise lone mothers as more or less deserving based on their marital status; their relationship to the state and its institutions, public attitudes and judgements by professionals and increasingly their relationship to the paid labour market. Single lone mothers have been depicted in negative ways in Irish society for decades; as sinful and immoral and thus deserving of the punitive treatment meted out by religious orders assisted by the state and civil society throughout the twentieth century (Luddy, 2011; Garrett, 2016). Since the 1990s in particular, lone parents have been viewed as a drain on state resources, as deficient parents and as calculating and conniving welfare recipients (Kiely and Leane, 1997). Engagement in the formal labour market of lone parents was traditionally not part of the Irish state's ambition for such parents and certainly not when the state first provided income support for lone-parent families in the 1970s. Traditionally in Ireland, there was the institutionalisation of a very strong male breadwinner regime and women's paid labour market participation was discouraged. These understandings of women's key role continued even when married women worked outside the home to enhance the family's income (Kiely and Leane, 2012).

One Parent Family Payment (OPFP) was the income support provided to lone-parent families in Ireland after its introduction in 1997, when it replaced a number of income support payments. Lone parents were entitled to receive the payment until their youngest child reached the age of 18 years (or 22 years if they were in full-time education). However, in the mid-2000s, as a step in the direction of activation, entitlement to state benefit started to be mapped on to the age of a lone parent's youngest child. For instance, the Department of Social and Family Affairs recognised 'parental choice with regard to care of young children but with the expectation that people will not remain outside of the labour force indefinitely' (DSFA, 2006: 9). This discussion paper promised voluntary rather than compulsory activation of lone parents, coupled with the vital package of supports, which it acknowledged would be required to accompany such a significant policy change (DSFA, 2006). These proposals were not instigated at that time. However, subsequently, the activation enshrined in the Social Welfare Act 2010 brought further implications for OPFP. In April 2011 new applicants could only avail themselves of payment until their youngest child was aged 14 years, at which stage they would have to move on to Job Seeker's Allowance (JSA) for activation purposes. Special provision was made to exclude from activation the category of lone parents who were bereaved, possibly indicating that this subset of parents were viewed by the state as more deserving than other categories. The Social Welfare and Pensions Act 2012 further reduced the period of cover for which lone mothers were eligible to claim One-Parent Family Payment. Low education attainment, no or minimal employment history, having poor health or a disability, or having care responsibilities for an older child with specific needs were all known barriers to paid employment for some lone mothers (Murphy et al, 2008). However, such factors were not recognised or catered for in the dependent child age category criteria set out in the 2012 legislation. After July 2015, this payment was no longer to be paid to recipients once their youngest child reached seven years, a development which prompted the '7 is too young campaign' by organisations representing one-parent families resistant to the measure. Thus, if in need of income support, from July of 2015, a mother whose youngest child was between 7 and 14 years had to apply for a Jobseekers' Allowance Transition (JST) Payment, requiring her to engage with the Department of Social Protection's case officers towards facilitating her movement towards the paid labour market. Failure to engage resulted in a lower rate of payment. Parents of children over 14 years who received the JSA payment could be penalised for not accepting a job offer or more hours of employment. In effect, a choice not to work outside the home was no longer afforded to lone mothers of schoolgoing children since they were incrementally reconceptualised as paid workers outside the home as their care work in the home was rendered invisible. As noted by Murphy (2020), the full-time labour market conditionality required of lone parents was not expected of their partnered or widowed counterparts, who could have been assessed as having greater capacity, capital, support and resources than the single lone-parent cohort to engage in paid work full-time. Irish research studies (Murphy et al, 2008; Society of Saint Vincent de Paul, 2014) provided much evidence throughout this period of welfare reform to challenge the premise that lone mothers required activation. They showed consistently high levels of motivation among lone mothers on social assistance to take up employment, training or education. The realities were such that lone parents had to reconcile paid work with their caring obligations and their material circumstances.

As the pursuit of the labour market activation of lone mothers continued unabated during austerity, key supports for lone-mother families were being curtailed or abolished entirely (Madden, 2014). Furthermore, the new range of supports promised by the government to facilitate what would be required for a 'careful' (Murphy, 2012: 3) model of activation (such as affordable childcare provision, were not forthcoming. Following Haney (2004: 340), this can be understood as a form of 'equality with a vengeance'. The lone parent was expected to become the ideal male citizen worker, whose household labour, care of children and others had to be done but could not get in the way of their breadwinning role. The pronounced vertical and horizontal gender segregation in the Irish labour market, as well as the gender pay gap, which increased lone parents' prospects of entering local, low-paid, insecure jobs, were ignored. This policy of activation was operationalised to coincide with commitments made as part of the Troika bailout (a three-year economic rescue programme implemented by the International Monetary Fund, the EU and the European Commission). However, it was not imposed by the Troika as it was one of a number of the policy reforms in the pipeline before the crisis (Hick, 2018; Millar et al, 2019).

Mothers and children in lone-parent families in Ireland were identified as experiencing the highest deprivation rate, a rate which increased rapidly after 2009, reflecting the impact of austerity measures on these families. Research conducted cautioned that the activation policy being pursued by the Irish government was likely to result in lone parents in paid employment being financially worse off (Millar and Crosse, 2016). According to Millar et al (2019) this research, originally used by government to appease opposition to the reform, was subsequently discredited when the findings did not provide the evidence base the government wanted. Subsequently, an independent evaluation by Indecon (2017) found that 53 per cent of lone-parent families reported being financially less well off by the activation reforms introduced, while 63 per cent reported being in full-time employment but struggling to afford basic items. An Economic and Social Research Institute (ESRI) study (Regan et al, 2018) further confirmed that the changes made to social welfare policy between 2011 and 2018 resulted in income losses for employed lone parents, predominantly attributed to the lack of affordable childcare and the concentration of lone parents in low-paid part-time employment. When the reforms and all other policy changes during austerity were taken into account, the income of both employed and unemployed lone parents had significantly decreased (Regan et al, 2018). The poverty rate of lone-parent families in Ireland actually doubled from what it was in 2012 to what it became in 2017 (Society of Saint Vincent de Paul, 2019). The Survey on Income and Living Conditions for 2018 showed that lone-parent families continued to be the poorest families in the Irish state with their deprivation rate at 42.7 per cent in comparison to 14.3per cent for families containing two adults and between one and three children (CSO, 2019). Leo Varadkar, the Minister of Social Protection at the time (2015–16), who later became the Prime Minster, paternalistically defended the policy reforms, seeming little concerned about the in-work poverty the government reform produced for families. He stated 'For reasons of confidence, mental health, self-respect and how they are considered in society, people are always better off working than on welfare, even if they might be a little better off on welfare' (Varadkar, 2016). Indeed lone parents' incidence of in-work poverty in Ireland was shown to increase dramatically from 8.9 per cent in 2012 to 20.8 per cent in 2017 (Society of Saint Vincent de Paul, 2019).

While the lack of disaggregated data on welfare penalties in the Irish context makes it impossible to know the level of penalties applied to lone-parent families (Murphy, 2020) who do not comply with activation requirements, there is evidence that the threat of penalties induces considerable fear and anxiety in this population (Zappone, 2016; Whelan, 2021). As noted by Murphy (2020) in the Irish context, lone parents now find themselves caught in the nexus of two related conditionality regimes (housing and welfare). They are problematised if they work part-time for nesting on in-work benefits and accused of 'gaming' the system when they seek the security of tenure associated with social housing rather than subject themselves to the insecurity of the private rental market (Murphy, 2020). While what is presented here is a distinctly Irish case study, the activation directed at lone parents and its impact in terms of contributing to the in-work poverty of these families mirrors research findings in several other country contexts (Knijn and van Wel, 2001; Ridge and Millar, 2011; Jaehrling et al, 2014; Wright and Patrick, 2019; Millar and Ridge, 2020). In many countries, categories of lone parents are a key target for an admixture of 'centaur state policy mandates' (Carey and Bell, 2020: 200), which construct them as workshy, irresponsible parent subjects in need of discipline and sanction via activation and, as is shown in Chapter 6, family support programming. The ratcheting-up of discourse and of powers to prevent and detect welfare fraud also merit attention as features of the centaur state (Wacquant, 2009a: 43) and these are given attention in the following section.

The pursuit of welfare fraud

While the policing of welfare fraud has always been a part of the welfare system (Kohler-Hausmann, 2007) the intensity with which welfare jurisdictions are pursuing the problem of fraud has increased in recent years (Chan, 2011) and in some countries (for example, the UK, the Netherlands) the pursuit is more intensive than others (for example, Germany) (Gantchev, 2019). Speaking of the British context, Larkin (2007: 311) described as a 'political obsession', Labour governments' preoccupation with eliminating social security fraud in the latter half of the 1990s and Connor (2007) depicted New Labour's *Targeting Benefit Fraud* Campaign initiated in 2000, as one of a set of measures designed to legitimate the employment first welfare state. While welfare fraud is typically punished by administrative sanctions, some countries (for example, the USA and the Netherlands) use criminal sanctions (Ranchordás and Schuurmans, 2020). In the USA, Headworth (2019) has strongly critiqued the welfare fraud unit's enforcement process, which converts the personal into the penal, by subjecting persons' private lives to considerable exposure and scrutiny in the interests of substantiating punishable offences. He has emphasised the damage this does to social capital in poor communities (Headworth, 2019). Recent trends have prompted justifiable concerns that the detection and prevention of welfare fraud are taking precedence over the procedural rights and welfare of persons investigated (Adler, 2016) and that welfare fraud discourse is feeding the stigmatisation of being on welfare. Certainly, there is evidence that despite the challenges involved in knowing the correct level of benefit fraud, members of the UK public tend to entirely overestimate the scale of the problem (Geiger, 2018). Indeed, there is evidence that welfare fraud campaigns and welfare fraud investigation work reproduce welfare stigma to such an extent that welfare recipients come to see themselves as the genuine exceptions among a group of predominantly guilty others (Headworth, 2019).

Britain announced it was going to war against welfare fraud in 2010. In Ireland, there was a renewed emphasis on the need to address welfare fraud after the economic crisis in 2008 by politicians on the left and right, which lead up to the high-profile 'Welfare cheats *cheat us all* campaign' in 2017 (Devereux and Power, 2019). The Irish war on welfare fraud has continued unabated. In 2020, the Irish Department of Employment and Social Protection investigators continued to participate in multi-agency vehicle checkpoints with the police and other agents to detect persons working when on welfare. In the same year, Department of Social Protection officials reported their intention to conduct some 700,000 claim reviews, inspections and investigations as part of their anti-fraud, compliance and control savings measures (€520 million) (Bray, 2020). The department's special investigation unit at the time comprised 114 officers and the additional 20 police officers on secondment from the Irish Police Service to the unit to bolster its investigative efforts (*Irish Times*, 2020). During the global COVID-19 pandemic, the Irish media reported that more than 2,500 pandemic unemployment claims were closed as a result of checks carried out by social welfare inspectors, who requested persons' social security/personal public service numbers at ports and airports (Horgan-Jones, 2020). These checks specifically targeted unemployed persons travelling abroad for what were considered to be non-essential reasons. However, following a wave of controversy challenging their legality, their discriminatory targeting and their punitive impact, the Irish Minister for Social Protection subsequently confirmed that persons on the payment travelling to COVID green list countries, would not have their payment stopped (Humphreys, 2020).

Welfare 'fraud' and the advance of the digital welfare state

Welfare fraud detection and investigation work are increasingly being outsourced by welfare authorities to other private entities. While in many countries citizens are relied upon to detect and report welfare fraud, a few countries' (for example, the Netherlands, Switzerland and the UK) authorities also employ private investigators (Ranchordás and Schuurmans, 2020). A host of countries (including the UK, Australia, Switzerland, the Netherlands, Belgium, the USA) have been experimenting with automated surveillance systems to clamp down on welfare fraud with, it would seem, limited information provided about their methods or little regard for welfare recipients' vulnerability, rights and privacy (Henley and Booth, 2020; Ranchordás and Schuurmans, 2020; van Zoonen, 2020).

For example, the digital risk assessment system ('SyRI') developed in 2014 for use by the Dutch government, was deployed in low-income communities. It applied a logarithm to link and analyse large amounts of personal data of citizens, held by diverse state agencies to identify what type of persons were more likely to abuse welfare, avoid paying tax and be non-compliant with labour laws and hence, to merit investigation. The District Court of The Hague ruled in February 2020 that SyRI violated the European Convention on Human Rights (ECHR) on the basis that it lacked transparency and had too few safeguards to protect persons' privacy (Henley and Booth, 2020). The court also raised significant concerns about its potential use to stigmatise and discriminate on the grounds of socio-economic or migrant status, because of its deployment in poor communities (The Public Interest Litigation Project, 2020). The implication of the ruling was that the system could no longer be used and the Dutch state did not appeal the ruling, claiming that the system had by that time shown itself to be inefficient, failing to add any value to fraud detection (The Public Interest Litigation Project, 2020).

The Online Compliance Intervention (OCI) – dubbed 'robodebt' – a debt recovery scheme introduced in Australia in 2016, prompted an ombudsman's investigation, a senate investigation and a strike by employees in the relevant administrative welfare department rolling out the scheme in 2017 (Whelan, 2020). The intervention sought to save the state time and money by outsourcing responsibility previously exercised by the service to welfare recipients themselves. They were requested by letter to submit documentation within a specified timeframe to explain discrepancies between benefits received and income declared to the tax office. After document submission by a welfare recipient, a positive outcome or a debt notification followed a period of waiting. Expanded data-matching by OCI links the relevant welfare support office (Centrelink) to the police and the courts. This means that outstanding arrest warrants may result in reduction or suspension of welfare payments for claimants (Whelan, 2020). It was widely challenged on many grounds including its incorrect assessments, its illegality, its mode of responsibilisation of welfare recipients, its communication and support deficits, its form of coercive debt collection and its damaging impact on democratic governance (Braithwaite, 2020). Despite investigations requesting that the intervention be put on hold, the Australian government continued with it and expanded it (Whelan, 2020). The government only announced its intention to disband it in 2020 after it was deemed illegal by the Australian Federal Court in 2019 (Staines et al, 2020). The opportunity to exercise greater visibility and surveillance of persons living remotely in Australia (predominantly Indigenous people) using welfare and employment services, is increasingly made possible by information technology (Fowkes, 2019).

In Denmark, where a shift has taken place from viewing single mothers as deserving in the 1990s to undeserving in recent years and particularly from 2010 onwards, they have been the focus of negative media coverage and targeted as the constituency of welfare claimants most likely to commit welfare fraud. Jørgensen (2018: 173) suggested that the shift in perception was possibly due to a concentration of poor undereducated ethnic women in this group, who are required to prove they are genuine singles to access a particular payment. They find themselves subjected to a paternalistic monitoring of their conduct for signs of irresponsible living. Identified as at greater risk of committing fraud, control units in local municipalities, which are responsible for investigating fraud, monitor their Facebook profiles, track movements in and out of their houses and employ a range of other intensive data-gathering and surveillance measures towards investigating if they are genuine singles. According to Jørgensen (2018) their treatment accentuates the perception of them as being criminal rather than in need of welfare and support.

Furthermore, as shown by Eubanks (2018) the data mining that such technologies permit, fuel culture of poverty theses. She highlighted the actions of a Republican governor's administration in Maine in the United States in 2014. His office compiled a list of transactions in which TANF (Temporary Assistance for Needy Families) recipients withdrew cash from ATMs in cigarette and alcohol retail outlets and out-of-state locations and then released this data to the public as 'evidence' of TANF families defrauding the system. This prompted legislative measures, requiring TANF recipients to maintain cash receipts for audit purposes and banning out-of-state ATM use for TANF recipients; measures which were neither practicable or enforceable. Eubanks (2018) argued that the legislation was immaterial as the impulse was to direct stigma at welfare provision by characterising its recipients as persons who were immoral, lazy, addicted spendthrifts. Eubanks (2018) also documented the many cases of automation and datafication, which have gone wrong in the USA, but which have led to wrongful accusations of fraud and the withdrawal of persons' and families' benefits, thus exacerbating their hardship. She compellingly argues, supported with evidence, that in contemporary societies we have established the 'digital poorhouse' from databases, algorithms and risk models to manage the poor and to evade our responsibilities to end poverty (Eubank, 2018: 12–13). The use of artificial information technologies is still relatively marginal to discussions about welfare reform and it is only emergent in critical social policy scholarship (Staines et al, 2020).

The response to COVID-19 relied heavily on digital innovations in so many ways and the evidence suggests they constitute a double-edged sword. In the field of public health, contact tracing, symptom-tracking apps, quarantine surveillance and digital immunity certification were all made possible with the assistance of digital technologies (Madianou, 2020). However, significant concerns are being raised about the use of these technologies beyond public health and for their deployment in future in ways not originally intended (Madianou, 2020). As a forerunner in the digitalisation of its public sector, Denmark's welfare encounters are increasingly digitalised and citizens are expected to be or become 'digital natives' (Schou and Svejgaard Pors, 2018). However, new patterns of exclusion are becoming evident as the most vulnerable citizens, such as homeless persons, the elderly, persons with disabilities, mental health problems and drug addictions, risk losing out on their entitlements due to the challenges they experience engaging with self-service solutions (Schou and Svejgaard Pors, 2018). The use of digital technologies in welfare advance privatisation agendas, make new forms of management and surveillance possible and in ways that can be more far-reaching than anticipated. These will undoubtedly require much greater scrutiny into the future in societies where reductive and stigmatising rhetoric about the lives of benefit claimants proliferates in the social and cultural spheres. It is this topic to which we now turn.

Culturalising poverty: the subjectification and stigmatisation of welfare recipients

Politicians and media interests who desire to treat all or categories of welfare recipients more harshly seek to manipulate public opinion accordingly. Moral opprobrium directed at categories of welfare recipients, poor and unemployed persons is a recognised feature of many country contexts' television, print and online media. In 2011 in the UK Prime Minister David Cameron reasserted his intention to go to war on welfare culture (Cameron, 2011b). In Ireland, Leo Varadkar, Minister for Social Protection, aspiring political party leader at the time and subsequently Irish Prime Minister, made clear his intentions to lead a party 'for the people who get up early in the morning' (Bardon, 2017).

Criticism of benefit scroungers and welfare cheats is relentless in UK political and media discourses (Hancock and Mooney, 2012; Jensen, 2013; Tyler, 2013; Jensen and Tyler, 2015; Hudson et al, 2016; De Benedictis et al, 2017) but it is also a feature of other country contexts. There has been a proliferation of 'poverty porn' in the last ten years through the media of reality television programmes and documentaries which serve to mobilise pathologies by making available for scrutiny and scorn, poor people' personal lives.[1] Constituting a form of moral tutelage, a host of TV programmes (for example, Nanny 911, Supernanny, The Jeremy Kyle Show) open up poor people's lives to moral scrutiny and judgement, hone in on their individual failings and refer them to the middle-class experts who help them to make themselves over, or to surmount their problems (Hancock and Mooney, 2012: 117). There is no end to the character props that stigmatise welfare recipients and narrate the case for more punitive welfare state reform to de-root a dependency culture in diverse country contexts. There is the 'welfare queen' in the USA, the 'dole bludger' in Australia, 'scroungers' and 'spongers' in Ireland, 'scroungers' and 'benefit broods' in England. As noted by Mink (1995) the icon of the 'welfare mother' or 'welfare queen' pathologised women's dependency on the state in the US context to such an extent that it provided in significant part the discursive reasoning for the neoliberal welfare reforms pursued. Jensen and Tyler (2015) tracked British politicians' use of media stories about families on benefits or the 'benefit broods' which provided them with the ammunition required to support cuts to welfare. In Denmark, Hansen (2019) documented the cases of 'Poor Corina' (2011), a parent depicted as flagrant and immoral for having material goods (for example, a flat-screen TV) and habits (smoker) perceived unbecoming of a welfare recipient and 'Lazy Robert' (2014), who stated his preference for welfare over low-paid menial work; both became 'folk devils' (Cohen, 1972). These gained public notoriety when they were used by politicians to generate public debate on welfare recipients' lack of deservingness and to propagate the view that the Danish welfare state was excessive (Hansen, 2019). In the wake of the 'scandals' of 'Poor Corina' and 'Lazy Robert', changes were made to Danish welfare policy to remedy the 'problems' made evident by these characters (Hansen, 2019). Recovering drug users and persons who have spent time in prison are among those cast as less deserving welfare recipients (Wincup and Monaghan, 2016). In 2016 in Ireland, an announcement that the Irish Health Service Executive and the Irish Prison Service had introduced a scheme to ensure that everyone leaving prison would receive a medical card (entitling them to access certain health services free of charge), generated negative media coverage. Some of it sought to whip up public controversy as to the unfairness of the scheme, suggesting it would anger families and groups (the terminally ill and so on) seeking medical cards (O'Brien, 2016; Shanahan, 2016).

In austerity Ireland, welfare cheats, unemployed persons, immigrants and single mothers were scapegoated and blamed for the 2008 economic crisis and called upon to bear the burden of austerity to a much greater extent than powerful banking and other interests, who actually had a case to answer (O'Flynn et al, 2014). Meade and Kiely (2020: 29) showed that, during austerity, Irish political and media narratives of the squeezed middle were used to denote middle-class hardship and to enable damaging myths about the unemployed to be propagated in the interests of bolstering 'ideological class warfare; legitimising neoliberal austerity and normalising unequal economic relations'. These narratives circulated at the same time as the ESRI, showing that between 2008 and 2013 real incomes for those at the bottom decile of income distribution fell by 22 per cent in comparison with 14.4 per cent for those in the middle-income bracket (Savage et al, 2015). As Jensen and Tyler (2015: 474) argued, the deliberate construction of 'undeserving' and 'immoral' welfare figures operate as 'technologies of control' aimed at disciplining the poor and 'technologies of consent' designed to propagate the required anti-welfare common sense required to justify punitive welfare reforms. The relevance of Jensen and Tyler's (2015) argument is supported by Philip Alston's (UN Special Rapporteur on Extreme Poverty and Human Rights) assessment of British social security policy as being one of the key contributors to poverty and social exclusion due to the value base, which underpinned its programme of austerity after 2010 (Alston, 2019).

A new welfare imaginary?

Notwithstanding complicated public attitudes to welfare provision – positive and negative as well as contested ideas pertaining to deservingness and undeservingness (Jensen et al, 2019), which also vary across countries (Hudson et al, 2016) – there are some reasons to be optimistic about welfare futures. Welfare states futures prompt much debate but there is evidence that they still enjoy public support in countries for diverse reasons (Hemerijck, 2011; Roosma and Van Oorschot, 2017; Taylor-Gooby et al, 2018; Curtice, 2020). While there are forecasts about welfare states' disassembly and possible demise (Rehm, 2020), there are also those who see strengthened and adapted welfare states as vital to addressing the key social, economic and environmental challenges that are confronting us (Ocampo and Stiglitz, 2018).

There is the existence of bottom-up activism and campaigning and no shortage of ideas from NGOs, academics (Williams, 2016; Patrick, 2018a; van Zoonen, 2020) and activists as to what first steps could be taken to move away from the worst excesses of punitive activation and welfare conditionality. In envisioning an alternative future against austerity and the particular orientation of the Conservative/Liberal Democrat coalition government's 'Big Society' agenda in the British context, Levitas (2012) articulated seven key principles as crucial to uphold. These were rethinking what counts as production and wealth, measuring what matters, making sustainability central, prioritising human wellbeing, promoting equality, addressing the quality of work; revaluing care and thinking in terms of the total social organisation of labour; providing universal child benefit and a guaranteed basic income or a citizen's income. Williams (2016) advanced the 7Rs as a repertoire of demands for advancing a future critical social policy. These are redistribution, recognition and representation rights, regulation, resource awareness and relational care or global justice on care. Basic income proposals, alternative conceptions of citizenship and sharing more broadly the overall supply of paid labour are just a few of the alternative approaches being put forward and some of these were given further impetus during the COVID-19 crisis.

There is a body of work by those who desire a future for capitalism but a form of capitalism that better serves people in a more just society (for example, Boushey, 2019; Case and Deaton, 2020). This may point to doors more open than others to instigate policy reform. For example,

Case and Deaton (2020), in the US context, propose a socialised health service, recognition of the role of trade unions, wage subsidies, increases in the minimum wage, better monitoring and regulation of corporations including big pharma and more strategies to prevent upward redistribution to the rich. Boushey (2019), more directly concerned with the impact of income inequality in the USA, advanced a solid set of proposals for much more equitable economic growth.

Political theorist Azmanova (2020a) posits taking the fight to precarity rather than income inequality. She presents precarity capitalism as the latest and more injurious modality of capitalism, which she claims has taken over from neoliberalism and has become more pronounced during COVID-19 pandemic conditions (Azmanova, 2020c). She argues that the structural conditions of precarity capitalism are such that real change is possible. This is because, as she sees it, a much broader alliance of actors can potentially organise around their shared discontent and sense of insecurity related to precariousness and impending loss of livelihood, despite their differential incomes and forms of employment. Therefore, Azmanova (2020b) envisages a way out of capitalism, not by expending energy seeking to overthrow it, but by engaging in a radical subversive pragmatic politics, which works unrelentingly to undermine the production of profit by the pursuit of universal unconditional welfare and investment in social provision and public services.

With reference to the poverty porn culture, Jensen (2014) highlighted the need to disrupt this moment of welfare commonsense and to bring welfare to life socially and culturally. This involved centring the experiences of those on low income and working collaboratively with them to formulate a new welfare imaginary (Jensen et al, 2019), researching up rather than down and using social and mainstream media to challenge welfare stigma and to support local forms of resistance against regressive welfare reform. Newman and Clarke (2009) argued that the values that make us wish to defend welfare states and public provision such as fairness, equality, social justice and citizenship, are co-opted and used in the service of neoliberalism to justify welfare conditionality, activation and to mobilise hostilities against welfare recipients, migrants and others. Part of the political discursive project requires a focus on such values and according to Newman and Clarke (2009), these have to be actively and continually wrestled and detached from their neoliberal articulations and reinvested with meaning.

Social media are being used in tandem with more traditional forms of activism to portray the lived experience of counter discourses to the portrayals of poor people and poor communities in TV and other media. Dole Animators (2013) (https://doleanimators.org.uk/about/), involving a group of benefit claimants working together on an animated documentary and other projects, provides one such example. In response to the TV series *Benefits Street*, there was the Parasite Street (2014) website and associated Twitter account and the 'Positively Stockton-on-Tees' campaign (2014), both of which challenged the media discourse and engaged public audiences (Feltwell et al, 2017). In Aotearoa/New Zealand the #wearebeneficiaries campaign initiated in 2017 by a group of artists achieved some political purchase when they sought to de-stigmatise welfare receipt and to promote solidarity (Meese et al, 2020). Lived welfare experiences gathered via research or related on social media platforms also hold potential for welfare myth-busting and for ill-informed views propagated in media and official discourses to be challenged (Brooker et al, 2015; Hudson et al, 2016). While it is important not to overstate the impact such interventions can have, reframing the narrative can help to galvanise support for public and political support for much-needed policy reform.

Future development of digital welfare looks like it will further hollow out welfare infrastructure and human service provision, advance privatisation of welfare and contribute to the further depoliticisation of poverty due to its emphasis on solutionism (Madianou, 2020). Investment approaches in both the social security and social services fields, can be expected to continue to give significant impetus to big data innovations. They will help along the integration and exchange of information between services, evidence-based service delivery as well as providing the metrics needed to underpin service performance review and accountability requirements. Their potential to create further knowledge for use in dividing practices/them and us, in discriminating against particular groups or subsets of these groups and in representing individuals' lives in ways which significantly diverge from the realities of people's lives, is considerable (Madianou, 2020). The part played by big data in social policy and particularly in governing poverty merits more critical attention in scholarship (Staines et al, 2020) and more public information and debate as to its contribution in advancing or undermining democratic governance. The question posed by Eubanks (2018): 'Does the technological tool being developed or applied increase the self-determination and agency of the poor and would the tool be tolerated if it was targeted at the non-poor?' seems apt in the context of some of the digital welfare innovations profiled in this chapter. There is also merit in her call for the same surveillance spotlight to be put on the dehumanisation and indignity wrought by public assistance, homeless services and child protection services as is being put on state policing of poor people.

In Scotland, a new social democratic social welfare imaginary is in development (Patrick, 2018a). It marks a three-pronged divergence from UK policy, first by its emphasis on less punitive, more comprehensive social security provision; secondly its propagation of progressive social values such as dignity, human rights, equality and fairness and thirdly in its pursuit of good democratic governance and accountability (Wiggan, 2017; Bradshaw and Bennett, 2018). The Child Poverty (Scotland) Act 2017 set statutory targets for Scotland to achieve in the reduction of child poverty – targets, which were abandoned by the British Westminster government (Bradshaw and Bennett, 2018). The Social Security (Scotland) Act 2018 recognises social security as a human right in itself and essential to the realisation of other human rights (Machin, 2020). It also defines social security as a social investment in the people of Scotland, encourages access and avoids sanctions entirely (Alston, 2019). The Scottish government has used the powers at its disposal to enhance benefits, introduce new grants and top up social security payments from those set by Westminster (Bradshaw and Bennett, 2018). It established an independent commission on social security (ScoSS) to hold the social security system and its relevant minister to account. Its new statutory Poverty and Inequality Commission advises the government on anti-poverty and equality policy and monitors policy progress. 'Experience Panels' set up in 2017 engage with 2,400 volunteers from among those who use the social security system, to ensure users have their say in the system's design and operations. The Social Security Charter bolsters the human rights principle at the heart of the legislation by making explicit what persons can expect from the Scottish social security system. While achievements may be modest, given that the Scottish government only has control over a small proportion of its social security and welfare benefits spending (Wright, et al, 2018), its departure from the dominant narrative and policy approach of the UK is very welcome. The positive influence seeping into other social policy fields (for example, immigration policy), as observed by Mulvey (2018), is also noteworthy. Most importantly, the Scottish approach provides a template for countries willing to break away from criminalising poor people via punitive social security policy.

Conclusion

A significant shift from the idea of a right or entitlement to welfare is well underway in some country contexts and there are indicators that anti-welfare policy formation has taken root in different ways and with particular groups in sight. New developments in welfare state regimes seem driven by the desire to control rather than to care, to surveil rather than to service, to stigmatise and punish rather than to assert persons' dignity and human rights. Such is the depth of suffering caused to UK claimants by welfare conditionality that the ' mandatory futile job search' has been likened to the Victorian treadwheel (Wright et al, 2020: 291) and Universal Job Match (Job Vacancy Portal) to the Digital Panoptican (Wright et al, 2020: 287) due to its punitiveness and entrenchment in sanctioning. Failed outcomes in relation to welfare conditionality and activation policies do not prompt alternatives but more of the same, sometimes made more punitive. It is difficult to identify a Western country context where there is no intent by politicians or media to define and divide the strivers from the skivers; to identify some groups of welfare recipients as criminally suspect and to stoke sufficient anti-welfare sentiment to justify more punitive measures cloaked in the language of justice and fairness. It is accepted that indulging in nostalgia narratives (see *Guardian*, 2021) makes little sense in the context of welfare's consistent history in the punitive regulation of poor people (Hudson, 2016), as discussed in Chapter 1. However, we have also sought to offer some tangible proposals for social security and welfare policy change towards better carving out a shared terrain for both crime and social policy futures and as an alternative to the criminalisation of social policy permeating contemporary welfare landscapes.

Note

[1]   'Poverty Porn' media include *Saints and Scroungers* (BBC, 2009); *The Scheme* (BBC Scotland, 2010–11); *We All Pay Your Benefits* (BBC, 2013); *On Benefits and Proud* (Channel 5, 2013); *Skint* (Channel 4, 2013–15); *Ireland's Dole Cheats: Paul Connolly Investigates* (Virgin Media, formerly TV3, 2013; *Benefits Street* (Channel 4, 2014) and *Britain's Benefit Tenants* (Channel 4, 2015); *The Big Benefits Handout* (Channel 5, 2016); *The Slum* (BBC2, 2016); *Benefits Britain: Life on the Dole* (Channel 5, 2014); *Struggle Street* (SBS Australia, 2015).

4

Criminalising Borders, Migration and Mobility

Introduction

The intense regulation of migration is a central feature of our contemporary 'world order' (Castles et al, 2013) and is, in its current form, closely intertwined with the development of the modern nation-state and the history of colonial imperialism (Soysal, 1994). As will be shown throughout this chapter, the principles of national sovereignty and citizenship and the corresponding attribution of rights to those who are seen to belong shape how welfare and social policy are organised vis-à-vis those who are considered outsiders. The privileging of citizenship when it comes to social policy provision is a largely unquestioned doxic paradigm in our contemporary social imaginary, albeit we know that experiences of belonging and membership are much more complex and contested than governmental practices usually acknowledge (Gonzales and Sigona, 2017).

As in the other chapters of this book, criminalisation is conceptualised broadly and therefore refers, on the one hand, to some of the overtly violent and punitive practices of border policing, detention and deportation, and, on the other hand, to how criminalisation occurs through the operation of the welfare state and liberal (at least on the surface) policies. Overall then, it is proffered that these distinct, yet interrelated forms of criminalisation, regulation and control for those who are deemed to be 'outsiders' of our 'imagined nations' (Anderson, 1983), are similar to the dividing practices deployed by neoliberal welfare states to determine deservingness amongst its citizenry: who is deserving of how much support, who is to be excluded from the circle of rights-holders and how do austerity-driven welfare states continuously refine exclusionary practices, rendering them simultaneously more invisible *and* more insidious and punitive?

The governing rationality of neoliberal governance, which is more 'termitelike than lionlike', 'boring in capillary fashion into the trunks and branches' (Brown, 2015: 35–6) of all aspects of our societies, is the foundational logic of exclusionary practices across all population groups, creating universal precarities beyond boundaries of citizenship. Yet the harmful impacts of exclusionary and criminalising processes affect migrants much more profoundly, as will be discussed throughout this chapter. The status of being a migrant intersects with other precarious social positions, particularly gender, ethnicity and social class, and doubly excludes and criminalises those experiencing migrant status vis-à-vis those who are categorised as insiders by virtue of citizenship. For example, poor migrants are, through their non-citizenship status, affected by an additional 'funnel of expulsion' in the areas of work and welfare (Johansen, 2013). Similarly, when migrants are convicted of a criminal offence, they are usually punished by the respective national criminal justice system, and subsequently also face deportation, therefore exposing them doubly to punitive measures (Stumpf, 2006; Chacón 2009, 2013). They are also excluded from rehabilitative aspects of punishment (Gibney, 2013; Zedner, 2013).

The inclusion of a chapter on the criminalisation of migration as a distinct area of criminalisation of social policy is an acknowledgement of the fact that migration and migrants are now affected by a continuously tighter and widening net of punitive and regulatory measures, while at the same time faced with 'mesh-thinning' imperatives across austerity-driven contexts. The fact that many of the processes discussed in this chapter have moved from the margins of 'migration studies' to the creation of a distinct field of 'crimmigration', 'criminology of borders' and 'criminology of mobility' literature (Stumpf 2006; Chacón, 2009, 2013; Bosworth, 2013; Sing Bhui, 2013; Barker 2017, 2018; Aliverti et al, 2019; Franko, 2019), further signifies the importance of considering the interconnections of punishment, exclusion, regulation and migration.

Similar to the other chapters in this book, it is important to point out that the particular histories, geographical locations and political economies of jurisdictions discussed in this chapter mean that any broad-brushed conclusions with regards to the criminalisation of migration necessarily miss nuance and specificity. Nevertheless, it will become apparent that the criminalisation of migration operates through universally promoted logics, resulting in similar practices of othering, regulation and criminalisation across different jurisdictions and contexts. One of these overarching logics is the continuous meeting of contradictory processes, such as occurs when the contradictory logics of de-bordering simultaneously meet re-bordering practices (De Giorgi, 2010). When it suits the interests of global capital, labour movement is encouraged and facilitated across borders, often under exploitative circumstances, while, on the other hand, nation-states re-border their territories through negating full access to citizen and sometimes even denizen rights, as a result imprinting exclusionary, criminalising and harmful practices on migrants' lives (Aliverti et al, 2019). Despite the various permutations of the criminalisation of migration across different jurisdictions, the criminalisation of migration represents a particular form of universal governance, which 'while institutionally embedded within the nation-state, transcends them' (Aliverti et al, 2019: 242).

The broad-brushed discussion of the criminalisation of migration in this chapter also highlights the way in which policy discourses and practices travel comfortably across the globe and between jurisdictions that usually would not be linked in the process of policy transfer to be drawn out (Dolowitz and Marsh, 2000). During the migrant reception crisis in 2015 in Europe for example, European politicians praised the now partially outlawed practices of detaining refugees on Australian immigration detention islands, even inventing new words in the German language ('Anlandeplatformen'/ 'Landing platforms') to make these problematic practices more agreeable. Again contradictorily, the global circulation of ideas and punitive practices around the criminalisation of migration seem to know no boundaries, while these same practices simultaneously govern through and reinforce imagined boundaries between those who are considered to belong and those who are not.

Finally, it is important to emphasise at this stage, that throughout this chapter, 'migrant' and 'migration' are intentionally used as terms that are not legally defined, but are meant to capture the broad array of experiences of persons who 'move away from their places of usual residence, whether within a country or across an international border, temporarily, and for a variety of reasons' (IOM, 2019: 132). Given the 'backdrop of the insistence on nation states' sovereignty as the underlying tenet of the international legal architecture' (Reyhani, 2020: 8), and as a consequence mirrored in different social policy architectures which remain firmly based on nation-state sovereignty, this chapter is interested in migrants who for *whatever* reason cross international borders. International borders are, of course, a man-made construct and in themselves problematic, as they 'are drawn by the winners in territorial contests with little regard for the cultural integrity or internal social relations of those they displace' (Singleton, 2008: 39).

This chapter will first turn to a discussion of how different nation-states strategically produce outsiders through applying the criminal law with its various punitive strategies to the social practice of migration (Stumpf, 2006), while at the same time making migration law more punitive. But even more than this, the contemporary quest for ever more security, means that the crimmigration project (Stumpf, 2006) 'takes the form of an ever-rising spiral' (Valverde, 2011: 4), resulting in an overall trend of over- or hyper-criminalisation of migrants (Chacón, 2009; De Giorgi, 2010; Bowling, 2013). The governing logic of crimmigration develops a life of its own, continuously adding new permutations to its exclusionary and punitive logics. This suits a neoliberal world order that depends on cheap, flexible and right-less labour forces (De Giorgi, 2010).

Secondly, this chapter will consider the detention and incarceration of migrants as an example of yet another punitive surface onto which even the most inclusive welfare states project their exclusionary bordering practices. Thirdly, we will consider how migrants are now affected by a continuously tighter net of punitive and regulatory measures reaching into all aspects of their life worlds, which are experienced as 'everyday bordering' (Yuval-Davis et al, 2018). Essential to this governmental enterprise is the 'criminalisation by proxy' (Walsh, 2019) that simultaneously involves an ever-increasing array of actors and institutions, such as schools, universities, ordinary civilians and even migrants' own communities, into webs of surveillance and policing. Then another strategy of nation-states jealously guarding their borders when it suits them will be examined, namely the 'criminalisation of solidarity' (Fekete, 2009), where citizens are penalised for opposing the violence of bordering practices by aiding migrants through various means.

Next, it will be shown how the ideology of 'welfare chauvinism' (Andersen and Bjørklund, 1990) has been trans-morphed into a more insidious and unnoticeable ideology of 'welfare nationalism' (Barker, 2017, 2018). This highlights how the imaginary boundaries of the nation and the associated welfare state are used to justify highly exclusionary practices in terms of social policy provision. Problematically, in an increasingly polarised world, this imagined relationship between territory, identity, citizenship and rights is shamelessly capitalised on across the political spectrum, through the construction and vilification of the 'crimmigrant other' (Franko, 2019). Before concluding this chapter, attention will be brought to how the neoliberal state also governs through dividing practices along ethno-racial lines (Bowling, 2013) that are easily activated in societies that are faced with the fallout of neoliberal austerity politics. Supposedly economically sound intentions of welfare nationalism that emphasise the importance of keeping national household finances in good health, provide ample room to deploy socially dangerous ethno-racial othering practices (Barker, 2018). Particularly in the context of the Global North, the discursive as well as materially and legally fabricated connections between terrorism, ethnicities and migration, stigmatise Muslim populations (Fekete, 2004; Galantino, 2020). Finally, against the currently relatively bleak backdrop of hostile environments, the building of walls and seeming normalisation of othering across different parts of our world, the chapter will schematically consider some proposals that transcend earlier calls for post-national welfare landscapes (Soysal, 1994; Isin, 2000), including the right to global mobility (Cassee, 2016). In the current atmosphere of retrogression to and shoring up of national and regional borders, this might seem like rather abstract and wishful thinking. However, the discussion of alternative futures might assist in keeping alive the hope that better global futures are possible.

The strategic production of outsiders: governing migration through criminal law

The term crimmigration was coined in 2006 by the American socio-legal scholar Juliet Stumpf, through which she sought to capture and analyse the increased meshing of immigration and criminal law in the USA over the past 20 years that has led, overall, to the more punitive treatment of migrants (Stumpf, 2006). Summarised succinctly, this 'crimmigration merger' (Stumpf, 2006: 380), means that immigration violations that are not violent or harmful, such as presenting false identity documents so as to be able to work, become reclassified as criminal acts, resulting in the creation of an 'ever-expanding group of outsiders'. Under crimmigration regimes, punitiveness is expanded by entitling 'the sovereign state with certain powers: the power to punish, and the power to express moral condemnation' (Stumpf, 2006: 367).

To illustrate this point it is worthwhile to consider that in the US context, 'by 2005, immigration-related matters represented the single largest group of federal prosecutions, outstripping drug and weapon prosecutions' (Stumpf, 2006: 369). In 2011, about half of all federal criminal prosecutions in the USA were of immigration crimes (Chacón, 2013: 614), with migrants serving as easily available fodder for the machinery of the prison industrial complex (Alexander, 2010). Detention rates for persons committing 'immigration crimes', which in substance are mostly 'misdemeanors', are higher than for those committing violent crimes or drug-trafficking offences (Chacón, 2013: 632), indicative of migrants' outsider status.

While the contentious nature between citizenship, rights and belonging is central in migration studies more generally (Brubaker, 1992; Joppke, 2010), the specific use of criminal law to assert state sovereignty is particularly interesting when thinking about the criminalisation of social policy. Going back to the mid-nineteenth-century US context, Stumpf shows how state sovereignty was appropriated in the context of violent colonialism through the very introduction of punishment through criminal law: 'Justice Taney located the federal government's power to prescribe criminal law within Native American tribal territory in the inherent sovereign power to control the territory within its boundaries' (Stumpf, 2006: 410). Criminal law was thus expressively used to subjugate Indigenous populations to settler rule and establish state sovereignty, rather than to deal with criminal behaviour. The inherent punitiveness of regulating migration is also evident if one considers how criminal law and immigration law both draw on the same expressive functions of punishment by appropriating 'the power to exact extreme sanctions and the power to express society's moral condemnation' (Stumpf, 2006: 410). Both civil immigration and criminal law fulfil the same social function of creating 'insiders' and 'outsiders' (Stumpf, 2006: 380). The rise of crimmigration regimes also parallels broader societal changes, moving punitive ideologies from the 'rehabilitative ideal' dominating the Global North until the early 1980s, towards the 'new punitiveness' of advanced liberal societies (Garland, 2001), which emphasises prevention and risk management.

Since the initial theorisation of the crimmigration paradigm, and fuelled by anti-austerity politics and securitisation agendas, one can observe further permutations and intensifications of the criminalisation of migration, resulting in what some scholars have coined the 'hypercriminalisation' (De Giorgi, 2010) and 'overcriminalisation' (Chacón, 2013) of migration, which is signified through the continuous adding on of new institutional and legal forms of criminalisation. Central to this observation is that 'core principles of the criminal law are imperilled by many immigration offences' (Zedner, 2013: 51), including principles such as fair warnings, culpability or most importantly the 'harm' principle: 'in respect of many immigration offences it is unclear what the harm, or putative harm, is. ... Taken together these lapses raise profound questions about the justifiability of criminalizing illegalities by immigrants where these do not meet the basic precepts of criminalization' (Zedner, 2013: 51).

Overcriminalisation has the effect that it is near to impossible for migrants to shed the labels or harmful experiences that they face as migrants. Aliverti et al (2019: 243) liken these deep and wide criminalisation processes as the imprinting of labels or tags on persons with migration experiences: 'like a mini barcode tags glued to travellers' suitcases, they are almost impossible to remove, and can be easily read at various checkpoints, such as immigration-criminal justice and welfare systems in the countries of destination'. Similarly, Yuval-Davis et al (2018) trace how overcriminalisation of migration is experienced as 'everyday bordering' by those affected by it. They argue how, for example, the 2014 UK Immigration Act introduced bordering processes which reached 'more deeply into everyday life', making it harder for irregular migrants to find work, engage in education or access health care (Yuval-Davis et al, 2018: 233). Importantly, these authors' interviews with London residents with different types of citizenship status show how everyday bordering, while more disproportionately affecting those from ethnic minorities, was experienced by all migrants, even those with privileged labour and citizenship status, such as EU nationals working as middle managers. Further, they argue that in a more invisible way than the post-9/11 securitisation agendas of UK immigration policy, contemporary forms of 'everyday/everywhere bordering', threaten 'to destabilise the conviviality of multiethnic metropolitan London, the rest of the UK and other European societies' (Yuval-Davis et al, 2018: 239).

But it is not only the intensification and diversification of the criminalisation of migration that leads to the overcriminalisation of migration. Migrants are also differentially affected by the criminal justice system itself, a system that is confined by the boundaries of nation-states. In the English and Welsh context for example, Aliverti et al (2019) show how immigrants faced with criminal charges are more likely to be handed down prison sentences and less likely to be sanctioned by various probation orders, due to their lack of social and family supports. Migrants' lack of connections and support networks make these alternative sanctions less attractive than incarceration to sentencing judges (Aliverti et al, 2019: 250). A local barrister cited in Aliverti et al's (2019) research explains how the criminal law is a priori limited by the outsider status of migrants: 'The judges and the criminal justice system have serious restrictions to deal with this population [people with irregular migration status, without family, address, regular work]. There are options not opened to them. The only option is to free them or to send them to prison, no option of granting a community order or a suspended sentence. (interview, defence lawyer 1)' (Aliverti et al, 2019: 250).

Similarly, Aliverti et al (2019) show how sentencing judges' lack of access to information about a person's past can be used against migrants in criminal trials. For example, they cite from an interview with a probation officer who reflects on their experience of writing a pre-sentence report for a young Vietnamese man, pleading guilty for the cultivation of cannabis: 'as far as one can establish, this is the defendant's first conviction, however it is always frustrating to the report writer that we do not have access to any potential antecedents overseas ...' (Aliverti et al, 2019: 249). The absence of information, 'casts doubts on the individual's past' (Aliverti et al, 2019: 249), because of their precarious status and unknown background, due to their migratory experiences.

By the same logic, migrants were also affected by the restructuring of the English and Welsh probation service from 2013 onwards. Under the 'payments by result' contractual modality for the newly established – and now abandoned – mostly for-profit-based community rehabilitation companies (CRCs), those perceived as more difficult clients were less likely to be offered appropriate supports by a thinned-out probation service. Overwhelmed with bigger workloads and impersonal but cheaper solutions like tele-supervision, migrants with possibly more complex circumstances and less local support could more easily fall through the net of support under different probation arrangements (Burke et al, 2018). The same applies to social reintegration after prison, where the absence of entitlements to welfare supports can mean that 'post-sentence supervision can be ineffective for achieving social reintegration and curving reoffending' (Aliverti et al, 2019: 250). Criminal justice systems, while limited by national and local contexts, thus have consequences for migrants that transcend these contexts across time and space. This is glaringly obvious in relation to situations where deportations are the consequence of criminal sanctions. Border control is prioritised over this incongruence: 'decisions made in local courts affect places and people far from where the crime was committed. In these cases, too, punishment reaches back into people's lives and forward into their futures, as their past successes, children, hopes or aspirations are all disregarded in the name of border control' (Bosworth, 2019: 82).

An exploitation of contradictions: the criminalisation of migration

It has almost become a truism to state that the criminalisation of migration is exemplified by the contradictions of an increasingly globalised world and a simultaneous shoring up of boundaries. The criminalisation of migrants and migration is closely intertwined with the idea of the nation-state, which, as a consequence, gives preferential treatment to those who are deemed to have close enough ties so as to also derive rights from it. The seemingly unbreakable, if also artificial, tie between nation-states, citizenship and access to rights, is underpinned by 'membership theory' (Stumpf, 2006). Membership theory, 'restricts individual rights and privileges to those who are members of a social contract between the government and the people ... [and] provides decision makers with the justification for excluding individuals from society' (Stumpf, 2006: 367). Ultimately therefore, the criminalisation of immigration is facilitated by the unfettered and continued belief in state sovereignty (Reyhani, 2020) and its associated powers to exclude and punish.

However, sovereignty is being severely limited by globalisation and the intentional deregulation of global capital and labour markets (De Giorgi, 2006). With this in mind, it is useful to conceive of the criminalisation of migration as a governmental tool used to supply and control cheap labour from global and regional peripheries to the Global North, while the same machinery simultaneously invents new mechanisms to intensify such criminalisation. The criminalisation of migration, is therefore best understood as a contradictory yet useful strategy for neoliberal welfare states: 'this punitive shift is part of an emerging framework of penal and extra-penal regulation of migrations in which the illegalization and the hyper-criminalization of immigrants work symbiotically toward the reproduction of a vulnerable labor force, suitable for the most exploitative sectors of the post-Fordist economy' (De Giorgi, 2010: 153). When suitable, migrant labour is welcomed and sometimes actively recruited and the 'increasingly flexible and de-regulated neoliberal economy' is activated to increase the wealth of capitalist classes (De Giorgi, 2010: 153). The operation of criminal law itself, combined with the marginal social positions of migrants, contributes substantially to the overcriminalisation of migrants. At the same time, the sovereign state maintains the right to exclude the vulnerable labour force that is produced through and considered 'suitable for the segmented labor markets of post-Fordist economies' (De Giorgi, 2010: 147).

While the activation of such contradictory logics is not entirely new, the subordinate and marginalised positions of migrants have been magnified by austerity politics pursued since the 2008 financial collapse. The Spanish government, for example, like those in many other European countries, responded with severe austerity measures in 2011 and 2012, which decreased labour rights, increased labour market flexibilisation and cut social benefits drastically, resulting in increased precarity of all workers' jobs, but which more severely affected migrant workers. Job losses affected low-skilled migrant workers much more severely (Wonders, 2017: 15).

Another interesting example that illustrates how crimmigration regimes continuously find new ways of projecting migration control issues onto new canvasses was the attempt by the French government to move the country's labour inspectorate from the General Directorate of Employment into the immigration ministry (Fekete, 2009). As a result of trade union protests, based on the argument that 'it was wrong for them [trade unions] to play an active role in the government's fight against illegal immigration or incorporate them into the Aliens Police Force' (Fekete, 2009: 89), the move did not come about. Nevertheless, it is indicative of the governing logic of advanced liberal strategies to criminalise migration, particularly in relation to workers. Another axis along which the themes of labour, criminalisation and migration intersect is the refusal to allow asylum seekers, who are usually faced with having no or very limited access to domestic labour markets, to work. By denying asylum seekers the right to work, states are engaging in a form of structural violence (Canning, 2017). Asylum seekers, often skilled and highly motivated, are condemned to poverty and an existence at the fringes of society. The juxtaposition of governments' efforts to activate the unemployed underclass of citizens into labour markets, as discussed earlier, is diametrically opposed to the denial of the right to work of asylum seekers. Access to labour markets, even more so in times of austerity, remains a highly guarded national treasure. Locating her arguments in austerity-ravaged England and Wales, Canning (2017: 68) aptly notes how in both cases of asylum seekers and citizens, austerity is the common denominator which stigmatises and criminalises both groups by limiting access to labour markets: 'Austerity is thus further used as a tool to divide not only the "haves and the have nots" in welfare terms but also, in the case of citizens and non-citizens, the "should haves and should have nots"' (Canning, 2017: 68).

The immigration raid on an agroprocessing plant in Postville, in the US state of Iowa in 2008, offers a good example showing how the precarity of labour intersects with an ever-tightening legal machinery of crimmigration. The Postville raid was at the time the biggest workplace immigration raid in the USA and was heavily militarised. Nine hundred Immigration and Customs Enforcement (ICE) agents were deployed, 'including armed officers and a UH60 Black Hawk helicopter, to arrest 389 employees, 98% of whom were Latino' (Novak et al, 2017: 840). Just over 300 workers from 1,000 present, the large majority Latino, were subsequently detained for prosecution. Faced with the fear of lengthy pre-trial detention and a two-year prison sentence, 297 of them entered into a mass plea bargain, pleading 'guilty to aggravated identity theft based on their use of false documents to obtain employment' (Chacón, 2009: 144). As a result of this mass plea bargain, the large majority of defendants spent five months in prisons before being deported. The use of demeaning practices, such as the reported chaining together of defendants during hearings, shows the violence used here by authorities in addition to already overly punitive practices. Chacón also showed how many aspects of the Postville trial did not satisfy the usual procedural standards and safeguards for the administration of justice: 'many of those who pled guilty to aggravated identity theft probably did not satisfy the mens rea requirement of the charge because they had no knowledge that they were taking the identity of an existing person' (Chacón, 2009: 144). One of the key markers of the crimmigration merger is indeed that for migrants, the 'basic values of due process, fairness and equality of treatment and outcome, are drawn into question. As a consequence, justice itself is transformed' (Bosworth, 2019: 83).

Subsequent research has tragically shown how the harms committed by the Postville raid and subsequent trial have literally been imprinted (Aliverti et al, 2019) on migrants' bodies. The traumatic raid offered public health researchers a quasi-experimental research context, in which they could investigate the direct effects of the raid on migrants' health, and compare it with previously available health data. As a result, they showed that in the state of Iowa, 'infants born to Latina mothers had a 24% greater risk of LBW [low birth weight] after the raid when compared with the same period 1 year earlier' (Novak et al, 2017: 839). The case demonstrates how vulnerable migrant workers, particularly women, are exposed to the violence of immigration control practices and how once the crimmigration machinery is in motion, it is difficult to halt. In the quest to make the machinery more effective, new permutations are added, intensifying the impact of criminalisation upon migrant workers.

It is important to keep in mind that it is the vast global and regional social inequalities which have been intensified through processes of globalisation, and which form the backdrop to the criminalisation of migration, particularly with impacts on vulnerable labour forces. Beneficiaries of globalisation have been able to capitalise on the 'de-bordering' (DeGiorgi, 2010: 151) of financial capital and labour markets, while poorer populations are increasingly regulated by a 'simultaneous re-bordering' across the Global North (De Giorgi, 2010: 151). The apparent crumbling of boundaries is accompanied by ever more intricate ways to regulate and penalise migration, affecting the global poor disproportionately: 'borders have thus resumed all their symbolic and material violence against specific categories of people (under-privileged, non-western, "Third-World" migrants) who, as a consequence of the marginal position they occupy in the transnational circuits of production, are locked in the lowest regions of what Zygmunt Bauman (1998: 69–76) has called the "global hierarchy of mobility"' (De Giorgi, 2010: 151).

Taken together, these examples show how the use of criminal justice systems to deal with the social problem of migration, the exploitation of vulnerable labour forces and the restrictive access to welfare, are interwoven through mutually reinforcing mechanisms: 'the functional equivalence and aggregate effect of seemingly unrelated state policies and practices regarding matters of welfare, employment and criminal justice ... bolster, simultaneously as well as cumulatively, migrants' exploitability in the labour market' (Cheliotis, 2017: 79). It is not only the continuous tightening and modification of criminal law that fortifies crimmigration regimes, but it is also the migrants' precarious social position that affects them when facing criminal law as it does when accessing social policy provision: 'the law operates in complex ways to produce the differential inclusion of certain groups' (Aliverti et al, 2019: 248).

The detention of unwanted bodies

When the shoring up of borders doesn't work, nation-states turn to the detention and incarceration of migrants. Contemporary prisons across all of our societies remain in large part 'poor houses', disposing of those members of society who are not able to compete in our neoliberal and highly unequal societies (Ruggiero, 2018). From this perspective, the detention of migrants has to be equally understand as the most extreme form (apart from death and torture) of criminalisation of social policy, in this instance of nation-states' take on migration and mobility. As can be seen globally, but particularly across the Global North, 'immcarceration' (Kalhan, 2010, in Bowling, 2013), or the incarceration of migrants, has become a normalised response to punish and contain mobility (Bloch and Schuster, 2005). Unwanted bodies are confined in makeshift camps in the near vicinity of popular holiday destinations, such as the infamous camps of Moria, confined on remote off-shore islands such as Nauru and Manus, or locked up in cages along the US/Mexican border. But even closer to home, immigration detention has become normalised through custom-built immigration detention centres – immigration removal centres – and is equally visible in the high incarceration rates of migrants across national prison estates (see Aas and Bosworth, 2013, esp. part II; also see Wadia, 2015).

One of the strong indicators of the intensifying carceral net of social control for migrants is that even in traditionally less punitive penal climates, incarceration and detention of migrants has been on the rise for the past two decades. Wacquant compares the over-incarceration of post-colonial migrants in Europe to that of black Americans in the US prison industrial complex: 'the massive over-incarceration of postcolonial immigrants in the EU ... turns out to be steeper in most member states than the over-incarceration of black Americans across the Atlantic-a revealing yet little-known fact that is either overlooked or denied by continental criminologists' (Wacquant, 2014: 1696). The stark rise from the early 2000s onwards in incarceration rates of migrants across European prisons, confirms this. De Giorgi (2010) constructs a 'hyperincarceration factor', comparing incarceration rates for citizens and immigrants. He shows, for example, that in 2007 incarceration rates of third country nationals across the EU were on average 6.2 times higher for migrants than for citizens of EU member states. Italy (14.4), the Netherlands (11.6) and Portugal (10.2) are the countries with the highest 'hyperincarceration' factor, followed closely by Greece (9.9) and Austria (6.9). Based on these figures, De Giorgi suggests that although European penal regimes are usually depicted as much less extensive in comparison with the USA, when it comes to the criminalisation of migrants, one can see 'an unusual intensity of penal practices' across the EU (De Giorgi, 2010: 155).

The strength of the contradictory 'system of inclusion and exclusion' (Bowling, 2013: 298) that contemporary welfare states have constructed vis-à-vis migrants, is further visible when we consider that even penal regimes which would traditionally be considered at diametrically opposed ends apply similarly punitive strategies with regards to the detention of migrants. In their comparative analysis of the phenomenon of dedicated prisons for foreign nationals in Norway and England and Wales respectively, Pakes and Holt (2017: 67–8) show how the percentage of foreign nationals in these separate prisons is much higher in Norway than in England. Whereas in England the percentage of foreign nationals in prisons rose from 8.5 per cent to 13.9 per cent in 2013, it rose from 12.9 per cent to a staggering 33.1 per cent in Norway. This means that every third person incarcerated in Norway is a foreign national. And while both countries saw an increase in their general prison populations in the same time period, the increase is much starker in Norway, where this rise amounts to 385 per cent for foreign nationals when compared to a 33 per cent increase for nationals (Pakes and Holt, 2017: 68). While segregation in prisons depending on national status is often the case, even without explicit prisons for migrants (Ugelvik, 2017), Pakes and Holt (2017) suggest that in the Norwegian case the dedication of a separate prison is indicative of the broader trend of separation and ejection, wanting to permanently exclude migrants, particularly migrants with criminal convictions from Norwegian territory. This is in stark juxtaposition to the usual assumption of Norway being one of the exponents of penal exceptionalism (Pratt, 2008). The janus-faced state (Barker, 2013) with a double vision (Ugelvik, 2013) deals with those who are seen as beyond inclusion using an entirely different penal and welfare landscape than applied to its citizens. The promotion of values of equality and tolerance are prioritised towards those who are seen as belonging to the nation-state. And although Pakes and Holt (2017) concede that prisons generally in Norway remain diverse, they conclude that: 'the prison has become a key site of crimmigration, at least in Western Europe, where foreign nationals are overrepresented in most prison populations' (Pakes and Holt, 2017: 73).

What is problematic about any institutional detention set-up for migrants, is of course that they criminalise migrants both symbolically, as well as materially, and thus fortify the popular image of migrants as others. Symbolically, by segregating asylum seekers into different types of group homes and detention facilities, where individual autonomy is restricted and levels of surveillance significant (Hewson, 2020). The message given by states is clear: you are not welcomed as an equal member in our midst, but are to be contained as cost-effectively as possible until you can *maybe* gain an advanced status of membership, through, for example, an officially granted refugee status.

Debates have emerged in the early twenty-first century as to the similarities and differences between immigration detention facilities and traditional prisons (Kaufman and Bosworth, 2013; Warr, 2016; Turnbull and Hasselberg, 2017). Bosworth (2019: 82) suggests that irrespective of the 'administrative nature of their confinement' 'detainees find many similarities between the two systems and assert over and over again that, "I feel like I'm in prison"'. Franko (2019) argues that crimmigration facilities or 'houses of banishment', are more punitive than traditional prisons, as they 'lack a legitimating discourse and the awareness of due process and rights' and are less transparent and accountable than prisons (Franko, 2019: 69). In addition to penal power, crimmigration institutions also yield productive power (Foucault, 1977) in producing non-citizens, those who are prepared to leave (Franko, 2019: 70). The purpose of punishment in immigration detention thus changes fundamentally from a focus on rehabilitation through disciplinary power, to a focus on deportation and expulsion: 'The panopticon of the prison is transformed into a "banopticon"' (Bigo, 2006) of territorial exclusion and banishment' (Franko, 2019: 70). Perhaps most importantly, one must remember that these outwardly less punitive-appearing institutions due to their location in administrative law and lack of explicit purpose of punishment, nevertheless are experienced as punitive and 'in doing so, they change the role and social purpose of penality' (Bosworth et al, 2018: 39).

Materially, migrants experience in different detention settings pains of imprisonment (Sykes, 1958), that are usually described in relation to the deprivations experienced in prisons (Dullum and Ugelvik, 2012). These deprivations are multiple and include the lack of privacy, the lack of autonomy and also the above mentioned denial of the right to work as direct acts of state violence (Canning, 2017). In the Irish context, research into the much criticised system of 'Direct Provision' shows that asylum seekers feel continuously surveilled (Hewson, 2020) and incentivised to reshape their selves into liberal subjects, while simultaneously being coerced to be actively involved in their self-surveillance (Conlon and Gill, 2013).

Detention centres for migrants are usually also not exposed to the same level of public oversights as prisons and if provided for, often lack credible consequences for the breach of detention standards (Nethery and Holman, 2016; US Department of Homeland Security, 2018). In Spain's Foreigner Internment Centres (CIEs) for example, reports have emerged that since the economic crisis in 2008 conditions in immigration detention have further deteriorated (Jarrín Morán et al, 2012). Detainees are waiting in limbo, sometimes being held without judicial approval and simultaneously with no intention of deportation. Lack of access to legal counsel, inadequate health care and poor facilities further exacerbate their situation (Jarrín Morán et al, 2012).

The pain-inflicting nature of immigration detention has been well documented in different pieces of research with detainees and such research generally agrees that migration detention is equivalent or worse than incarceration (Bosworth, 2013) and experienced as a contradictory form of hostile hospitality (Khoshravi, 2009). Bhatia's (2020) research into the narratives of detained asylum seekers in Britain shows how immigration detention can exacerbate earlier traumas experienced by many asylum seekers and refugees, making the state directly complicit and responsible for 'injuries inflicted' (Bhatia, 2020: 36). One of Bhatia's research participants, Moulay from West Africa, incarcerated for using a fake passport out of fear of being refused asylum, explains how the experience of immigration detention rapidly worsened his health conditions and re-traumatised him: 'I keep on having nightmares. Even when people talk to me, I sometimes cannot hear what they are saying: the noises of prison, people banging the doors, all run in my head – and my head wants to explode at that time … that's why I get panic attacks all the time … I used to have flashbacks in past, but prison made it worst for me. (Interview with Moulay)' (Bhatia, 2020: 40). Similarly, in her research on the detention of migrant women in the UK and in France, Wadia (2015) shows how women feel extremely isolated in immigration detention, due to the often remote location of detention facilities, experience an extremely sparse environment with very little recreational opportunities on offer, are exposed to often inhumane and degrading treatment by staff and generally suffer from violent and insecure conditions. These experiences clearly show through the voices of migrants how immigration detention penalises those who were unlucky in the geographical lottery of birth.

Expanding the carceral net through criminalisation by proxy

In line with neoliberal governing, crimmigration regimes do not exclusively rule by force, but seek to activate partners across civil society in their enterprise of governing the perceived social problem of migration. Through this mode of neoliberal 'nodal governance' (Bayley, 1994), which means that governance does not emanate from one central point, but from and through multiple sites and actors, the state yields its power not by sheer force, but by 'enlisting assistance from non-state entities', 'to undertake previously state monopolized activities' (Walsh, 2019: 333). Civilians, NGOs, schools, universities and employers to name a few are responsibilised into the enterprise of criminalising migration and are thus repositioned as migration control agents 'by proxy' (Walsh, 2019). This produces particularly insidious effects that deepen the criminalisation of migrants significantly, and that regulate all aspects of migrants' life worlds, introducing 'everyday bordering' practices (Yuval-Davis et al, 2018) into the most benign social interactions. By deploying the dividing practice of including citizens in its net of control, regulation and surveillance, resistance and subversion to such bordering practices becomes all the more difficult. The neoliberal crimmigration state also expands its punitive tentacles into citizens' personal and deeply private moral decisions, by penalising when and how it is permissible to help migrants in distress.

In the US context, the strategy of different states and cities designing laws and ordinances that are harsher than federal immigration laws require is not only indicative of the entrenchment of crimmigration ideologies, but, in terms of governance mechanisms, also an example of criminalisation by proxy. Under the 2006 'Illegal Immigration Relief Act Ordinance' issued in Hazelton, Pennsylvania, for example, 'local officials enacted an ordinance that prohibited landlords from renting to noncitizens without legal authorization and also allowed for the revocation of the business licenses of any business owner who employed an unauthorized worker' (Chacón, 2009: 621). Subsequently hundreds of US cities followed suit with similar ordinances and legal provisions, effectively activating citizens to partake in a governmental exercise of criminalisation. Although many of these ordinances did not come into effect and were eventually successfully disputed before higher courts, they are indicative of the hostile anti-immigration environment created and actively driven across different North American cities (ACLUPA, 2014).

In another instance, the State of Alabama issued what became known as the toughest state measure on illegal immigration, the so-called Alabama HB 56 Bill. HB 56 envisaged the criminalisation of every aspect of undocumented migrants' social lives and effectively encouraged migrants to 'self-deport'. Infused with anti-Hispanic racist sentiments (Chacón, 2009), the bill was exemplary in deploying 'governing by proxy' strategies that 'obliged citizens of Alabama to participate in both the shaming of the undocumented migrant and the maintenance of the affective boundary keeping the undocumented migrant body from citizenship' (Lechuga, 2014: 83). In particular, these included the criminalisation of employing or renting property to undocumented migrants and the nullification of any type of contracts when involving undocumented migrants. Providing any type of transport to undocumented migrants in cars, meaning mundane acts such as, for example, offering a lift to a neighbour with undocumented status, were also criminalised under the Alabama HB 56 Bill. Students with an undocumented status were to be banned from attending public colleges and universities. Although the bill stopped short of limiting children's access to public schools, it mandated all schools to report information on enrolled students' immigration status. As such, HB 56 offers an exemplary case of governing by proxy, responsibilising citizens and various public institutions in the enterprise of policing and criminalising migration.

Internationally, the HB 56 Bill became infamously known, as high-profile business managers were arrested under its provisions that furnished the police with powers to demand identification of anyone suspicious of being an undocumented migrant (Pilkington, 2011). Although HB 56 has experienced a 'legal rollback', and many of its provisions were blocked by various courts (Mohl, 2016), its impacts on migrant communities were devastating:

Latinos across the state pulled their children from schools and abandoned their jobs in agriculture, poultry, construction, landscaping, restaurants, and service industries. They packed up cars and pickups with their belongings and disappeared into the night, when they were less likely to be stopped by police. In HB 56, there was no account made for 'blended' families in which one spouse held citizenship, or of undocumented immigrants with children who were native-born American citizens. All were equally targeted as undesirable minorities ... Many also remained, living in difficult circumstances under the radar of enforcement agencies. (Mohl, 2016: 48)

The damaging effects of HB 56 also affected migrants' health adversely. Public health researchers showed that not only were Latina immigrants mistreated by clinic staff, the bill had also 'adversely affected access to care for Latina immigrants and their children across multiple dimensions' (White et al, 2014: 398). Criminalisation by proxy through its far reach into local communities' fabric, therefore has to be understood as a very harmful, yet very effective strategy to criminalise and exclude migrants from all aspects of life.

Another prime example of the criminalisation through proxy is the activation of universities as agents made responsible for the governmental enterprise of regulating migration. Education becomes another 'bordering scape' (Yuval Davis et al, 2019: 120) through which governments are attempting to solve the contradictions inherent in neoliberal rule. Contemporary universities generally benefit from and depend on the internationalisation of education, particularly in contexts where universities are increasingly dependent on non-state funds. Walsh (2019) shows how in the USA, the UK and Australia, three of the 'leading recipients of international students' (Walsh, 2019: 327), universities have been enlisted 'within expansive and officially orchestrated infrastructures of surveillance', reflective of 'the public's growing insertion within security networks, outcomes which widen the state's gaze, reach, and disciplinary powers' (Walsh, 2019: 327–8).

The de-bordering and re-bordering logic of late capitalist rule repositions universities as partners in migration control. In the UK context for example, Walsh (2019) shows how the assignment of surveillance duties to universities from 2009 onwards, was part and parcel of a whole raft of measures, including a new Tier 4 visa for non-EU students and mandated check-ins with local police to name a few. As a result of government pressures, some universities have included measures such as introducing electronic card systems and even fingerprinting systems in some, to 'authorize students' capacity to remain within the national space' (Walsh 2019: 332). In this enterprise, lecturers are transformed into proxy immigration officers, who are required to 'act as informants, monitor attendance, and report absent students, with the

CRIMINALISING BORDERS, MIGRATION AND MOBILITY

University of East London automatically deregistering students missing one-quarter of their classes' (Walsh, 2019: 332). Neoliberal governance through responsibilisation and 'membershipping' rather than coercion, is exemplified in these arrangements and 'represents an admission that authorities are incapable of independently detecting illegality and require private actors to shoulder some of the burden' (Walsh, 2019: 334). The contradictory late capitalist logic of bordering and de-bordering permeates contemporary societies at different levels, including international student bodies. On the one hand, national governments have pushed internationalisation agendas 'as a critical means of positioning their countries with the circuitry of the global economy' (Walsh, 2019: 336), while, on the other hand, clamping down on international students' mobility, 'transforming the landscape of international education from a climate of reception and hospitality to one of suspicion and hostility' (Walsh, 2019: 337). Later in this chapter it will be shown how the criminalisation by proxy is also activated as a governance strategy in community-based approaches to terrorism prevention, another key site where civil society institutions are repositioned in the governmental enterprise of criminalising migration.

The criminalisation of solidarity

When governments deploy the strategy of governing by proxy through criminalising solidarity (Fekete, 2009) and securitising their borders, the stakes seem somewhat higher, considering that showing solidarity with migrants who face life-threatening circumstances, can decide over life or death. By criminalising solidarity with migrants as part of their border-shoring strategies, nation-states enter deeply into the soul of their citizens, requiring them to subsume their personally held ethical norms to the stubborn ideology of borders.

The criminalisation of solidarity with migrants is indeed nothing new and has a history that in Europe has become particularly pronounced since the early 2000s, when the EU adopted the 2002 EU Directive and Framework Decision on 'Strengthening the penal framework to prevent the facilitation of unauthorised entry, transit and residence' (Council Directive 2002/90/ EC of 28 November 2002), the so-called Facilitator package. The Directive was primarily/officially aimed at curbing human trafficking and 'required member states to create offences of directly and indirectly aiding the unauthorised entry, movement or residence of non-EU nationals' (Fekete, 2009: 84). However, as a result of the broad definitions used in the Directive, numerous jurisdictions have seen initiatives and practices taking hold that penalise both individuals as well as organisations who practise solidarity with migrants, often by offering essential and life-sustaining support (Macanico et al, 2018; Resoma, 2020). A whole variety of acts of civil disobedience, including sea and land rescues of migrants, airport deportation protests and even the provision of medical assistance have been criminalised in these broad sweeping attempts to fortify the borders of Europe. The Directive also enabled states to criminalise shelters and service providers, charging small fees or donations for their services, ranging from individuals providing lifts or shelters to NGOs and volunteers in border zones providing the most basic services, including the provision of food, shelter, showers, medical assistance and access to justice and so on (Resoma, 2020: 2). In France, for example, an official decree of 2007, although later altered, contained a provision that allowed data to be stored on persons 'providing accommodation to foreigners with no authorisation to stay and on anyone visiting foreigners in detention centres' (Fekete, 2009: 85).

In Greece, Médecins Sans Frontières (MSF) closed its humanitarian project on the island of Lesvos when migrants were poisoned after 'drinking contaminated water from rusty and mouldy pipes' (Fekete, 2009: 88). The Greek authorities had intentionally underserviced the refugee camp on Lesvos, thus undermining the work of medical humanitarian organisations such as MSF. In Spain, a new law was passed in 2009, designating severe fines for those 'who facilitate the irregular stay of a foreigner after having provided them with a letter of invitation to travel to Spain' (Domínquez–Mujica et al, 2014: 119). In line with neoliberal governing, the criminalisation of solidarity demands every citizen join in the governing project of criminalising migration, or otherwise risk punishment: 'The objective of criminalization of these forms of migrant solidarity is to intervene in existing social relations, creating the condition for every citizen to become a border guard, responsible for checking the immigration status not only of their tenants, employees, students and patients, but also of the people they meet on the street, exchange a meal with, host in their houses' (Dadusc and Mudu, 2020: 20).

In Europe, this criminalisation of solidarity has become even tighter and more heavily militarised since the refugee reception crisis of 2015, when millions of displaced migrants tried to reach Western Europe (Rea et al, 2019). Systematic legal and discursive attacks portraying, framing and persecuting solidarity with migrants, have seen a hostile environment emerge all across Europe. The European research platform ReSoma (Research for Social Migration and Asylum) identified that by 2019 at least 171 persons have been criminalised in at least 60 cases and criminal prosecutions for showing solidarity with migrants across 13 member states of the EU (ReSoma, 2020). The large majority of these were based on the crime of 'facilitation of entry or transit', followed by 'facilitation of residences' as causes for prosecution.

In Italy, the Salvini Decrees of 2018 and 2019, named after the anti-immigration Italian interior minister at the time, introduced extremely harsh and punitive anti-immigration measures, penalising both migrants as well as, particularly, those who manned sea rescue boats. The 2018 Salvini decree abolished the so-called humanitarian protection permit, which 'contributed to an increase in negative decisions on asylum applications from 67 percent in 2018 to 80 percent in the first 10 months of 2019' (HRW, 2019). The 2019 Salvini decree introduced fines of up to 1 million euros for sea captains failing to obey orders of police or navy ships defying a ban to enter Italian waters (HRW, 2019). In her letter to the Italian authorities, the UN High Commissioner of Human Rights (OCHCR) expressed stark concern that the 2019 Salvini decree was in breach of international human rights law and 'represented yet another political attempt to criminalise sea and rescue operations' and that it intensified 'the climate of hostility and xenophobia against migrants' (OCHCR, 2019: 2–3).

A prominent example of the criminalisation of solidarity was the arrest in 2019 of the German sea captain Carola Rackete, when she decided to enter into Italian waters with the NGO sea vessel *Sea-Watch 3*, to bring 42 rescued migrants on shore. Rackete was arrested for defying orders issued by Salvini as well as for 'violence against warships' (Maritime Executive, 2020). Shortly before, the European Court of Human Rights had rejected the migrants' appeal that would have granted them safe harbour (EFE News Service), indicating the strength of the wider European bordering consensus. Showing very clearly the populist appeal of the criminalisation of solidarity ideology, Salvini at the time commented live on his social media platforms that Rackete would have to face consequences for her decision to save human lives. Italy 'was not a travel agency' and Italy was 'ready to block any kind of illegality' and the 'ship captain will pay the consequences' (EFE News Service, 2019). Rakete was released from house arrest before long and subsequently Italy's Supreme Court of Cassation upheld the release (Maritime Executive, 2020).

The securitisation agenda of European borders has indeed become so dominant that even military priorities have become subsumed under its auspices. In March 2019, the EU decided to cancel the naval mission 'Sophia', which used boats to patrol the Mediterranean between Libya and the EU to conduct military surveillance of the arms embargo on Libya (Amjad, 2020). The EU decided to shift its military surveillance from a sea operation to air and drone surveillance. It was argued through a very warped logic, that the absence of the sea vessel would deter further migrants from trying to make their way to Europe and therefore contribute to saving lives. In an official statement, Frontex suggested that 'all parties involved in SAR operations in the Central Mediterranean unintentionally help criminals achieve their objectives at minimum cost, strengthen their business model by increasing the chances of success. Migrants and refugees – encouraged by the stories of those who had successfully made it in the past – attempt the dangerous crossing since they are aware of and rely on humanitarian assistance to reach the EU' (Frontex, 2017: 32, cited in Dadusc and Mudu, 2020: 18). The vilification and criminalisation of human traffickers has become such an accepted logic in mainstream political circles (Pickering and Weber, 2013; Prosinger and Thomma, 2017) that its suppression is prioritized over saving human lives.

It seems plausible to also consider the argument that governments engage in the criminalisation of solidarity so as to render their own lack of solidarity invisible. The activist group Alarm Phone, for example, explains governments' concerns of being surveilled when 'illegal returns of refugees under the eyes of Frontex and NATO are more likely to happen in the absence of civil rescue boats who can document human rights violations on the sea' (Alarm Phone, 2019). Others suggest that 'civil society actors aiding border crossers in Greece are criminalized because they challenge and interfere with state policies and practices of hostile hospitality' (Schack and Witcher, 2021: 477). In doing so, civil society organisations become repositioned discursively and materially as criminal entities as observed by a MSF representative:

> Since the beginning of our mission, MSF was accused of being a pull-factor, and of undermining maritime safety and security. We were very concerned about the impact of this dominant narrative of NGO search and rescue (SAR NGOs) being a pull-factor (parents would send more unaccompanied children to Europe, and so on) which began in 2016 ... We also saw for ourselves how this criminalisation was manifesting itself through a kind of legal persecution ... But it's very strange to see how EU states respect that law but disregard all other international and European laws. They disregard the Geneva Convention for refugees, they disregard European laws about family reunion, and so on. The same disregard for international law applies in other contexts – beyond Europe. It is something that is becoming global. And it is obvious in a securitised approach to borders in all high income States, the Global North, whatever we like to call it. (Webber, in Fekete, 2018: 69–70)

Criminalising through welfare exclusion

The 'internal logics' of the welfare state always 'depend on exclusion' (Barker, 2018: 18); however, for migrants, these exclusionary practices are more manifold and the 'accumulating effects of borders' (Aliverti et al, 2019: 254) shape social policy for migrants, and in particular poor migrants, more restrictively. The overlap between the regulation, exclusion and criminalisation of migrants is, as for social policy subjects in other parts of this book, very fluid.

Franko's (2019) term of 'bordered penality' is useful when considering how contemporary welfare states and regional entities such as the EU continuously express the outsider status of migrants through ensuring that benefits and rights exist exclusively for those who are considered to belong. Although ethno-racial discourses and right-wing ideologies usually underpin practices of bordered penality, its governing logic reaches much deeper, appealing to the mostly unquestioned link between the nation-state, citizenship, identity and belonging. As a consequence, 'bordered penality' is now also routinely used by the political mainstream, symbolically upholding the sense of the nation, albeit this also is an imagined concept (Anderson, 1983). Franko's work on 'bordered penality' is undertaken in the Norwegian context, which has one of the strongest welfare rights regimes globally, thus making the emergence of this concept all the more interesting. She questions how a nation-state which is particularly keen on values of equality and inclusion can justify the exclusion of non-nationals from the rights it so strongly defines as core to its identity. Franko explains that these exclusionary practices allow the nation-state to assert its dwindling authority in the global context of neoliberalism and apparent threats to national identity, but importantly also to reassert its authority against those who do not possess citizenship. 'Bordered penality' expresses the 'intrinsic boundedness of the welfare state, where its normative framework of social equality and inclusion reveals itself to be universal exclusively within the boundaries of citizenship' (Franko, 2019: 110). Limited access to welfare rights for migrants therefore asserts this boundary *both* materially as well as symbolically.

Even in the context of the EU, where freedom of movement forms such a central pillar of the political consensus, the freedom is primarily reserved for workers, and it is severely limited in terms of social rights (Pennings, 2015). What this means in practice, is that European citizens from poorer European regions are a priori less mobile than their wealthier counterparts, putting into question claims that we may be moving towards any form of post-national citizenship in the EU (Soysal, 1994; Sassen, 2002).

The prioritisation of economic over social citizenship in the EU context was clearly reflected in a landmark ruling involving a 25-year-old Romanian single mother, living in Germany and in receipt of some minimal benefits for her young child. The European Court of Justice ruled that the refusal to pay unemployment benefits to her was justified, as she couldn't prove that she was looking for work, and therefore the anti-discrimination rules of the EU did not apply (Meingast, 2014). The ruling thus reaffirmed the foundational linkage between work and access of rights with regards to the European freedom of mobility. Even in a relatively limited geographical and cultural, yet highly unequal, space, this shows how welfare rights remain deeply contested and firmly in the hands of nation-states. Just as the pursuit of curbing welfare cheating has become a central strategy in many national contexts, as outlined earlier in this book, EU member states' concerns over welfare tourism have become so significant that they are fast eclipsing the free movement principle in the EU (Hansen, 2015). In the aftermath of austerity politics, we have indeed witnessed the emergence of a political consensus amongst wealthy European nations, that poor migrants from the periphery of Europe are unwanted, unless they are required by labour markets (Hansen, 2015). In a joint letter to the Irish EU presidency of 2013, Austria, Britain, Germany and the Netherlands, explicitly addressed their unease with European social citizenship, framing it as a problem of 'poverty migration': '[t]his type of immigration burdens the host societies with considerable additional costs, associated with the extra provision of schooling, health care and adequate accommodation'. The letter requested that concrete measures be taken: '[a]ll necessary measures need to be taken to deal with the consequences of this type of immigration and to fight its causes. This includes legal as well as financial measures' (Letter to Mr Alan Shatter, 2013).

What becomes clearly visible here, is how European bordered penality towards peripheral regions globally is mirrored vis-à-vis poorer regions within its own political entity: 'In fact, these safeguarding manoeuvres towards Africa, on the one side, and the EU periphery, on the other, should be conceived as constituting two sides of the same neoliberal trajectory, such that migration and free movement policies are dissociated, or disembedded, from questions of social incorporation and citizenship' (Hansen, 2015). Just as bogus claimants and welfare cheats are politically and discursively constructed by populist political and media discourses within nation-states, so are welfare tourists accused of the same moral transgression across boundaries. What is comfortably forgotten is, of course, the vast global and regional inequalities that in many instances result in wealthier regions relying on and intentionally attracting cheap labour forces when they so require.

It is also important to remember that migrants' lack of rightful belonging to a particular nation-state means that they are often the first to be hit by welfare retrenchment, as they are not perceived as rights-holders at an equal level as citizens. In Spain, for example, the austerity-ridden government introduced harsh measures in 2012 that reduced access to health care for migrants, by introducing a co-pay system for medicines and removing free health care for irregular migrants, producing a situation that 'was literally life-threatening since irregular migrants often waited to seek medical care until their condition was a crisis' (Wonders, 2017: 18). In Denmark, the Danish People's Party, between 2001 and 2011, introduced social reforms which disproportionately affected migrants: 'These reforms were primarily conducted in the areas of (means-tested) social assistance and (universal) family allowances, and have been instrumental in pushing the universalist Danish model towards a more multi-tiered system in which labour market participation (and hence social insurance mechanisms) becomes more important for determining benefit level' (Kvist and Greve, 2011, in Ensser-Jedenastik, 2018: 308).

The use of bordered penality in social policy measures is also well exemplified by the federal Australian Status Resolution Support Service (SRSS) scheme for asylum seekers, introduced in 2015. Set up as part of a 'gradual shift' (Aliverti et al 2019: 251) to accommodate asylum seekers, more specifically so-called illegal maritime arrivals, in the community, rather than in detention centres, it was designed as a system of support for asylum seekers while their status was being determined. Under the SRSS scheme, asylum seekers receive rudimentary welfare supports according to a classification into different 'bands', including a basic living allowance, casework support and access to torture and trauma counselling services (Australian Refugee Council, 2019). The operation of the scheme has been outsourced to NGOs and is 'marked by extreme complexity, uncertainty and discretion' (Aliverti et al, 2019: 252). Emblematic of neoliberal governance by proxy, case workers are repositioned as surveillance officers, who have to report 'major health events, unaccompanied minors missing school, or SRSS recipients being a victim, perpetrator, or witness to a crime' (Aliverti et al, 2019: 253) to immigration authorities. The support scheme can therefore have a clearly punitive effect, as the surveillance and reporting practice of supporting officers can negatively affect migrants' asylum approval processes. More recently, a behavioural contract has been added to the scheme which recipients have to sign, requiring asylum seekers to comply with very vaguely defined 'acceptable behaviour' that is in line 'with the expectations of the Australian community' (Aliverti et al, 2019: 254). Aliverti et al argue that this further 'injects a quasi-criminal dimension into welfare provision for this group' and means that the 'scheme operates as an internal bordering practice, mediated through federal welfare provision and backed up by the sanction of detention' (Aliverti et al, 2019: 254).

From welfare chauvinism to welfare nationalism

The exclusion of migrants from welfare regimes due to policymakers' pandering to public moods in relation to migrants' deservingness of social rights, has produced rich empirical data over the past two decades (see Ensser-Jedenastik, 2018: 295 for a good overview). Generally, the emphasis is placed on understanding which different principles, for example merit, need or equality, motivate different attitudes towards migrants' deservingness. What can be seen from this literature is how migrants are excluded in the popular imaginary, and therefore easily targeted for exclusion by policymakers as well. Migrants have become the new undeserving poor across many different national contexts (Bommes and Geddes, 2000; Larsen et al, 2018). An interesting qualitative focus group study conducted in Germany in 2016 for example (Heuer and Zimmermann, 2020), identified that the deservingness of migrants was not considered to be a priority across different publics, including the middle class, working class, young and old people. Across all focus groups taken together, immigrants' deservingness was ranked behind that of family, the elderly, low-income and unemployed, and was only followed by a lower ranking given to the 'well-off'. Interestingly, amongst both working-class and elderly focus group participants, migrants were ranked below the 'well-off' in their level of deservingness. The study authors were particularly interested in the reasoning behind these categorisations and noted that the 'rather low deservingness of immigrants was justified with references to (lack of) identity and (lack of) reciprocity, whereas social investment arguments were frequently utilized to justify higher deservingness, but seem to have barely influenced the final ranking of this vignette' (Heuer and Zimmerman, 2020: 397).

A climate of austerity and feelings of deprivation amongst socially excluded populations seem to further intensify these attitudes towards migrants across different EU member states: 'symbolic boundaries between "us" and "them" are more outspoken when a scarce pool of welfare resources is at stake among those who are the most vulnerable' (Reeskens and van Oorschot, 2012: 132). Political parties, particularly amongst the political right, but more increasingly also amongst more centric parties, exploit these feelings of 'welfare envy' by linking the ideas of 'deservingness' to social insurance-based, that is, 'earned', welfare rights benefit payments, versus reserving tax-funded, that is, non-insurance-based, 'compensation benefits for citizens' (Ennser-Jedenastik, 2018: 308).

Traditionally, the concept of 'welfare chauvinism' (Andersen and Bjørklund 1990: 212) seemed useful, as it could explain the symbiosis between right-wing political parties, public attitudes and limited generosity towards migrants as welfare recipients. The term in itself might appear somewhat contradictory, in so far as it captures both 'a leftist welfare stance towards natives with a rightist position as far as non-natives are concerned' (Ennser-Jedenastik, 2018: 294). What can, however, be seen since 2010, is that welfare chauvinism is deployed both by mainstream political parties and also in generous welfare states, making it necessary to broaden our understanding towards a wider concept of welfare nationalism, that is, the intertwining of national identity and welfare rights in mainstream political discourse.

In the Finnish context, for example, Keskinen (2016) shows how political discourse across the party spectrum, that is, not only amongst the political right, commonly uses welfare nationalism to justify differential social welfare provisions for migrants. This seems to be supported by the majority of the population, who tend to be 'less willing to provide welfare benefits to migrants unconditionally and a larger share deem citizenship a central criterion for such benefits than their fellow Nordics' (Keskinen, 2016: 354).

Similarly, Barker's (2017, 2018) work on welfare nationalism offers a more variegated analysis to widely accepted 'neoliberal accounts' (Barker, 2017: 126) of hollowed out welfare states (Wacquant, 2009a). Rather, she argues that welfare nationalism does not only operate in residual welfare states or where austerity dominates, but as part of the construction of the welfare state sui generis. Welfare nationalism seeks to 'keep the welfare state solvent for members' (Barker, 2017: 126–7), but for members *only*. In particular, Barker shows how Roma populations are criminalised and othered in contemporary Sweden, underpinning not only right-wing but also mainstream political strategies. Despite being EU citizens, these populations are 'considered outsiders on two dimensions, first as beggars who are considered not to be legitimate workers but potential drains on the welfare state, and second as foreigners with limits on solidarity as fellow citizens' (Barker, 2017: 127). Much more subtle than overtly exclusionary practices, welfare nationalism operates through othering, which, in the context of more universal welfare regimes, such as in Scandinavia, seems contradictory or counter-intuitive.

The contradictions of welfare nationalism and exploitation of migrant labour become particularly apparent when one considers the recent indexation of child benefit rates in Austria. In 2019, the leading conservative party initiated the indexing of family benefits and family tax relief for children of EU citizens living in other EU member states to their respective national living standards. Appealing to a conservative and right-wing electorate, the government promised that this would save the taxpayer roughly 114 million euros (Kronen Zeitung, 2018). As in most other European countries, residential tax payers in Austria are entitled to a scaled benefit payment ranging from 114 to 165 euros of child benefit per child, depending on the child's age. It is important to note that non-Austrian EU citizens residing in Austria pay social security contributions and taxes equivalent to Austrians. It appears that Austria's indexation move was based on a previous concession by the European Council under pressure from Britain's pre-Brexit referendum negotiations, that confirmed that the indexation of social benefits for EU citizens was compatible with European treaty law (Blauberger et al, 2020). The essential freedom of movement of workers had become undercut by concerns over welfare tourism.

The architects of the Austrian indexing legislation defended their move with little regard of the lived realities of people, arguing that child benefit was a social policy measure and not an income support measure and therefore excluded from European equality legislation. The Austrian child benefit indexation meant that parents of children residing in countries with higher living expenses, such as Switzerland and Belgium, were due a raise of 40 per cent in their monthly child benefit payment, while for those from poorer European countries, such as Romania, faced a 40 per cent reduction in monthly child benefit levels. For example, from 1 January 2019 onwards, a Bulgarian working in Austria received only 51.30 euros in child benefit/ *Familienbeihilfe* compared to 114 euros earlier, or if the child was living in Austria (Blauberger et al, 2020).

The indexation therefore 'mostly affects EU citizens in the low wage sector, for whom generous family benefits constitute a wage subsidy and who may be perceived as a threat in terms of job competition' (Blauberger et al, 2020: 940). Romanian workers in Austria, for example, work mostly in the care and agricultural sectors (AMS, 2016), two sectors, which are nearly entirely dependent on non-Austrian workers (Marhold and Ludvik, 2020). It is also important to highlight that other countries have requested similar moves towards indexation. In 2017, both Irish and German ministers wrote to the European Commission president, requesting that 'indexation should be an option for Member States, and with no reciprocity required', with a somewhat contradictory justification: 'we explicitly support the principle of freedom of movement in the EU. However, we believe that it is necessary to adjust rights arising as a consequence of this principle to reflect changing circumstances and to ensure that this will continue to enjoy acceptance amongst our EU citizens' (Doherty et al, 2017). It is notable that both ministers were from centrist and social democratic parties respectively, suggesting that welfare nationalism appeals across a wide political spectrum.

Quite worryingly, such indexation moves in a political union clearly indicate a different valuation of different parts of Europe. Independent of the actual outcome of the current European Commission-initiated infringement procedure against Austria, such initiatives can be best understood as attempts of national governments to apply their dividing practices across the separation lines of nationality, even in contexts where European legislation explicitly forbids this. Welfare nationalism exerts its powers and regulates access to welfare rights much more stringently for those who are deemed to not fully belong as citizens. But more than this, it shows how European citizens from poorer regions are treated in a differential manner from those from richer regions. As in national social policy, social class and status, and with this the regulation of access to welfare, operate with stigmatising features (Spicker, 2011: 16). In the debates leading up to the indexation of child benefit, welfare recipients from Eastern European countries were represented by political parties of the centre-right and tabloid newspapers as welfare tourists, trying to exploit the Austrian welfare state (Blauberger et al, 2020), rather than the valuable contribution that they make to Austrian society being emphasised. Ironically, the shortage of care and agricultural workers from Eastern Europe was acutely felt during the Corona Crisis in 2020, to such an extent that the Austrian government organised several chartered flights for Romanian workers. The demands of the low-pay labour market in times of restricted European travel made this move politically defensible. The fact that the differentiation in child benefit payments happens in the EU where, under other circumstances, such heavy emphasis is given to the link between work and mobility (rather than citizenship rights more broadly), shows how nation-states seek to retain power over 'everyday bordering' practices (Yuval Davis et al, 2018), so as to reassert their sovereignty and exclude non-citizens.

The deployment of ethno-racial dividing practices

The racialisation of migration policies, everyday bordering and bordered penality in different national contexts are important to highlight as specific and added layers of criminalisation deployed as further dividing practices in different national contexts (Kabir, 2005; Gibney, 2013; Maguire, 2014). To justify ever-increasing and fine-tuned versions of criminalisation of migrants, the 'myth of migrant criminality' (Chacón, 2013: 629) is connected to deeply rooted ethno-racial prejudices and beliefs. Chacón (2013), for example, shows in the US context how several federal states, who have clamped down on unauthorised migration, were actually experiencing a decrease in crime rates. She argues that this indicates the unnecessary activation of criminal law, signifying the intentional spreading of 'the myth of migrant criminality, sometimes tinged with (or even steeped in) racism or nativisim' (Chacón, 2013: 629). Quite pessimistically, Melossi (2013: 288) argues that the vilification, exclusion and criminalisation of migrants is immanent to the capitalist logic and part of 'deep-seated cyclical processes'.

The ethno-racial element of crimmigration has become more strongly pronounced since 9/11, with the 'war against terror' resulting in increased hostility towards migrants and particularly Muslims in various jurisdictions (Burnett, 2017; Patel, 2017; Nguyen, 2018; Evolvi, 2019). One could observe how the discursive construction of causal linkages between migration, race, terrorism and crime served as a suitable strategy deployed by policymakers to justify bordering practices of a material as well as symbolic nature. The creation of an ever-increasing group of outsiders through establishing these causal linkages, suits the shoring up of boundaries and other penal bordering practices and represents 'a fundamental passage in the process of social construction of migration as a threat' (Galantino, 2020: 1). Across the globe, we see this particularly through the insertion of national terrorism-prevention agendas into policy and programmatic priorities that reach deeply into the fabric of social life. The insertion of crime control priorities along ethno-racial lines de-centres the importance of social policy priorities of inclusion and creation of opportunities for marginalised persons. This results in a stronger emphasis on the securitisation of social policy, and prioritises crime prevention and particularly terrorism prevention, which are steeped in ethno-racial assumptions about those being targeted.

The community-based Countering Violence Extremism (CVE) programme in the United States offers an interesting example to consider the activation of ethno-racial imaginaries in the name of security and crime prevention. Just like many other strategies of criminalisation of social policy – and in contrast to the stark and overtly displayed racism of Trump's anti-Muslim travel bans from 2017 for example – neoliberal governing operates much more subtly, through consent and under the guise of progressive liberalism.

The CVE programme was initiated under the Obama administration in 2016 and relied on the 'largest and only congressionally appropriated budget for countering violent extremism initiatives' (Nguyen, 2019: 323). Under the CVE, community-based organisations in partnership with local law enforcement agencies could apply for grants to implement terrorism-prevention programmes. Communities were selected for participation in the CVE programme based on their ethnic composition (American-Somalis, Muslim minorities and so on), therefore carving out these population groups as problematic a priori and establishing the race–migration–terrorism nexus. Community partners were asked to 'identify and report individuals at-risk of violent extremism, enhance community resilience to terrorist radicalization, and thwart the online presence of terrorist recruiters' (Nguyen, 2019: 328). Not by force, but through communities' active participation, terrorism prevention repositions individuals as proxies, reaching deep in the social fabric of communities, in some instances encouraging 'family members and friends to tip off the police, if worried about a person's behaviour' (Nguyen, 2019: 329). In her research, Nguyen shows how even schools become sites of terrorism prevention, adjusting curricula to security concerns, for example by replacing baseball players with snipers in mathematical formulas and placing students on internship programmes in the security industry.

Problematically, as in all crime-prevention initiatives, any type of behaviour, in this case racial optics deviating from euro-centric norms, can arbitrarily be classified as 'risk factor' to be intervened upon or watched out for. In the context of the CVE programme, this ranges from signs of 'acculturation-related stress', growing beards or saying 'inshallah', which are all 'treated as precursors to criminal violence, despite recognition that there are no scientifically proven indicators, warning signs, or risk factors of violent extremism' (Nguyen, 2019: 332). Nguyen also argues that efforts to paint terrorism-prevention initiatives as anti-racist and inclusionary can contain epistemic contradictions, as racist discourses are replaced with other essentialised versions of ethnicities and cultures, including 'orientalist depictions of the Middle East as a dangerous and lawless breeding ground for terrorism' (Nguyen, 2018: 842).

Nguyen further suggests that American Muslim communities' active participation in the CVE programme can be explained by the fact that it represents one of the few state-sponsored opportunities through which they can demonstrate good citizenship and develop a sense of belonging (Nguyen, 2019: 334). Such repositioning of local communities as partners in crime prevention is, of course, emblematic of wider neoliberal governance strategies, discussed above, 'giving local police legitimacy, credibility and access to targeted communities' (Nguyen, 2019: 330) and repositioning civil society as 'force multipliers' (Nguyen, 2018: 841).

In a very similar way to the American CVE programme, the UK-based CONTEST terrorism-prevention programme offers another example of governing by consent along ethno-racial lines. In 2015, the so-called Revised Prevent Duty Guidance (UK Home Office, 2015) set out a legal duty for educational settings to prevent young people from being drawn into terrorism. Under the Guidance, schools were required to keep a risk register of students and staff, to report suspicious students to the police and to work with the police and 'Prevent officers' as part of multi-agency teams. Patel (2017) suggests that although formulated in a supposed 'post-racial' context, racist assumptions are heavily veiled in this anti-terrorism-prevention context, justifying the 'heavier focus on members of the Muslim population' as 'proportionate to the threat' (Patel, 2017: 3). According to Patel (2017: 3), the promotion of fundamental British values implicitly paints migrants as undemocratic and uncivilised. How effective the programme is in terms of refocusing the 'gaze' of participating entities becomes apparent when considering that the Department of Education's evaluation of it reported that schools 'were deemed to be overzealous in their referrals' (Chisholm et al, 2017: 6). Schools were successfully repositioned as partners in terrorism prevention, and in some instances have even become champions of terrorism prevention. Some schools, for example, brought issues such as school policies on the use of hijabs to the attention of Prevent teams. In one instance, a mother and her children's departure into a war zone was intercepted at the airport, based on a school's notification to the authorities. The potential security threat was considered higher as the welfare of the children, who did not receive child-friendly treatment during the event. Chisholm et al (2017) conclude that the Prevent Guideline offers opportunities to transmute social issues into topics of crime control, when they were previously not: 'This particular issue seems to make schools behave in a way ... that means they don't necessarily follow the normal procedures around talking to parents before making referrals and seeking their concerns. Quite clearly in neither of those cases [discussed during this interview] was there an immediate safeguarding risk ... yet they acted as if there was at the highest level' (Chisholm et al, 2017: 27). Criminalisation of migration through community-based crime and terrorism prevention means that social behaviours are catapulted into the realm of crime control with clear ethno-racial inflections and cultural racism, which are all too easily projected onto the canvas of terrorism prevention.

A new impetus to the othering and criminalisation processes of migrants in the UK context was, of course, the Brexit referendum. Built on the previous promotion of a hostile environment through various government policies, Brexit discourses intensified racist violence against migrants generally and Muslims in particular. According to Burnett (2017), the Brexit referendum, which 'became a proxy for a debate about who should or should not be in the UK, and if so under what conditions', played out at the 'intersection of anti-migrant and anti-Muslim racism'. Both migrants and Muslims were portrayed routinely as 'societal antibodies' (Burnett, 2017: 88). Brexit served as a platform to shift discourses that previously belonged solely to the far right into the political mainstream (Burnett, 2017: 89), and matters over entitlement, citizenship and belonging became re-bundled in an exemplary exercise of welfare nationalism.

Quite predictably, the gendered aspect of ethno-racial elements of the criminalisation of migration is particularly visible, considering how once again women's bodies have, in many different contexts, become suitable objects onto which the concerns of securitised social policy can easily be projected. The wearing of headscarves and hijabs have been matters of public debates across different jurisdictions for a longer period of time, but one could see the re-emergence of concerns over women's choice of dress after several terrorist incidences across Europe in 2015. In Austria, for example, the centre-right government of 2017 introduced, under the guise of wanting to support migrant women's integration, a law that criminalised all 'whole-face coverings' ('Gesichtsverhuellungen'), except for particular purposes, such as very cold weather or cultural events (festivals) (BMEIA, 2017). The colloquially called 'burka ban' attaches a fine of 150 euros to transgression of the law. Given that there are only an estimated 300 burka wearers in Austria, the officially stated goal of integration seems somewhat bizarre, not to mention the lack of cultural sensitivity towards women who wear the burka for a range of different reasons (Khan, 2020). The images on the poster explaining the 'burka ban' are visible at airports and all public offices in Austria, clearly depicting Muslim women with different versions of face coverings, with big red crosses across them. It is difficult to not to interpret these images as a wielding of symbolic power against Muslim women.

Around the same time, the banning of 'burkinis', swimwear used by some Muslim women, covering the entire body and head, offered another canvas onto which the nexus between migration, race and risk could be projected. In the summer of 2016, around 30 French cities banned burkinis from beaches and public swimming pools, claiming that the burkini was 'unhygienic, a uniform of Islamic extremism, and a symbol of women's oppression' (Evolvi, 2019: 469). In the German city of Koblenz, the city council banned women from wearing burkinis in municipal swimming pools (Cranmer, 2019). Although these different versions of burkini bans were eventually overturned by higher courts, the projection of security concerns on Muslim women's dress has to be understood as an instrumental strategy to 'present Muslims as the *enemy within* who pose a threat to *our liberal way of life*' (Patel, 2017: 3). Post-race state accounts of cultural practices such as a dress style 'overlook many of its religious and cultural meanings in favour of an emphasis on its connections to gender inequality and terrorism' (Evolvi, 2019: 470). Dress styles are constructed 'as active choices, and this view allows for victimization blame to be firmly laid at the feet of Muslims, with the premise that they are responsible for actively choosing to wear markers of difference and in doing so reject and offend mainstream society' (Patel, 2017: 3). These various bans on Muslim women's dress offer a prime example of the criminalisation of social policy. Debates about 'counter-terror, immigration and citizenship' 'become blurred, with one policy being used to support the other' (Patel, 2017: 3).

Conclusion: a world without borders?

The process of othering and dividing between the deserving and undeserving is central to social policy provision, if also pronounced to different degrees in different types of welfare states. Yet the argument was pursued in this chapter that these fault lines are harsher and potentially more harmful for people on the move, asylum seekers, refugees and migrants. Again, these groups were treated with broad brushstrokes in this chapter, despite their differential legal status and related privileges, resulting in a variety of experiences of mobility. Nevertheless, the argument remains the same, namely that the very practice of social policy provision can be likened to a drawing of borders, which is further accentuated when it comes to migrants and particularly the most marginal groups of migrants. Othering, stigmatisation and criminalisation are closely intertwined processes that shape migrants' access to services and rights in fundamentally different ways than for citizens of affluent welfare states. As legitimate outsiders in welfare landscapes, limited by the horizon of nation-states, migrants' exclusion from services and rights is often accepted without too much controversy. As social policy provision is widely considered to be within the remit of the nation-state, a diminished right of access to social policy provision has become a rarely challenged paradigm.

Rather than concluding this chapter by thinking about administrative technicalities or international rights' frameworks that could improve the mobility experiences of migrants, we conclude by thinking about what might seem completely utopian: a right to global mobility and the possibility of open borders (Casey, 2010). Shah (2020: n.p.), taking the long view of history, reminds her readers that our societies 'have always depended on free migration' and she passionately argues that 'migration is not the crisis, but the solution'. In his philosophical plea for open borders, the Swiss philosopher Andreas Cassee (2016), argues that the right to global mobility is not utopian, but that from a moral perspective all migrants should have the same access to rights as the 'resident' population of any given territory (Cassee, 2016: 210–13). This might appear at first sight as a very controversial position, but Cassee convinces that from a global ethics perspective immigration controls are not justified and access to equal rights for everybody is entirely justifiable (Cassee, 2016: 213). He imagines an ideal world where inequalities between different regions and territories of this world would be so minimal that migration would equally be minimal and restrictions therefore not necessary. However, he concedes that in our current non-ideal world, dominated by stark inequalities in terms of wellbeing, peace and quality of life, more stringent mobility restrictions are necessary. Nonetheless, Cassee concludes that we should put all of our efforts into working towards the 'ideal' scenario, where mobility of movement would not be penalised anymore (Cassee, 2016: 278), rather than thinking about how to institute more efficient mobility restrictions. Similarly, Bauboeck (2014), argues that from a 'normative perspective' access to multiple citizenships, and therefore also access to multiple sets of rights, is desirable.

One could argue that the move away from borders, bordering practices and conditionalities for access to different types of membership, as wishful and utopian as it sounds, would counter one of the fundamental logics of neoliberal governing: dividing practices. Rather, it would recognise the increasingly visible interdependence of our various social challenges. Chinese artist Ai Weiwei's words seem an inspiring alternative to the multiple bordering practices shaping our contemporary societies and in a way serve as a reminder of the roles each one of us could play in the dismantling of borders: 'Establishing the understanding that we all belong to one humanity is the most essential step for how we might continue to coexist on this sphere we call Earth. I know what it feels like to be a refugee and to experience the dehumanisation that comes with displacement from home and country. There are many borders to dismantle, but the most important are the ones within our own hearts and minds – these are the borders that are dividing humanity from itself' (Weiwei, 2018).

5

Criminalising Homelessness and Poverty through Urban Policy

Introduction

The struggle over the 'Right to the City' (Lefebvre, 1970), intensified through late capitalist developments of gentrification, privatisation and hyper-surveillance of public spaces, has markedly differentiated outcomes for homeless persons and other marginalised populations in the city. In this chapter, it will be shown how the management and criminalisation of perceived problem populations have intensified across contemporary cities and is achieved through an increasing array of different exclusionary legal mechanisms, interventions and technologies manifested in urban policy. While the historical continuities in both the criminalisation of homelessness and the deployment of urban policy to exclude marginalised populations is acknowledged, it is argued that contemporary developments have accelerated and extended the impacts of these processes. Across contemporary urban spaces, the contradictions of neoliberalism, manifested in the 'centaur state's' (Wacquant, 2009a: 43) active deregulation and facilitation of private capital markets' rights to the city, are clearly visible. Simultaneously, regulation, penalisation and behavioural management of the poor and the disenfranchised through more intricate legal and policing and urban planning mechanisms are expanded. These impacts are particularly experienced in what Manuel Castell's defined as the 'Fourth World' of urban poverty, where 'people and places are characterised by the erosion of the welfare state and intense social and spatial exclusion' (Castells, 2000: 168). Guiding the conceptualisation of the criminalisation of social policy in urban contexts is Loïc Wacquant's observation that areas of intellectual concern, namely class fragmentation in the city, ethno-national classifications and penal policy, have remained in separate silos amongst analysts but are, however, closely interdependent in shaping the experiences of the racialised urban precariat (Wacquant,

2014). Throughout this chapter, it will be shown how the 'neo-liberal Leviathan' projects its punitive powers through the three vectors of class, race and the deployment of punitive policies; how spatial regulations impact on every aspect of 'agents in everyday life', but particularly those marginalised by poverty, social class and ethnicity; and how social policies are enrolled by the state to help produce urban hierarchies through their 'classifying and stratifying agency' (Wacquant, 2014: 1699). The targeting of homeless populations through endlessly refined and new layers of civil ordinances excludes them from public spaces but also changes and loosens the protections usually accorded in legal processes (Ashworth and Zedner, 2014). The logic underlying the intensifying regulatory grip on homeless populations is similar to that applied to other groups considered outsiders, such as drug users, migrants or the long-term unemployed. However, whereas under the disciplinary state these would have been targeted for reform and reintegration (Foucault, 1977), the newly devised exclusionary mechanisms are deeply reflective of our devaluation of certain human lives, representing 'the widespread denial of our shared moral status as human beings' (Bosworth, 2019: 93).

Drawing upon a wide range of international contexts, the chapter traces the intersectionality of criminalisation and urban policies in five interlinked areas. First, it will demonstrate how the increased codification of provisions located in civil law adds to the width and intensity of social control in urban centres. This significantly affects homeless populations, who most visibly break the 'unwritten codes of conduct' (Bergamaschi et al, 2014: 4). Secondly, interlinked urban processes such as the privatisation of urban spaces, gentrification and the entrepreneurial agenda (Harvey, 1989) of neoliberal urban policy and their effect on homeless persons' daily lives, restricting their right to the city (Lefebvre, 1970), will be considered. Thirdly, it will be argued that the dominance of CPTED signifies the securitisation of urban policy agendas, problematically extending more widely into urban communities, including schools and youth clubs. In the securitised city, design and 'hostile architecture' are used to control areas of public life perceived as a threat to consumerism, and are further intensified through the use of new surveillant technologies reducing the anonymity of street life. Fourthly, the relationships between homeless people and the police are addressed, tracing the ever-increasing frontier of police intervention, the cynical and often racialised redeployment of urban planning and social policy against the homeless and their unintended criminalisation by apparently benevolent housing and social reintegration policies. Fifthly, it will be shown how governmental efforts to counter territorial stigmatisation and attempts to address the iniquitous use of social and spatial policy can lead to the opposite effect of actually deepening territorial stigmatisation. Finally, this chapter will conclude by considering alternatives to conditional and criminalising modes of urban and homelessness policy.

Deepening and diversifying the criminalisation of homelessness

Homelessness is neither a morally transgressive or harmful act, yet homeless persons have for many years been labelled as outsiders who 'don't respect the rules of public space and who cause disorder' (Bergamaschi et al, 2014: 4). Historically, vagrancy and poor laws of the nineteenth century in different national contexts have combined various measures of criminalisation with low standards of care (see O'Sullivan, 2012 82–4, for a good summary of the debates). The lack of privacy and merging of private and public life when living on contemporary streets means that homeless persons' daily activities are conducted in public under intense scrutiny. Daily acts of survival and living, such as begging, food scavenging, loitering, urinating in public or sleeping in the 'wrong' place have been criminalised since the early beginnings of urbanisation (Creswell, 2001). Historically, in an attempt to prevent unwanted behaviours and offer charitable support to the 'vagrants' and 'vagabonds' of the modernising city, preventive instincts in tandem with the establishment of modern police forces were swiftly complemented by more punitive legal provisions that 'targeted the homeless and designated them as prima facie suspicious on little more ground than that they were too poor to find shelter' (Ashworth and Zedner, 2014: 41).

The relationship between policing and homelessness remains fractious, with contemporary policing practices continuously feeding the social problem of homelessness into the criminal justice system. One can observe across many jurisdictions how the growth and diversification of new community–police partnerships and seemingly more progressive and softer policing practices have resulted in distinctively new forms of surveillance and coercive care of homeless populations. But even beyond homeless populations, policing of cities is highly stratified across racial and classed lines, affecting marginalised populations much more deeply than others. What gives the criminalisation of homelessness a particular shape in contemporary societies is the sheer increase in different types of legislation, ordinances and regulations that criminalise various aspects of homeless people's lives (Misetics, 2013; Persak, 2016; Du Verteuil, 2019; Mc Elroy and Werth, 2019 NCLHP, 2019). Importantly, this increase is accompanied by the diffusion of the neoliberal governing rationality of managing and containing social problems, rather than addressing the underlying causes. This management is achieved in the legal arena through the design of civil ordinances, resulting in a 'blurring of boundaries' (Cohen, 1985) between the criminal and civil law. This blurring results in a loosening of legal restraints and protections usually accorded by the criminal law, in the name of crime prevention, security and gentrification. As a result, what can be seen in neoliberal cities is arguably a more intensified version of the criminalisation of homelessness. Bergamaschi et al show that in the Italian city of Verona this even extends to the penalisation of solidarity with homeless persons: 'offering a drink or something to eat to a homeless person could mean paying a fine of 25 to 500 euros' (Bergamaschi et al, 2014: 8).

The United States, like other prototypical minimalist welfare states, illustrate intense diversity of urban socio-legal strategies that have, overall, actually deepened the criminalisation of homelessness. The National Law Centre on Homelessness and Poverty (NLCHP) has documented in great detail the growth of homelessness related offence types and categories over the past 20 years across American states and cities. The list of different kinds of offences homeless persons can be charged with is mind-boggling. It ranges from 'camping bans', 'evictions of encampments', 'sleeping bans', 'sitting and lying down restrictions', 'living in vehicles bans', begging and loitering bans, but also public urination/defecation, scavenging and dumpster diving laws (NCLHP, 2019: 37). The NCLHP's systematic survey of 187 cities across the United States bears evidence to the strong upward trend of criminalisation of homelessness between 2006 and 2019. Over this period, 45 new laws across the United States prohibiting sitting and/or lying down in public have been created, signifying a 78 per cent increase since 2006 and a 17 per cent increase between 2016 and 2019 (NCLHP, 2019: 42). Similarly, the NLCHP demonstrates a 50 per cent increase between 2006 and 2019 in the enactment of laws prohibiting sleeping citywide and a 29 per cent increase in laws enacting sleeping bans in particular places (NCLHP, 2019: 41). Bordering on inhumanity, some cities, such as Honolulu in Hawaii, enforce a total sitting and lying down in public ban for most hours of the day, making it impossible for homeless people to lawfully rest in public (NCLHP, 2019: 49). As Du Verteuil (2019) notes, findings such as these squarely oppose claims that we have moved towards 'post-revanchist' cities.

Equally, across the Atlantic, Hungary has, since the coming into power of Viktor Orbán's right-wing government in 2010, clamped down on homelessness and severely tightened its grip on homeless populations. As in other jurisdictions, the criminalisation of homelessness in Hungary has historical precursors, both during and after communist rule (Misetics, 2013). However, most recent years have seen criminalisation of homelessness 'intensified ... codified and systematic' (Misetics, 2013: 103). Orbán's government could already lean on a whole raft of opportunities to criminalise street homelessness and poverty through measures such as the criminalising of scavenging and begging (Misetics, 2013). However, in addition, Orbán's government in 2012 introduced hefty fines of roughly 213 euros per 'rough-sleeping misdemeanour' and on top of that the possibility for homeless persons to be incarcerated for up to 60 days after two such 'rough-sleeping misdemeanours'. Coupled with the legislation's rationale, which outlaws residing in all public places in the entire country, the shift from stigmatisation and exclusion to criminalisation occurred despite widespread protests in civil society, and was successfully achieved in a short time. When even the Hungarian Constitutional Court deemed the legislation unconstitutional, the government clenched their fist even further and introduced a Constitutional Amendment to contravene the Constitutional Court's ruling (Podoletz, 2016).

In England and Wales, the introduction of Public Spaces Protection Orders (PSPOs) in 2014 (United Kingdom, Anti-Social Behaviour, Crime and Policing Act, 2014) under the Conservative/Lib Dem government offers another example of the state's 'uncontrollable addiction' to 'manage social problems without eliminating them' (Gilling, 1997: 15). Under the PSPO regime, the government devolved authority and responsibility to local authorities in regulating ASB. The PSPOs' introduction has to be understood as the latest variation in a two-decade-long string of initiatives, leading steadily to the 'hyperregulation of public space' (Brown, 2017) in England and Wales. Since the mid-1990s consecutive governments had introduced different mechanisms aimed at controlling incivilities in public spaces. Most famously, the Crime and Disorder Act 1998, section 1 (repealed) had introduced Anti-Social Behaviour Orders (ASBOs), which linked a serious of fines to vaguely and eternally elastically defined forms of anti-social behaviour. A few years later, the Criminal Justice and Police Act 2001 (sections 12–16), introduced the 'Designated Public Places Disorder', which provided the police with powers to deal with anti-social drinking in specific areas, marked by local authorities as designated areas (Home Office, 2009). Like the previously introduced mechanisms of ASBOs, it has also been critiqued for disproportionately targeting vulnerable populations (Brown, 2017). Therefore, PSPOs are best understood as the latest version of the same impulse, namely to penalise urban outcasts and expand the reach of crime control in the regulation of social life. While PSPOs are in themselves civil orders, the breaching of PSPOs' conditions constitutes a criminal offence, with the maximum penalty of 1,000 pounds, therefore shifting perceived incivil behaviour into the criminal realm.

There are several commonalities between these three examples of criminalisation of public spaces and homelessness, and they provide a good idea of the contemporary contours of this phenomenon. One can observe, in each case, a clear predominance and protection of commercial and private interests over the interests of marginal populations. What is reflected in all instances of overcriminalisation of homelessness is the outcome of a battle, where middle-class and business owners' 'lifestyles, values and norms' prevail (Bergamaschi et al, 2014: 6). In the 'entrepreneurial city' (Hall and Hubbard, 1996), private business owners feel emboldened to claim their rights to the city over those of precariously living persons, even using litigation. In the city of Olympia, Washington, for example, 'local businesses filed a lawsuit against the city for opening a sanctioned encampment for unhoused people rather than aggressively enforcing the city's trespassing and nuisance laws' (NCLHP, 2019: 54). The classed nature of the criminalisation of homelessness also means that outwardly benign-looking ordinances, such as 'camping citations', are applied differentially. In Colorado, camping citations between 2017 and 2018 were used mainly against homeless persons. Only three citations were issued to people actually camping (that is, sleeping beneath an actual tent or tarp). All the others were used to further police homeless persons: '45 citations (46% of total) were issued to people who were sleeping under a blanket or in a sleeping bag, and 32 citations (33% of total) were issued to people sleeping on the ground without any cover whatsoever' (NCLHP, 2019: 38). Due to the differential use of public space and the involvement of crime control agencies such as the police and private security companies, people of colour, Travellers, Roma and LGBTQ + people are all disproportionately affected by these criminalisation measures.

Moreover, it is essential to point out that all these measures, independent of their legal nuances, tend to combine the worst of both civil and criminal law. The criminalisation of incivilities (Persak, 2016) penalises homelessness with bans, orders, fines and ultimately possibly incarceration, but at the same time lacks the usual safeguards of the criminal law. The fact that many legal instruments devised are located in the realm of civil orders can often lead to a lack of rights and accountability for homeless populations: 'There is often no formal hearing, people have no right to a lawyer, and the burden of proof is very low. Notably, the discretionary powers given to police forces in enforcing these orders are problematic: to move the problem off their beat and onto someone else's further isolating and immiserating the people they target' (Vitale, 2017: 141).

In his investigation into the English and Welsh PSPO regime's legal and human rights standards, Brown (2017) shows how, similarly to other anti-social behaviour regulation mechanisms, PSPOs lack the scrutiny and other oversight mechanisms that usually safeguard against excessive criminalisation. Challenging PSPOs in the courts, for example, is made very difficult by the lack of access to civil legal aid supports and the exclusion from judicial review proceedings (Brown, 2017: 563). Rather, PSPOs allow local authorities to regulate and potentially criminalise behaviours which may not be 'directly or even remotely harmful, offensive or immoral' (Brown, 2017: 549).

Therefore, criminalisation is not used as a last resort, but PSPOs allow local authorities to criminalise unwanted behaviour already criminalised through other bylaws. This means additional possibilities to be penalised when poor. A similar process can be identified in the Hungarian context, where the newly introduced anti-begging legislation has not been accorded the usual safeguards of the criminal justice system to homeless people before the courts: 'So in general, the Code of Infractions creates a scenario, where it is possible to be given a prison sentence without a court looking into the detail of the offence' (Podoletz, 2016: 79). Rodger (2008) explains that the design of public order and ASB legislation through civil law mechanisms is a suitable strategy for governments looking for measures that allow for quicker remedies, lower standards of proof and a flexible combination of surveillance and behavioural change. However, the state reserves itself the right to 'recourse to criminal law' 'as the ultimate threat to force conformity through the back-door mechanism of enforcing a criminal sanction against anyone found guilty of breaching a civil law order' (Rodger, 2008: 10). What is achieved through the raft of civil law measures against all types of anti-social behaviour is that 'social policy strategies targeted at issues that may have deep-seated social causes are replaced by a focus on medium-term goals' (Rodger, 2008: 9).

In the US context, some legal challenges have been successfully taken against the criminalisation of homelessness provisions, often successfully confirming their illegality vis-à-vis constitutional principles such as the Eighth Amendment (the right to be free from cruel and unusual punishment) or the Fourth Amendment (the right to protect people from unreasonable searches and seizures by the government). Even the First Amendment (the right to free exercise of religion) has been invoked in establishing the unconstitutionality of criminalising homelessness (NCLHOP, 2019). For example, the city of New York wanted to disperse homeless individuals sleeping on Fifth Avenue Presbyterian Church property. This was ruled against by different courts on the grounds of freedom of religion: 'because preventing the church from using its own property to provide shelter for the homeless burdened its protected religious activity' (NCLHP, 2019: 79). The fact that the right to religious activity has to be invoked in defending the protection of homeless persons is indicative of such persons' deeply excluded and stigmatised status in contemporary cities.

Further, it is interesting to note a similarly paternalistic attitude underlying the officially stated rationales of more intensive regulatory and criminalising measures affecting homeless populations across different national contexts. After all, policymakers don't want to be seen as agents of repressive systems or ideas. Consequently, one can notice that the introduction of punitive measures is justified in the name of the concerned person's 'own good'. In the English and Welsh case, Brown (2017) shows how this rationale was combined in the city of Newcastle's justification for the introduction of a PSPO: 'Beggars often need long term help, and support rather than short term donations; [begging] can be intimidating to the public; [begging] can be detrimental to businesses by putting shoppers off entering shops where beggars congregate' (Newcastle City Council, 2016). However, punitive logic was combined with this caring paternalism. Rather than justifying the need for a PSPO for aggressive begging, the PSPO was interested in reaching further and encompassing all kinds of begging.

This intensified criminalisation of homelessness across cities in different jurisdictions is emblematic of the neoliberal logic of governing, characterised by an endless cycle of fine-tuning legislation to address a social problem that cannot ultimately be solved through criminalisation. Gilling's (1997) observation on the fate of the policy concept of crime prevention can be seamlessly applied to the criminalisation of homelessness. He observes how prevention has become a parameter so broad and vague that it 'widened the scope for preventive intervention immeasurably' (Gilling, 1997: 20). These observations also resonate with more general post-structuralist views on government where the failure of government is part of the immanent logic of governing: 'governmentality may be eternally optimistic, but government is a congenitally failing operation' (Miller and Rose, 1990: 10). Faced with this congenitally failing operation, that is, the inability to solve the problem of homelessness and crime control in public spaces, governments, states and cities across many different national contexts engage in a resurrection, diversification and intensification of punitive regimes of street life.

Gentrification, inequality and criminalisation

Urban policy shapes how cities are experienced. Despite geographical variations, urban marginality and criminalisation of homeless persons and other disenfranchised city dwellers are intensified in contemporary urban landscapes. In the entrepreneurial city (Harvey, 1989), which is characterised by its focus on private business interests and the enabling of enterprise, the city is envisaged as a shop window, prioritising values such as 'competitiveness, beauty, safety and useability' (Bergamaschi et al, 2014: 5), which become focal points of public investments. The simultaneous and resulting exclusion of poorer residents vis-à-vis other more affluent city users such as tourists and 'place-mobile capitalists' (MacLeod, 2002: 605), is one of the main features of entrepreneurial cities. The entrepreneurial city offers spaces for consumption, leisure and cultural production for these privileged groups, making the streets meaner for those who can't participate. Emblematic of neoliberal capitalism, disciplining in the entrepreneurial city is universally present, yet manifests itself though sometimes seemingly banal interventions. Disciplining occurs through a 'range of architectural forms and institutional practices so that the enhancement of a city's image is not compromised by the visible presence of those very marginalised groups' (MacLeod, 2002: 602).

Additionally, critical analyses of gentrification processes argue that what is often presented as revitalisation of urban areas entails harmful outcomes for those already living on society's margins. Urban renewal processes tend to sharpen socio-economic inequalities and further exclude already marginalised groups. While it remains hotly debated as to who wins and who loses through gentrification processes (see, for example, Schlichtmann et al, 2017), some have argued that gentrification is couched in 'revanchist' politics that combine strategies of policing, displacement and criminalisation, aimed at sanitising and indeed fortifying entrepreneurial cities (Smith, 1996 Wacquant, 2000). Ultimately, no generalisations are possible, as the 'geography of gentrification' (Lees, 2012) literature points to the importance of paying attention to marked geographical differences when considering the workings and effects of gentrification. As a result, this has created many 'nuanced accounts of how global flows of capital come to matter through grounded histories, institutions, and imaginaries', resulting in 'geographies of commodification and displacement' (Mc Elroy and Werth, 2019: 879).

Generally, however, the 'European model of control and regulation of public space' is based on a 'less punitive and pervasive approach than in American cities', given its particular social, political and cultural background (Bergamaschi et al, 2014: 8). In Europe, urban control measures tend to be targeted mainly against immigrants and, rather than actual control of homeless persons, are characterised by 'reassurance policies' (Bergamaschi et al, 2014: 8). Nevertheless, even in European contexts, it has been shown how gentrification leads to an 'assault on the poorest sections of the urban population', 'heralding the erosion of spatial justice' (MacLeod, 2002: 609). MacLeod's analysis of urban politics in Glasgow suggests that Glasgow's revanchism tends to be 'minor-league compared to the perspective's "home base" of New York' (MacLeod, 2002: 603). Nevertheless, he maintains that we can see a 'selective appropriation of the revanchist political repertoire' (MacLeod, 2002: 603) emerging from the mid-1990s onwards. He contrasts the reinvention of parts of inner-city of Glasgow, symbolic of its 'renaissance as a postindustrial city' (MacLeod, 2002: 612), with removing a long-established homeless hostel in the middle of gentrified Buchanan Street. MacLeod is careful to suggest that more theorisation is needed to understand the relationship between gentrification processes and the revanchist city. Nevertheless, he concludes that a relationship exists between entrepreneurial modes of governance and urban revanchism (MacLeod, 2002: 617).

The phenomenon of the creeping private use of public spaces is another interesting phenomenon that shows how the change of land use affects the surveillance of and control over urban areas. A *Guardian* cities investigation from 2017 (Shenker, 2017) mapped the startling spread of over 50 pseudo-public spaces ('pops') across the UK capital. Pseudo-public spaces are essentially large urban areas which appear similar to public spaces but are actually owned by large corporations such as Mitsubishi or J. P. Morgan. Unlike other cities such as Rotterdam, New York and Toronto, these pseudo-public places are not subject to the same bylaws as other public areas in the city, but how they are regulated remains unclear. As a result, members of the public are not informed of what is permissible (taking photographs, sitting down) and private security companies are often authorised to police these spaces. The presence and lack of public regulation of pseudo-public places are problematic as the public has no way to know how these spaces are governed and regulated.

The steadily increasing privatisation of Vienna's property market offers another example of a European city's experience with gentrification, where in the process undesirable persons are removed from visibility. Vienna is considered one of the most socialised European cities, with two-thirds of the housing stock operating on a publicly subsidised basis (Mocca et al, 2020). Increasingly, however, many parts of the city are experiencing the privatisation of housing stock; the stock thus falls outside the remit of the otherwise tightly regulated rent control system, returning healthy profits for investors and landlords. Looking at different indicators of gentrification, such as education levels, housing stock, housing standards and so on, in the 15th district of Vienna, the European research project 'Beyond Gentrification' (2016) arrives at nuanced views as to the slowly creeping gentrification processes in this socially diverse and formerly working-class district. Interestingly, however, the authors of the project pinpoint the 2011 citywide ban on street prostitution as a turning point in the district's public image, as well as increased 'confidence' levels of residents to push the 'NIMBY' (not in my backyard) agenda. In interviews with residents, researchers found that the ban on street prostitution in the name of public safety was very much pushed and welcomed by residents (Beyond Gentrification, 2016). Liberal elites are interested in their privileges being protected, even if this means compromising their supposed principles of equality and social inclusion (Vitale, 2017; Bloch and Meyer, 2019). Also worthy of note is that criminalisation of street prostitution immediately attracted an enormously increased police presence and simply pushed sex workers into apartment-based prostitution. The contentious connection between gentrification and exclusion of perceived risky persons, and equally the displacement rather than solution of the perceived social problem, are visible in this example (Beyond Gentrification, 2016).

The outcome of gentrification processes seem to be 'imprinted more dramatically upon urban landscapes of North, Central, and Latin America' (MacLeod, 2002: 602), with the racial history and politics and violent policing practice deserving particular attention. In addition to acknowledging the connections between racialised policing, incarceration and homelessness, some commentators suggest that the deeper signification of gentrification has to be understood in the historical context of racial oppression: 'Culturally, I think the way that a lot of African American and Latino people experience gentrification is as a form of colonisation ... the gentrifiers are not wanting to share – they're wanting to take over' (Butler, 2017). The intricate connection between gentrification and policing, given longstanding police violence and racial profiling in many different national contexts, cannot be overlooked. To prove this empirically, Laniyonu (2017) correlated spatial econometric models from New York City, showing how as 'cities pursue growth strategies designed to appeal to members of the so-called "creative classes", they increasingly adopt punitive policing strategies, such as order maintenance policing' (Lanviono, 2017: 898). Yet, even within the United States, local specificities of gentrification processes and outcomes are varied. In their study of gentrification in Oakland, California, Mc Elroy and Werth (2019: 879) argue that transposition of 'flat comparisons' of gentrification processes from other tech-colonised US cities overlook the 'multiple histories and geographies of ongoing racialised dispossession and refusal' in Oakland (Mc Elroy and Werth, 2019: 880). In particular, they highlight the link between land-use protections and policing of cultural spaces along racialised lines and admonish us to be aware of layered specificities when discussing gentrification. Resonating with the criminalisation of incivilities (Persak, 2016), so central to the criminalisation of social policy and highlighted throughout this book, they show how Oakland's Nuisance Eviction Ordinance has been used disproportionately to evict tenants for mundane nuisance violations, rather than, as envisaged, for violent crime, sex work and drug-related activity (Mc Elroy and Werth, 2019: 886). These nuisance evictions, they highlight, were concentrated in East Oakland, 'an area already targeted by redlining, foreclosures, mass incarceration, and other technologies of racialised dispossession' (Mc Elroy and Werth, 2019: 887). Importantly, their research also shows the Oakland Police Department's central role in the enforcement of what is essentially gentrification legislation, that is, in closing down 'legally permitted cultural spaces'. Contrasting downtown nightclubs owned by Black and Latinx operators with others, they show that these were disproportionately closed down 'due to intense surveillance and prosecution by the City' (Mc Elroy and Werth, 2019: 889). Crucially, they interpret this as a continuation of practices 'foreclosing the social pleasures and spatial practices of young people of colour since at least the rise of the Black Panthers' (Mc Elroy and Werth, 2019: 889).

Designing homelessness out the entrepreneurial city

The entrepreneurial city also engages in physically designing marginalised people out of its midst. Although some would say that situational crime prevention is not a coercive tool (Ashworth and Zedner, 2014), it is suggested here that the increasing technologisation and sophistication of urban design that often goes unnoticed and arguably affects everyone, does disproportionately affect homeless persons and indeed others, such as young people, who would use non-commercial public spaces more frequently than others. Different applications of the CPTED paradigm offer prime examples of how an instrument of crime control, once invented, becomes an ever-evolving, fine-tuned and expansive vehicle, not necessarily malignantly aimed at poor persons, but continuously affirming their status as unwanted bodies.

CPTED has its origins in British Home Office research from the 1960s and heavily draws on the city planner Oscar Newman's concept of 'Defensible Spaces' (Newman, 1972). Newman developed several principles, including territoriality, natural surveillance, image, milieu, safe adjoining areas and defensible spaces, with the overall aim of preventing crime and victimisation. Newman's idea of Defensible Spaces was subsequently developed into the crime-prevention paradigm of CPTED, which has gained significant traction amongst urban planners, police departments and national and international policy-making bodies. Emblematic of advanced liberal governance, urban safety is managed through 'nodal governance' (Bayley, 1994), involving individuals and communities in thinking about and acting towards crime prevention. In line with neoliberal governing rationality, the emphasis on responsibility for one's safety was central in Newman's original definition of a 'defensible space' as 'a residential environment whose physical characteristics – building layout and site plan – function to allow inhabitants themselves to become key agents in ensuring their security' (Newman, 1972). In the struggle over public spaces between different interest groups, the CPTED paradigm can, in best-case scenarios, protect, for example, women's and girls' use of public spaces by providing appropriate lighting, visibility and CCTV surveillance. Critiques of CPTED cannot, therefore, be oversimplified, and it is vital to consider the political and ideological contexts in which particular measures are implemented. However, what can be seen as emerging in the context of the entrepreneurial city is how CTPED is instrumentally deployed to deter undesirable persons from spaces that are increasingly organised around consumption.

For example, the use of noise-emitting devices as a form of public policing in the style of pest control merely redistributes risks and does not reduce the occurrence of the unwanted behaviour. So-called mosquito-repellent noise devices were initially designed to emit noise at a frequency that affects under 25-year-olds, an age group often considered particularly problematic when gathering in groups and defying the norms of the entrepreneurial city. The manufacturer subsequently lowered the noise frequency to affect older persons as well (Little, 2015). Today, the device's leading manufacturer distributes the system widely across nine European and ten global countries outside the EU (Compound Security, 2021). In the Canadian city of Winnipeg, the device was installed in 2020 as a pilot project to deter homeless persons from congregating. City officials had justified the introduction of the noise-emitting devices after several fires lit by homeless people had threatened to damage bridges. After an outcry by homelessness organisations, the pilot project was discontinued. The major of Winnipeg publicly declared his dissatisfaction with the lack of scrutiny by the city government over the installation of the devices and acknowledged that it would further stigmatise homeless persons: 'part of the concern that I have, and I know others are sharing it, is the stigmatization that does exist for those members of our community that are affected by homelessness, and what it communicates to the broader community' (Keele, 2020). While resisted in some national contexts, the Mosquito device offers a prime example of the exclusionary and criminalising nature of environmental crime prevention. Similarly to other civil law mechanisms aimed at ASB management, CPTED measures sweep across all members of particular social groups, not only those who behave 'undesirably', and physically displace a perceived problem rather than significantly address it. Legal safeguards against such devices are more or less non-existent for users of public spaces and the fact that they are privately available without regulation (Little, 2015) while targeting the 'usual suspects' is highly problematic.

How an environmental crime-prevention tool, once invented, continuously seeks to attach itself to new surfaces is also apparent when one considers the use of such tools in social settings such as schools. The use of CCTV surveillance in schools is, of course, more generally indicative of society's failure to create safe spaces for children and young people. The securitisation of school spaces usually also attracts closer partnerships with police forces and private security firms, enabling the reach of crime control actors to extend more deeply into the social fabric of communities. An interesting case study of the net-widening tendencies of CPTED is offered by the EU-funded Cooperation in Science and Technology (COST) action on Crime Prevention through Urban Design and Planning, which operated between 2012 and 2016 (COST Action TU1203, 2017). As part of the COST action, Serbian partners set up a CCTV surveillance project in a number of primary and secondary schools across Belgrade, with headmasters of involved schools sending their video footage directly to the police. While the project report emphasises the importance of data protection and privacy rights, there seems to have been no awareness of the blurring of boundaries between social control and welfare.

In addition to attaching itself to new surfaces, the CPTED paradigm has also lent itself to appropriating a harsher character by engaging in strategies of defensive or hostile architecture and exclusionary design (Bader, 2020). Starolis (2020: 57) argues that a 'war on sitting' has emerged in the gentrified city, where 'seating options have shifted from subtly uncomfortable to outright "aggressive"'. These interventions are characterised by their banality and their near invisibility, yet punitive and exclusionary impacts on marginal populations (Bergamaschi et al, 2014). Through observing the implementation of hostile seating architecture in three public spaces in Philadelphia, including two parks and the windowsill of a bank on a busy intersection, Starolis (2020: 57) concludes that 'almost every observation revealed that these interventions do very little to stop the behavior that had been deemed undesirable in each site'. Rather, what she observed was that the interventions had a 'way of alienating the majority of users, reaching far beyond the specific groups or behaviors that prompted hostile interventions in the first place. Efforts to prevent certain uses or users have, in turn, made spaces uncomfortable or unusable for all people' (Starolis, 2020: 57). Paradoxically, the attempt to remove unwanted or risky bodies from public spaces therefore contributes to the lowering of the quality of public spaces for all.

In their analysis of the use of hostile design and urban furniture in the Italian city of Bologna, Bergamaschi et al consider how 'anti-homeless' benches have been installed by the city council as a response to citizens' complaints about 'improper occupation of public space' (Bergamaschi et al, 2014: 12). These benches are typically designed, either through a choice of materials or shape, to discourage resting or lying down. The design of benches 'passes completely unnoticed by the ordinary citizen, the tourist or the suburban visitor who all gravitate to the spectacularized inner city' (Bergamaschi et al, 2014: 12). Yet for homeless and poor persons, this hostile architecture results in a city less accessible. As they 'cannot be eliminated or institutionalised, they are removed from places under the public eye, they become invisible, they are out of sight' (Bergamaschi et al, 2014: 13).

Policing homelessness in the revanchist city

In its extreme manifestation, shored up by policing powers and practices, the gentrified city is realised through highly punitive and marginalising practices, resulting in what Neil Smith (1996) famously coined the 'revanchist city'. Urban middle-class populations of affluent Western cities, priced out of property markets through gentrification processes and affected by the decline of the welfare state, feel threatened by the arrival and spread of the urban 'underclass':

> More than anything the revanchist city expresses a race/class/gender terror felt by middle- and ruling-class whites who are suddenly stuck in place by a ravaged property market, the threat and reality of unemployment, the decimation of social services, and the emergence of minority and immigrant groups, as well as women, as powerful urban actors. It portends a vicious reaction against minorities, the working class, homeless people, the unemployed, women, gays and lesbians, immigrants. (Smith, 1996: 208)

Central to the ruling elites' and white middle class' response to the perceived threats of unwanted populations, is a turn towards crime control, rather than to a stronger welfare state: 'Crime, in particular, has become a central marker of the revanchist city, the more so as the fears and realities of crime are desynchronised' (Smith, 1996: 209). The relationship between gentrification, policing and further entrenchment of inequalities is central to the concept of the revanchist city. What aggressive gentrification projects of urban areas that have become 'valuable areas for real estate development' (Vitale, 2019: 189) mean for the criminalisation of street homeless populations can be very well exemplified by the 'Safer Cities Initiative' launched in the Skid Row area of Los Angeles in 2006. The politics, practices and outcomes of the Safer Cities Initiative exemplify the interplay of racialised policing, the failings of the minimalist welfare state and the contribution of conservative criminology in producing an expensive, yet destined to fail, intervention.

The historic Skid Row area in Los Angeles was originally created as a 'kind of ghetto of social services for the very poor in order to keep them out of other residential neighbourhoods' (Vitale, 2017: 189). Geographically, LA Skid row is a very small area of inner-city Los Angeles (0.85 square miles) and at the time of the launch of the Safer Cities Initiative in 2006 had a very high density of homelessness, namely 42 times the citywide average in both Los Angeles County and City. In absolute numbers, this meant that roughly a maximum of 1,400 homeless people were counted on Skid Row's streets. The homeless population on Skid Row could be characterised as chronically homeless, facing significant mental health issues and addiction problems, with black men being overrepresented amongst their numbers (Blasi, 2007: 5). In the absence of a robust welfare state response and other social policy measures, the Skid Row Safer Cities Initiative was designed as a 'quality-of-life policing' intervention with some rather patchworked and ineffective social service provisions primarily set up to soften the public image of the initiative. Heavy policing investment was an integral element of the Safer Cities Initiative. An additional 50 police officers were deployed to the Skid Row area, leading to a disproportionate increase in policing interventions, resulting in raised citations and arrest numbers. For example, in the first year of the Skid Row Safer Cities Initiative, the LAPD issued over 12,000 citations for pedestrian violations (walk/don't walk), which was between 48 to 69 times higher than the city average (Blasi, 2007: 6). The majority of arrests in the first year of the initiative involved drug-related offences (over 50 per cent of the 750 arrests per month). Whereas the median amount of drugs seized was very small (2.5 grams), and was mainly for personal use or survival dealing, a large proportion of those charged ended up behind bars (Blasi, 2007: 6). In conjunction with the Safer Cities Initiative, a concurrent district attorney's plea bargain initiative meant additional criminalisation for homeless drug addicts. Whereas previously a conviction for minor drug offences would have meant access to court-mandated drug treatment and other services in lieu of incarceration ('Proposition 36 drug treatment and other services') (Blasi, 2007: 7), the plea bargain initiative meant that a conviction for even a small quantity of drugs would most likely result in incarceration. Notably, this meant incarceration in notoriously underserviced prisons, failing to provide the most basic health and mental health-care services for incarcerated persons. To further add to and fully close the circle of criminalisation, the initiative also meant that prisoners upon release were deemed 'illegible for many federally subsidised housing programs and ineligible for food stamps when they are released back to the streets' (Blasi, 2007: 6). In search of solving a social problem, the Skid Row Safer Cities Initiative clearly contributed to the feedback loop between the criminalisation of homelessness and incarceration.

A really interesting in-depth UCLA Law Department study into the LA Skid Row Safer Cities Initiative (Blasi, 2007) reveals the politically conservative tough-on-crime politics and 'broken-windows' policing approach adopted throughout the initiative. The study showed how the initiative was, from its very initial stages, designed as a law-and-order campaign, rather than a welfare campaign aimed at supporting street homeless persons. In line with the neoliberal emphasis on individual responsibility and diminishing attention paid to social contexts, the researchers showed how, in the very first multi-stakeholder agenda-setting meeting, the focus was placed entirely on the crimes directly related to homelessness, such as sleeping or camping on the sidewalk, and entirely ignored the lack of available shelter or sufficient facilities (such as toilets) for Skid Row residents. In line with neoliberal responsibilisation, the individuals, but not the lacking social supports, were problematised, even by attending charities, and chiming with this, the security-oriented policing focus was adopted (Blasi, 2007).

It is also interesting to note that the Skid Row Safer Cities Initiative relied on the consulting services of George Kelling, at the time Professor of Criminal Justice at Rutgers University and Senior Fellow at the conservative think tank the Manhattan Institute (Blasi, 2007: 24). Kelling's name will ring a bell with avid criminology readers. Together with James Wilson from UCLA, he had published a famous paper on the 'broken-windows' theory (Wilson and Kelling, 1982), which posits a link between visible disorder or uncared property and the attraction of further disorder or crime. Similarly to the situational focus of CPTED, 'broken-windows' theory has been criticised for facilitating heavy-handed and intrusive policing practices (Delgado and Stefancic, 2016; Deuchar et al, 2019; Vitale, 2019), while at the same time being welcomed by policymakers for its apparently easy solution to crime. Vitale (2019: 221–2) aptly explains that broken-windows' policing connects to a 'larger arc of urban neo-conservative thinking going back to the 1960s'. This is really important, as it provides a sense of one of the key ideological ingredients underlying the criminalisation of social policy. According to Vitale, the proponents of broken-windows policing 'believed strongly that there were profound limits on what government could do to help the poor. Financial investment in them would be squandered; new services would go unused or be destroyed; they would continue in their slothful and destructive ways. Since the root of the problem was either an essentially moral and cultural failure or a lack of external controls to regulate inherently destructive human urges, the solution had to take the form of punitive social control mechanisms to restore order and neighbourhood stability' (Vitale, 2019: 221–2). Kelling seems to have been very much aware of the contentious nature of broken-windows policing, as documented in the minutes of the first Skid Row Safer Cities Initiative meeting, contemplating how the image of the initiative could be defended in public: 'Quality-of-life policing is not going to look good and it is not going to feel good but we have got to gain the moral high ground. How we gain the moral high ground is by getting the media on our side' (Kelling, cited in Camp and Heatherton, 2016: 286).

In terms of reaching its goal of crime reduction, the Skid Row Safer Cities Initiative was only partially successful. While, overall, crime rates seem to have gone down significantly in the inner-city area, this trend was much more strongly pronounced outside the Skid Row area, indicating that the downward trend was not a result of the Safer Cities Initiative. In fact, violent crime had reduced more significantly outside the Skid Row area, quite a sobering result given the disproportionately intensive policing presence in Skid Row (Blasi, 2007). In addition, and in tune with the neoliberal turn in social policy, the social provisions envisaged as part of the Safer Cities Initiative, the so-called Street or Services programme, were makeshift and only symbolic rather than substantial in nature. For example, 'the promised additions to the supply of shelter and supportive housing have primarily been limited to keeping open a warehouse-style-shelter to which homeless people are bussed from Skid Row in the afternoon and returned to Skid Row early the next morning' (Blasi, 2007: 7). Coupled with the additional criminalising effects of the broken-windows approach to policing, Skid Row Safer Cities Initiative illustrates how social policy operates in tandem with criminal law in the revanchist city. Vitale's (2010) damning conclusion suggests that state intervention in this case not only led to the displacement of vulnerable people, but, quite paradoxically, even deepened the problem of homelessness: 'the SCI may have succeeded in displacing people from Skid Row, but it has not reduced homelessness. In fact, it has made it more difficult for many people to escape homelessness. The heavy reliance on arrests, especially those that involve charges of drug dealing, make it more difficult to access social services, employment, and permanent housing' (Vitale, 2010: 869). The Skid Row Safer City Initiative serves as a prime illustration of different elements of criminal justice and social policy converging and imprinting itself quite violently on the lives of most marginalised homeless persons.

Managerial policing and benevolent care

The debates around urban revanchism have moved along since their inception. De Verteuil (2019), for example, argues that any blanket interpretation of urban policies as 'revanchist' must be an oversimplification, as revanchism doesn't take into account the 'increasing disconnect between national-level revanchist rhetoric excess since the mid-2010s, and a more local, on-the-ground reality that is alternatively supportive and ambivalent' (De Verteuil, 2019: 1056). He argues that after legal and activist challenges by the American Civil Liberties Union (ACLU) and other Skid Row institutions, the mid-2010s saw a series of more supportive measures emerge. Los Angeles has seen 'policy developments that suggest a criminalising "war on the homeless" has all but petered out', as well as an increasing appetite for more 'liberal attitudes towards urban poverty', expressed in the support by city management and civil society of several 'Housing First' types of initiatives (De Verteuil, 2019: 1057). However, even if one accepts that urban revanchism is at times characterised by inflections of liberalism brought to the fore by different gentrifying communities, the underlying punitive attitude towards homeless persons and other urban outsiders remains firmly intact. Liberals, and even social activists, in the context of material and ontological insecurity, are driven to 'call on local governments to "get tough" on homeless people in their midst', and call for the 'removal of homeless encampments by police in New York and San Francisco' (Vitale, 2017: 98). NIMBY initiatives are not driven by neo-conservative law-and-order citizens, but supported by a variety of different communities, including from working-class Latino communities, gentrifying beach communities or mixed immigrant communities (De Verteuil, 2019: 1058).

One can also clearly detect the continuing war on homelessness in the following two examples of policing in gentrifying US neighbourhoods, which are particularly interesting, as they are cloaked under the guise of liberalism. They demonstrate how alternative and supposedly more subtle and supportive forms of policing can be just as harmful and exclusionary towards urban outcasts. Herring's (2019) research on what he describes as 'pervasive', 'third party' and 'complaint-oriented policing' in San Francisco, analysed 3.9 million 911 (emergency), and 311 (non-emergency City and County of San Francisco number) call records and also conducted participant observation alongside police officers, social workers and homeless men and women residing on the streets of San Francisco. His research traced the punitive nature of 'complaint-oriented' policing, which refers to policing that responds to the public's complaints, including calls from citizens, organisations and government agencies (Herring, 2019).

Herring's research shows how homeless populations are intensely policed and exposed to possible criminalisation through an additional layer of surveillance and complaints. As part of this complaint culture, 'law-abiding' citizens and very often people who think they are doing good, while in fact they may be contributing to 'displacing them [homeless people] spatially, temporally, or bureaucratically – forcing homeless people into new spaces or reclassifying the "homeless problem" as an issue for another agency or institution' (Herring, 2019: 771). 'Pervasive policing' (Herring, 2019: 785), then, is enabled by the power given to citizens to make complaints against the usual suspects in highly unequal and racially stratified societies. Pervasive policing is an immensely symbolic action, as it takes place even when it is not effective and does not make any sense for participants, either police officers or homeless persons. The following narrative of Herring's research illustrates this point very well:

> At the conclusion of another move-along order I experienced while camping with a group in tents outside a municipal bus yard, the officer apologised: 'I don't know why they're calling, I mean this seems like an ideal spot, out of the way, and you all are keeping this spot clean. I mean, I know this is pointless, but you gotta move.' One of the homeless men replied, 'Yeah, it's a bummer. It's all good. I know you're just doin' your job. It's a shitty job.' The outcome of these interactions was a constant churning of homelessness in public space. (Herring, 2019: 785)

Herring's work reminds us that we have to move beyond the binary distinction of aggressive versus therapeutic policing and understand that supposedly benevolent forms of policing can be experienced as equally harmful.

Again in the US context, Bloch and Meyer's (2019) study on white residents' engagement with so-called civil gang injunctions in a gentrifying city neighbourhood of Los Angeles offers fascinating insights into the amalgamation of apparently contradictory liberal concerns around police violence and civil rights by white residents who are, at the same time, actively participating in intense policing practices. They suggest that we have to move away from our 'traditional understanding of revanchism as a decidedly vengeful repossession of territory' (Bloch and Meyer, 2019: 1102). Rather, neoliberalisation of space, coupled with longstanding ethno-racial othering and policing practices, results in less visible, yet equally intrusive, forms of what they term 'implicit revanchism'.

Bloch and Meyer's study is located in Echo Park, a 'high-rent hipster haven', (Bloch and Meyer, 2019: 1103) that, however, has maintained its diverse population. So-called gang injunctions have been in operation in Los Angeles since the 1980s, but the combination of this civil law mechanism with the gentrification of Echo Park shows how ethnic minorities are targeted and excluded from gentrifying neighbourhoods. Essentially, the injunctions allow the courts to put restrictions on so-called gang members movements and association with each other, in designated areas. Once classified as a 'gang member', civil acts such as 'standing, sitting, walking, driving, gathering, or appearing anywhere in public view, in a public place, or any place accessible to the public' (Bloch and Meyer, 2019: 1111) can be used by police officers to monitor and reprimand behaviour which is not criminal, or even 'incivil', but may be observed as threatening by white hipsters. Classified as nuisance complaints, such gang injunctions, as the authors show, are based on 'a multisensory and subjective reading of others' (in)appropriate behavior and demeanor', operating as a 'moral geography ... of what is deemed by ascendant community members to be out of place, disruptive to the senses, and potentially dangerous' (Bloch and Meyer, 2019: 1105–6). As a consequence, and despite its ethnic diversity, Echo Park is policed as a white space. The fact that liberal concerns around police violence allow for the simultaneous participation in policing (for example, through complaints made at community fora and requests made for the activation of gang injunctions) is a key feature of liberal modernity, a 'co-constitutive element of a politics of (in)security that forms the very heart of liberalism's project of social order' (Bloch and Meyer, 2019: 1110).

Crucially, such 'implicit revanchism' is exemplary of many similar processes that one sees in operation throughout different thematic areas of the criminalisation of social policy. While the 'punitive edge of policy has occasionally been blunted, such "softer" social policy continues to target the homeless and drug users in progressive cities, and we maintain that such supportive or even apparently "compassionate" approaches are no less embedded in broader assemblages that continue to violently dispossess and exclude these and other marginalised groups' (Bloch and Meyer, 2019: 1109).

On the basis of this kind of evidence, one is therefore admonished to be cautious when the increased involvement of communities in policing and, indeed, other social interventions are promoted as unequivocally positive developments (Cohen 1985; Shapland, 2008). Given the inherent power differential between those who usually complain and those who are complained about, the supposedly progressive practice of including communities in policing can therefore lead to increased criminalisation. A good example of this is a 2014 amendment to the British Anti-Social Behaviour, Crime and Policing Act 2014 (UK Government, 2014, section 104), through which the role of communities in policing ASB was strengthened. The amendment introduced the so-called 'community trigger' mechanism, which was designed to give victims and communities a say in the way ASB is dealt with. Community members who feel that their concerns about ASB have not been responded to after three complaints have the right to activate the 'community trigger'. It appears that community triggers have been activated relatively sparingly, nevertheless the inclusion of the trigger signifies a clear move towards complaints-oriented policing, with all its problematic features. It also shows how, once in motion, we are likely to observe a continuous recycling and intensification of criminalisation processes, difficult to contend with.

Cohen suggested that the resulting boundary-blurring between fields of social welfare and social control was neither a negative nor a positive value in itself and it could go either way: 'they can easily lead to the most undesirable consequences: violations of civil liberties, unchecked discretion, professional imperialism' (Cohen, 1985: 257). Subtle ways of crime control and supposedly benevolent methods of care towards homeless persons, in particular, can be experienced as coercive and possibly lead to criminalisation further down the line. Inventions such as 'homeless courts' in the USA, aimed at improving 'efficiency in judicial proceedings, match[ing] sanctions and services to offenders, and build[ing] bridges between public and private agencies that serve offenders', can further criminalise the poor. In line with other research into how advanced liberal states prefer to intervene in social problems (Gray, 2011), Vitale (2019: 103) concludes that homeless courts in the US context 'almost never include stable housing, much less permanent housing with support services. Instead, they keep people involved in a series of social service and court appointments that rarely resolve their underlying problems. And even when that does happen, this does nothing to expand the available supply of housing for those with very low or no income. In essence, they are rearranging who gets a particular unit, rather than addressing the structural lack of affordable housing.' This mirrors Gray's (2011) observation on youth resettlement support for young people leaving custody in England and Wales. She shows how the emphasis of programmes and resource allocation prioritises interventions aimed at changing young people's behaviour, rather than supporting them in accessing resourced supports which might offer them a chance of altering their material life circumstances.

Territorial stigmatisation and criminalisation

In addition to the material hardship experienced through punitive and exclusionary urban politics, 'territorial stigmatisation' (Wacquant, 2007: 15) denotes specifically how reputational damage is attached to various locations, affecting those associated with them. The emphasis in the penultimate section of this chapter is placed on how the deployment of state-led measures, in the name of de-stigmatisation, can paradoxically intensify stigmatisation and exclusion. In their study on urban regeneration initiatives in Limerick, Ireland, Power et al (2020: 18), for example, conclude that 'both territorial stigmatisation and "official" efforts at de- stigmatisation deploy discourses in the service of sustaining the status quo'. State investment in urban regeneration of schooling and housing in stigmatised places is justified by drawing on the very same discourses that produce territorial stigmatisation in the first place: 'Rather than understanding the challenges faced by disadvantaged neighbourhoods as the product of global structural shifts in the distribution of economic activity, and the failure of the State to prevent these exacerbating pre-existing class inequalities, policy approaches have located the problem to be addressed in the physical and social composition of the estates themselves' (Power et al, 2020: 16).

A particularly crude yet illustrative example of the punitive nature of efforts of de-stigmatisation are various versions of consecutive Danish governments' efforts to de-segregate public housing areas, characterised initially as disadvantaged, and ultimately outspokenly as 'ghettos'. Since the mid-1990s, the coming together of multiple social problems in public housing areas with high levels of migrants as residents were understood to be a result of government housing policies, lack of state investment in good-quality housing and lack of sensible urban planning, resulting in increasingly secluded neighbourhoods amidst gentrifying areas in the centre of Copenhagen (Oliveira e Costa and Tunstroem, 2020). However, gradually, the language became harsher as well as policies much more punitive. The conservative government of 2004 introduced the term 'ghetto' in a national policy strategy document (Oliveira e Costa and Tunstroem, 2020) and classified five to ten such areas as 'ghetto areas'. Measures introduced were not yet overtly punitive, although they already targeted 'migrants from postcolonial origins' (Wacquant, 2014: 1688), and 'gave public housing companies the option to deny a rental contract to people on social benefits' (Oliveira e Costa and Tunstroem, 2020: 55). The measures were formulated as responses to 'ghetto residents'' own shortcomings, particularly in relation to low employment levels, 'making their situation seem like a choice or individual failure while overlooking the wider structural biases that worked against these individuals in society as a whole' (Seemann, 2020: 11). By 2010, the overt racism had become inserted in an expanded policy that targeted a longer list of now 29 'ghettos', that were described as lacking in 'Danish norms and values' (Oliveira e Costa and Tunstroem, 2020: 56). While some emphasis remained on the role of the built environment in these 'ghettos', a wide range of social welfare recipients, including those on social assistance, unemployment benefits, sickness benefits and early retirement schemes, were not offered housing in these areas, a clear indication of the exclusionary strategies deployed by the measures.

While the ghetto policy was downplayed by the social democratic government between 2013 to 2018, who changed the term ghetto to 'deprived areas', it was resurrected with full vengeance by the incoming right-wing government from 2018 onwards. Under the No Ghettos in 2030 policy initiative, and under the guise of 'equality promotion', immigration, identity and non-Danishness, particularly that of non-Western and Muslim migrants, were reframed as the key problems of 'ghettos', and the 'number of "non-Western immigrants *and descendants*" was a novel criterion used in the identification of "ghettos"' (Seemann, 2020: 12, emphasis added). The ghetto list was extended to over 40 areas, and a tiered system of classification, identifying different levels of ghettos, including 'hard ghettos', was set up. Public housing bodies were not only given the option of ending tenancies of 'ghetto residents', but they could now be forced by the state to decommission entire housing units if they did not fulfil the task of integration, albeit such 'integration' was extremely vaguely formulated (Oliveira e Costa and Tunstroem, 2020: 59).

Outrightly punitive and stigmatising measures were introduced, meaning that 'ghetto residents' are subject to entirely different laws than others. For example, children have to attend a 25-hour weekly mandatory pre-school programme from age one, to ensure their integration into Danish society and its social norms and values. The introduction of increased punishment zones means that offences such as violence, vandalism, burglary, drug offences or threatening behaviour attract twice the length of sentences for those living in 'ghetto areas'. In 2020, the UN OCHCR accused Denmark of ethnic and racial discrimination, in particular in relation to the selling off of a publicly owned housing project (Mjølnerparken), as a direct result of the 2018 'Ghetto list policy', where 98 per cent of residents are immigrants or are born to immigrants: 'We call on Denmark to respect its obligations under human rights law based on the premise that all people, simply because they are human beings, should enjoy all human rights without discrimination on any grounds' (OCHCR, 2020). Under the guise of supporting the de-segregation of poor public housing areas and vying for profitable sales of inner-city land to private investors (Overgaard, 2020), different versions of Danish 'ghetto list' policies can only be described as punitive and segregationist. Research has also shown how the ghetto lists produced mental health challenges, particularly for children, and are unsurprisingly experienced as overtly punitive (Gulis and Safi, 2020). Danish 'ghetto' politics in the name of de-segregation offer a prime example of the criminalisation of social policy and how 'social citizenship is increasingly conceptualised and shaped in relation to geographic entities (*spatialisation*), which in turn are defined, *inter alia*, by ethnicity (*ethnicisation*)' (Seeman, 2020: 2).

Conclusion: in search of solutions …?

As this chapter has touched upon a number of interrelated issues, often dealt with in separate spheres in policy terms, it is difficult to select one particular positive example of how the criminalisation of homelessness, the overregulation of public space and territorial stigmatisation could be countered. This chapter therefore concludes with two examples that can provide food for thought for alternative visions when it comes to thinking about the criminalisation of homelessness in particular, although this re-visioning might also impact how one considers the control of marginalised populations and the criminalisation of public spaces more generally.

First, one can turn to the often cited 'best-practice' example of the 'Housing First' paradigm, which originated in the American Pathways Housing First model but has been most successfully applied within Finland (Y Foundation, 2017: 9). At the core of the model is a rights-based and unconditional approach to housing, where housing is provided in a highly supportive environment that operates services for organisations for homeless persons that 'do not want to get rid of their clients. Instead, the purpose is to provide clients with a permanent dwelling – that is, a home' (Y Foundation, 2017: 15). Importantly, Housing First signifies a shift away from punishing or criminalising homeless persons, towards a transfer of a sense of fulfilment through home ownership, often resulting in a sense of safety, but also self-esteem for the majority of those who are rehoused, opening up further avenues for positive life changes. This is squarely opposed to the traditional model of housing provision for homeless persons, the so-called staircase model, where the homeless person 'earns' their own home based on fulfilment of prerequisites, often related to substance abuse management or good behaviour in homelessness shelters. Once these conditionalities are fulfilled, they are then provided with a home. It seems fairly obvious to state how infantilising such conditionalities can be and how they perpetuate the distinction between the deserving and undeserving poor through the need for performative 'good behaviour'.

As a result of adopting the Housing First approach in 2008, which included significant investments in the construction of new homes, Finland is the only country in the EU within which homelessness rates are falling steadily (Kaakinen, 2018). Correspondingly, street homelessness has nearly been eradicated, and in the capital Helsinki only one 50-bed night shelter remains. The city of Helsinki owns its own construction company to build social housing, and one in seven residents live in city-owned housing. Official housing policy demands that areas of new housing development must provide a strict balance of housing that limits social segregation. In addition, Helsinki owns 70 per cent of the land within the city limits, and as part of its current social housing strategy is providing 7,000 newly built homes a year. This is in stark contrast to the Republic of Ireland, for example, where, despite its government's adoption of Housing First in 2018, only 6,000 new homes were built by the Irish state in the entire country in a year (*The Journal*, 2019). In the Australian context, Clarke et al (2019) show, quite disappointingly, how Housing First initiatives perpetuate the very problem that they purport to address: housing conditionalities. Under the label 'Housing First', regional governments' policies 'require service providers to transition their most complex clients through temporary accommodation to ensure housing readiness' (Clarke et al, 2019: 955). As a consequence, some of the 'most vulnerable clients' are submitted to 'indefinite warehousing within inadequate shared accommodation facilities, or, in some cases, excludes them from accommodation altogether' (Clarke et al, 2019: 955). The important conclusion is that a progressive ethos and programme such as Housing First does not unconditionally lead to a 'paradigm shift', but that it is context-dependent on the broader socio-political context.

A second interesting concept to consider when thinking about alternative approaches to housing is cooperative housing, 'an umbrella term that comprises a wide range of collectively self-organised and self-managed housing forms' (Czischke and Huisman, 2018: 158). Although bottom-up cooperative housing developments are not new, top-down cooperative housing developments seem particularly promising 'in addressing some pressing contemporary social concerns, including the environmental, care and refugee reception crises' (Czischke and Huisman, 2018: 158). Czischke and Huisman (2018) describe how the Startblok project, initiated in 2015 in Amsterdam as an innovative approach to provide housing for newly arrived refugees, offers a hopeful alternative to the usual warehousing of refugees in European cities. As part of the collaboration between the Amsterdam Housing Cooperation, the city of Amsterdam and a Dutch refugee support NGO, retrofitted housing containers on a former sports field on the outskirts of Amsterdam were repurposed to house over 500 young adults, aged between 18 and 27, half of whom were Dutch and half refugees. Czischke and Huisman's (2018) preliminary findings show that the collaborative housing project has facilitated social bonding 'across ethnic and cultural backgrounds by virtue of belonging to the same age group and household type' including the 'creation of social bridges between refugees and Dutch tenants' (Czischke and Huisman, 2018: 165). Significant public investment by the city of Amsterdam, including the building of roads and sewage outlets, demonstrates the need of official support for such initiatives, but also shows how housing can be designed so as to engender a sense of care and mutuality, and can ultimately intensify social solidarity.

6

Policing Parenting, Family 'Support' and the Discipline and Punishment of Poor Families

Introduction

This chapter starts with the premise that the state's targeting of poor families for intervention is nothing new and indeed has a very long history. However, it does contend that in recent years there has been intensification in the policing of working-class families. This has happened due to the reification of particular knowledge, worked into selective evidence-informed programmes and practices adopted in different country contexts, which are negatively interventionist. This policing epitomises features of a 'centaur state' (Wacquant, 2009a: 43) with its 'worried frown' (Flint, 2019: 263) directed at poor families and, more particularly, poor parents. It is argued in this chapter that the intensive policing of poor families firmly locates the problems of poverty and inequality in poor families and serves to obscure states' responsibilities to address social inequalities and to really improve the material conditions of poor people's lives. The chapter draws on conceptual insights provided by the criminalisation of social policy in Chapter 2, parenting culture studies (Faircloth and Lee, 2010; Lee et al, 2014; Jensen, 2018) and critical social policy and social work (Featherstone, 2006; Featherstone et al, 2014b). It puts under the microscope 'state–family–capital relations' in a period characterised by rising social and economic inequalities, neoliberalisation and ethno-nationalism (Rosen and Faircloth, 2020: 14).

In 1979 Jacques Donzelot developed his thesis on the policing of the 'modern' family in the service of twentieth-century capitalism. He argued that since the late nineteenth century there was a shift in the government of families to a government through families, which impacted all families, albeit differently depending on their class positioning. He claimed that while the state, aided by the social professions, makes significant incursions into family life in general, poor families were in 'a vice of tutelary power' (Donzelot, 1979: 97). As noted by Donzelot (1979), the 'helping' professions, comprising psychologists, psychiatrists, doctors, nurses and social workers were ideally positioned to regulate families in states' interests, comprising as they did the 'psy' complex. Donzelot (1979) was writing about France but the implication of Donzelot's thesis had relevance for other country contexts. More importantly, it was prophetic in its forewarning of neoliberal states' desire to reduce spending to remedy class inequalities and to provide unconditional family support in favour of adopting standardised, targeted family interventions such as the ones identified in this chapter, which are aimed at improving the moral character and functioning of 'problem' or 'troubled' families.

Donzelot's legacy has been recognised in the field of parenting culture studies (Bristow, 2013), which has directly addressed the rise of intensive mothering/parenting since the mid-1990s. In 1996 Sharon Hays, a sociologist, proffered the concept of 'intensive mothering' to capture at the time the enormity of the ideological expectations being put on mothers to rear their children (Hays, 1996). This observation prompted a body of work on analysing parenting culture, which focused first on mothers (Hays, 1996; Wall, 2010; Faircloth, 2013), then on fathers (Shirani et al, 2012) and, more recently, on couples (Faircloth, 2020), to document and analyse the ways in which societies have come to demand so much of parents. Indeed, the assumption that parenting has the potential to determine a child's future and to secure or jeopardise national prosperity is one that has become increasingly hegemonic in many country contexts (Gillies, 2020). Its influence is evident in the field of youth justice. While there is a long historical tradition of viewing parents as responsible for their children's offences, this was more directly incorporated into legislative measures in the UK throughout the 1990s and the 2000s (Arthur, 2010) and in Ireland as a result of the Children Act 2001. More direct sanctions and requirements were made available to courts to administer to parents in instances where their children committed crimes. Just as parents are lauded when their children succeed, they are blamed for poor parenting when their children behave badly or experience poor outcomes, regardless of their income levels or resources (Furedi, 2001; Bristow, 2009).

Cohering with intensive parenting is intensive childhood, which captures the kind of investment children are now considered to need from their parents and other experts to overcome their vulnerability and risk and to grow into self-reliant and productive citizens (Prentice, 2009; Rosen, 2018). Parents in families with resources can more easily engage in concerted cultivation (Lareau, 2011) or the kinds of enrichment opportunities (Smyth and Craig, 2017) to maximise their children's positive outcomes as objects of expert knowledge, policy-making and practice. However, working-class parents have simply fewer resources to draw on to achieve the standards expected. Parenting culture theorists have also noted that in contemporary societies political concern with family structure (for example, two-parent family) has declined, as concern with family relations, parenting competencies and practices (how parents and children relate to each other and what they do) has become more pronounced (Gillies, 2005a). As shown in this chapter, a kind of neoliberal familialisation has been increasingly extending its tentacles into households and particularly low-income households (Gillies, 2014; Rosen, 2018). After the financial crisis in 2008, this coincided with universal welfare entitlements and child and family income cash supports in many countries being withdrawn (Daly, 2020).

Bodies of knowledge travel or are imported from particular sites of production into child welfare, social work and family support policies, practices and decision-making. They give politically chosen policy and programmatic choices 'epistemic authority' and legitimacy. What Donzelot (1979) called the 'psy complex' has come to exercise considerable influence in the field of child welfare, dwarfing other disciplinary knowledges, which accommodate the 'psy complex' and yield to its explanatory power in the field (Brannen, 2020). Agents of state in many country contexts are increasingly intervening in family life in the name of prevention science, a field of interdisciplinary research which has matured over a 30-year period and which draws from a broad range of disciplinary knowledges, but particularly epidemiology, medicine, biology, neuroscience and psychology. Prevention science has within its capacity the generation of knowledge to enhance equality, to reduce disparities in health outcomes and to impact at a population level to improve the social conditions in which people live their lives. However, the knowledge or evidence being harvested most readily from prevention science for policy-making and practice is that which chimes with neoliberal conceptions of poor children and their parents (Featherstone, et al, 2014a; Edwards, et al, 2016; White, 2017). When politically the problems are perceived to be the parents and the quality of their parenting, the proper locus for early intervention is the family, in an effort to reduce their burden on the state as its members move through life. The invocation of selective knowledge from science and its simplification and codification for policy-making and intervention has been explored in detail in the work of others (Featherstone et al, 2014a; Macvarish et al, 2015; Beddoe and Joy, 2017; Gillies et al, 2017; Wastell and White, 2017; White, 2017). For the purpose of this chapter, the focus is on growing influence of ACEs research in the child and family welfare fields; two family support interventions; the concerning tends in child protection practice; and, more specifically, the issues raised by the political pursuit of non-consensual adoption of looked-after children.

Adverse Childhood Experiences (ACEs): 'We have the science to act but do we really?'

The research on adverse childhood experience pioneered by Felitti, Anda and colleagues in 1998 in California in the USA (Felitti et al, 1998) catalysed a huge body of research in this field, inspiring what many have called an ACEs and a related Trauma-Informed Care movement (Craig et al, 2019). To put it in perspective, Kelly-Irving and Delpierre (2019) noted with reference to the Web of Science database that there was only one paper published on ACEs in 1985 but over 200 in 2018. ACEs research, its discourse and the movement it has inspired, have become very influential in the USA, and somewhat influential in other country contexts (Spratt et al, 2019) and in fields as varied as public health, paediatrics, early childhood education, family intervention work and child protection social work. Felitti et al's (1998) research involved over 17,000 predominantly white, middle-class, educated persons, who, while receiving physical examinations, completed survey questionnaires requiring them to retrospectively report on their childhood experiences and on their health status and behaviours at the time of survey. As a result of the research, evidential connections were made between experience of childhood adversities and subsequent negative health outcomes. The foundational ACEs study (Felitti et al, 1998) has been followed by extensive research. Some of this has focused on the intergenerational consequences of ACEs via the transmission from mothers to offspring (Madigan et al, 2017; Letourneau et al, 2019) and the negative impact of ACEs on children's developing brains and bodies and their future wellbeing (Cprek et al, 2020; Hughes et al, 2017; Javier et al, 2019).

That childhood adversities could produce poor adult outcomes is not surprising; however, the appeal of Felitti et al's (1998) research and some of the studies that followed is that they allowed something very complex to be simplified and made measurable in a way as to make it appealing to researchers, policymakers and practitioners (Lacey and Minnis, 2019). Determining what qualifies as an adversity and what does not, for whom, when, in what circumstances; knowing how adversities combine and interact and what ones are worse than others are all challenges. How to take account of the severity or otherwise of adversities and how they may be experienced subjectively in different ways, at different times, in different circumstances and over time and so on, is also not easy. In this context, boiling down childhood adversity in all its considerable complexity into a ten-item yes/no response questionnaire or a set of questionnaires and adding up adversities are appealing and helps make a highly complex area of investigation accessible, not only to researchers but also to individual professionals. For example, on the website of the American magazine *Psychology Today* it is advised that 'The primary means for practitioners to determine whether adverse childhood experiences might be taking a toll on an individual is to administer the 10-question ACE Questionnaire.' Allowing professionals to add up a person's adversities to generate an ACE score that can then be used to predict their cumulative risk of experiencing poor outcomes is very attractive in its simplicity. However, the notion that one would add up points based on a group of heterogeneous questions requiring yes/no to obtain an individual cumulative ACEs score, which has the status of a 'diagnosis', has been very strongly challenged (Kelly-Irving and Delpierre, 2019; Lacey and Minnis, 2019; Anda et al, 2020; McLennan et al, 2020). As noted by McLennan et al (2020):

> One of the most commonly used ACEs questionnaires is a ten-question version (ACEs-10), that is composed of two clusters – one asking about different types of child maltreatment and the other asking select questions about household challenges. Unfortunately, both this questionnaire and its derivatives have substantial drawbacks that warrant careful consideration about their use. ... Given these deficiencies, we recommend that these limitations are addressed before further use of ACEs-10, and its derivatives, for either clinical or research purposes.

This limited instrument is used to inform the care and clinical intervention that follows. ACEs routine enquiry, ACEs screening, the call to practitioners and individuals to be ACE aware or to individuals to find out their ACE score have proliferated, but they have all been challenged on different grounds. There is a lack of evidence showing the positive impact of their use (Ford et al, 2019; Anda et al, 2020; Campbell, 2020). Meriting attention also is the fatalism and the determinism that can be associated with an ACEs 'diagnosis' and practitioners and services' capacities to respond to the issues arising in the most beneficial ways (Finkelhor, 2018; Lacey and Minnis, 2019).

Macvarish and Lee (2019) have noted how much of the ACEs research is used in the service of propagating a moralising discourse that is implicitly gendered, raced and classed. There is a cultural proliferation of popular ACEs discourse and media (TED talks, videos) propagating simplified messages pertaining to ACEs, enforcing stereotyping and stigma and conveying the inevitability of poor outcomes unless individuals/families succumb to ACEs-inspired interventions. For example, paediatrician and proponent of ACEs research in the USA, Nadine Burke Harris, in her TED talk, uses the metaphor of the 'the bear in the forest' to represent a violent father (the bear). As related by Burke Harris, he returns to the family home each night and his behaviour activates severe and repeated stress in his child, to cause profound health damage and detrimental outcomes. She advocates multidisciplinary treatment, parent education and, if necessary, medication to prevent ACEs and to address the impact of high ACE scores. Burke Harris is California's Surgeon General, and in January 2020 California became the first state in the USA to introduce screening for ACEs, targeted at children of families on Medi-Cal (health insurance for families on low income) reportedly at a cost of $160 million (Underwood, 2020). The Welsh Public Health Network Cymru produced an animated video cartoon of a boy suffering abuse, who relates his story as a child, then a teenager and later as an adult, who has poor health outcomes and who bears witness to the damaging outcomes for his own children. This is available on YouTube and is reproduced on websites of services that work with low-income families. Youngballymun is an area-based childhood programme (ABC) in a disadvantaged community in Dublin in Ireland. Part of its work involves creating awareness of ACEs by showing a resilience documentary, providing workshops to explore ACEs and devising collaborative strategies to support families in the community. The following was published on the website of this organisation, which is in a poor community, ravaged by austerity, and which had the highest concentration of lone-parent households in the country of Ireland in 2000 at 43.6 per cent (Ballymun Local Drugs Taskforce, 2000):

> The most reliable way to produce an adult, who is brave and curious and kind and prudent is to ensure that when he is an infant, his hypothalamic-pituitary-adrenal axis functions well. And how do you do that? It is not magic. First, as much as possible, you protect him from serious trauma and chronic stress; then; even more important, you provide him with a secure, nurturing relationship with one parent and ideally two. (Tough, 2012: 182, cited in Youngballymun, 2021)

ACEs research, its discourses and movement can be rightfully lauded for putting ACEs on political agendas in a way that they never were before; however, there are significant problems with ACEs' conceptions, discourses and in the translation of their research findings into policies, diagnoses, treatments and practices. For example, as mentioned, child-rearing is 'scientised' in ACEs discourse (Macvarish and Lee, 2019: 75) and ACEs are rooted in a conception of child welfare as biological and cultural rather than material. In this manner, rather than bringing any significantly new insights to bear, ACEs can be viewed as proliferating an old idea packaged as a new one (Lee et al, 2014). They propagate an understanding of poverty as an outcome of household adversity as distinct from a cause of that adversity – people are poor because of the households they grow up in, which are dysfunctional, and because their brains and their bodies are damaged and they have been born to brain- and body-damaged parents. Intergenerational poverty is divorced from its social context, constructed as having genetic and biological antecedents, transmitted from parent to child via their own personal failings, poor choices, faulty socialisation practices, norms and habits.

> ACE counts correlate with worse health, criminal justice, employment and educational outcomes over the life course. The impacts of ACEs on criminality, violence, early unplanned pregnancy and retention in poverty means those with ACEs are more likely to propagate a cycle that exposes their own children to ACEs. (Bellis et al, 2014: 5)

The foundational ACEs study (Felitti et al, 1998) mentioned earlier in the chapter restricted samples to predominantly white, adult, middle-class, educated persons and adversities to ten items, which were behavioural, relational and rooted in household dysfunction. Subsequent studies (Ye and Reyes-Salvail, 2014; Finkelhor et al, 2015) sought to address this limited operationalisation by adding questions about other potential adversities and about the social and environmental conditions that cause adversity. However, these did not lead to a broader conceptualisation of adversity and its social distribution in an unequal society, or to policy-based approaches that could complement medicalised and therapeutic responses to adversity's effects (Metzler et al, 2017; Lacey and Minnis, 2019; McEwen et al, 2019; Walsh et al, 2019). Nonetheless, to date ACEs research has been considerably influential, despite its unready state as scientific evidence (Lacey and Minnis, 2019). It is being used to drive policy and service provision in the direction of individual and family-level interventions and psychosocial therapies (for example, trauma-informed care) and away from actions needed at community, regional, national and international levels (Hartas, 2019; McEwen and Gregerson, 2019). Redistributing wealth, challenging precarity and low pay, addressing housing shortage, improving housing conditions and enhancing living environments are pushed down the public policy priority list in helping families to improve their lives. Alternatively, an excessive focus is put on households, on child–parent relations and on upskilling parents so that they may better cope with the circumstances of their lives and buffer their children from the socio-economic inequality and deprivation likely to be their lot. As researcher Kelly-Irving commented in the *Irish Times* newspaper:

... If someone is living in poor-quality, noisy, overcrowded housing without access to green spaces, these are material conditions that need to be tackled. Therapy and interventions alone are a patch, but it's still a lot to ask a child to be resilient if they are going home to a damp and hungry house. (Kelly-Irving, cited in McGuire, 2019)

While ACEs research's potential to build up population-based data may be useful for population-based actions, it is unfortunately finding a comfortable home in the area of diagnosis and in service-level provision/intervention design for, predominantly, poor children and their families (White, et al, 2019). While proponents of ACEs lament resistance to the ACEs message, almost no policy or practice area engaging with poor people or their families is left untouched by ACEs research, its discourse and its relations (for example, toxic stress, trauma-informed care). Spratt and Kennedy (2020) identified a host of recent social service developments in the UK and Ireland inspired by ACEs-related research findings. Notwithstanding the proliferation of ACEs research in the USA, Scotland is proudly presenting itself as an ACE-aware nation and it resourced a full-time governmental post to progress the ACE agenda. Very similar research to Felitti et al's (1998) was conducted in Britain by Bellis et al (2014) and the first national ACEs study was undertaken in England in 2013. The British NHS initiated an ACEs hub to progress national actions on ACEs and grew its number of ACE-based interventions. In Northern Ireland, ACEs has gained significant traction and in the Republic of Ireland there are ACEs online communities, training for child welfare personnel and so on. Joy and Beddoe (2019) noted that the ACE questionnaire was being circulated in trauma-informed practice education for social workers in New Zealand, though at the time they were writing, it had yet to permeate social work practice in any significant way. They raised concern about its proliferation in New Zealand, considering that it was a tool that seemed not to be attuned to the societal structural impacts of racism, poverty and colonisation.

ACEs research is helping along a slew of surveillant and behaviour change-based family interventions, which seek to make persons resilient to the awful conditions of their lives. Parents, more often mothers and more specifically poor and lone mothers, are the core of targeted interventions, constructed somewhat paradoxically as the cause of ACEs and the solution in ACEs research (Macvarish and Lee, 2019). ACE-informed interventions do not challenge or disrupt the excessive focus on parenting in a climate of intensive parenting. Rather, they put pressure on working-class parents, including solo/lone mothers, with limited economic and cultural resources, to produce and rear children with outcomes comparable to their middle-class counterparts (Macvarish and Lee, 2019). ACEs research has yet to exert the significant influence it has in the USA outside of that country. However, given that decision-makers in most country contexts seem to have a penchant for checklists, assessment tools and cookie-cutter approaches aimed at standardising professional practices, it is difficult to imagine that it will not take greater hold. Furthermore, as will be shown in the following section, ACEs research could find another comfortable home in a family support landscape, in which a variety of social ills impacting families are also boiled down to deficits in parenting capacity.

Family 'support' via programmatic interventions

While family support should never be romanticised because it has always had its authoritarian, controlling, stigmatising and paternalistic strains (Donzelot, 1979; Rose, 1990; Van Wel, 1992; Welshman, 2017), it has undergone a metamorphosis in recent years into something quite distinctive and worrisome. Helping professionals have become increasingly tied into delivering more transferrable, standardised, evidence-informed, responsibilising programmes (for example, Head Start, Sure Start, Family Intervention). These in turn have been displaced by even more targeted, intrusive and controlling interventionist projects of government (Nurse Family Partnership, Family Nurse Partnership (FNP), Troubled Families Programme (TFP)). This metamorphosis is not particular to any one country context as the trend towards more muscular forms of family policy and practice intervention have been documented in many country contexts (Ball et al, 2016). These include England (Welshman, 2017; Crossley, 2018), France (Join-Lambert, 2016), Denmark (Dannesboe et al, 2018), Sweden (Lundqvist, 2015; Widding, 2018), Germany (Ostner and Stolberg, 2015), New Zealand (Beddoe, 2014) and more recently Norway (Malmberg-Heimonen and Tøge, 2020). An increase in child poverty in Norway from 7 per cent in 2006 to 10.8 per cent in 2017, attributed to inequality due to limited growth in incomes of immigrant families, prompted the introduction of a targeted low-income family support programme (HOLF) in 2015 to reduce the likelihood of intergenerational poverty transmission (Malmberg-Heimonen and Tøge, 2020). This marked a new departure for Norway, where traditionally enhanced universal services and better income redistribution, rather than targeted family support, would have been the more likely policy responses (Malmberg-Heimonen and Tøge, 2020).

Furthermore, there are new sites in which the surveillance of parenting is taking hold. For instance, in Ireland, government-funded family hubs, the shared living spaces provided for homeless families, many of which are lone-parent families, apply strict rules of conduct (curfews, visitor bans, physical restrictions on movement, obligations to search for private rental accommodation). Families living in the hubs have their parenting actively monitored to the extent that long-term residents, both parents and children, compared them to prison-like institutional settings that undermined independent family functioning (Hearne and Murphy, 2017; Ombudsman for Children's Office, 2019). Each of two programmes (Nurse Family Partnership and the TFP) the following sections of this chapter focus on, share features. These are: close monitoring of families, predominantly female-headed households; a focus on individual parental responsibility as a solution to structural inequalities; and a concentration on fostering aspiration for a better future to be achieved via labour market engagement (Crossley, 2016, 2018). They are intensely interventionist and moralising, employing as they do the social 'classing gaze' (Finch, 1993). Each seeks to address the 'intergenerational' disadvantage confronted by families, but in a way which allows the depoliticisation of such disadvantage (Crossley, 2016, 2018). As shown in the following sections, they considerably obscure states' obligations to address social inequality, poverty and institutional failings or to improve the social conditions that make poor people's lives, particularly parents' and families' lives, much more difficult.

Nurse Family Partnership/Family Nurse Partnership

The Family Nurse Partnership (FNP) was introduced in England by the Department of Health in 2006 and was adapted from the US-derived Nurse Family Partnership programme developed in the 1970s. This US programme has also been modified for use in many countries including the Netherlands (the Voorzorg Nurse Family Partnership) (Mejdoubi, 2015), Scotland (Cannings-John et al, 2018), Canada (Jack et al, 2012), Northern Ireland (Smyth and Anderson, 2014), Germany (Kliem et al, 2018) and Australia for implementation with First Nations mothers and babies (Zarnowiecki et al, 2018). NHS England transferred the programme to local authorities in 2015 and it was then provided in over 100 local authority areas (Corbacho et al, 2017). FNP is a fee-based programme available only under licence, with intellectual property held by the University of Colorado.

On the FNP website in England, it is stated that the FNP team is comprised of a supervisor and eight nurses, each of whom engages with a cohort of clients and an administrator. It comprises a voluntary home visiting programme for first-time low-income young mothers aged 19 years or under. A specially trained family nurse visits the young mother regularly, from the early stages of pregnancy until their child is two years old. By using a psycho-educational approach and a focus on positive behaviour change, FNP provides ongoing, intensive support to young, first-time mothers and their babies as well as fathers and other family members if mothers would like them to take part (FNP website). The psychological theories underpinning the programme are also described on the website – human ecology theory (Bronfenbrenner, 1979), attachment theory (Bowlby, 1969) and self-efficacy theory (Bandura, 1977) – while the visiting nurses are trained in motivational interviewing techniques.

Randomised controlled trials (RCTs) of the programme in the USA reported positive results, such as extended spacing between pregnancies, increased maternal employment and self-sufficiency, reduced criminal activity by mothers, improved pregnancy behaviours, and reduced child abuse and neglect (Olds et al, 1986, 1997, 2002, 2007, 2019). An RCT of the programme (VoorZorg) in the Netherlands reported positive outcomes in the domains of child protection, home environment and child behaviour (Mejdoubi et al, 2015). The FNP was subject to a formative evaluation in England (Barnes and Henderson, 2012) and subsequently a RCT, which was accompanied by a cost-effectiveness evaluation conducted alongside (Robling et al, 2016). This found that there was no effect on the short-term outcomes measured. A key boast of the programme, as is common to most early intervention initiatives, is that its early intervention orientation saves the state money in the long term by reducing the demand for foster care and residential care. However, when economically evaluated in England it was not found not to constitute a cost-effective intervention (Corbacho et al, 2017) and the case was made, based on the evidence, to discontinue the programme altogether (Robling et al, 2016). However, rather than being discontinued, the programme was enhanced in England in response to the RCT findings.

The FNP integrates two key principles of criminal justice: early intervention into 'failing' families and the reinforcement of parental responsibility and self-sufficiency. The programme's distinction as, in part, a crime-prevention intervention was originally elaborated by its creator David Olds, who wrote:

> The Nurse–Family Partnership (NFP) is different from most mental-health, substance-abuse, and crime-prevention interventions tested to date in that it focuses on improving neuro-developmental, cognitive, and behavioral functioning of the child by improving prenatal health, reducing child abuse and neglect, and enhancing family functioning and economic self-sufficiency in the first two years of the child's life. (Olds, 2007: 206)

It aims to change behaviours not material circumstances, as the focus is on providing advice and practical support but not financial aid. Indeed, David Olds, in the 'David Olds' story' on the programme website (Nurse–Family Partnership, 2020) is credited with saying that it is with the help of a well-trained nurse supporting a woman during pregnancy that she can overcome obstacles like poverty in her life:

> There is a magic window during pregnancy… it's a time when the desire to be a good mother and raise a healthy, happy child creates motivation to overcome incredible obstacles including poverty, instability or abuse with the help of a well-trained nurse.

In Australia, the significant socio-economic deprivation experienced by many in the FNP target group (Aboriginal mothers and their children) was identified as a huge factor undermining the value of home visiting programmes and underscoring the urgent action need to address the social determinants of health. Some home visits had to take place in cars or other settings because the mothers participating did not have homes for professionals to visit (Zarnowieki et al, 2018). Unstable living conditions and crowded housing were factors which explained programme attrition in the USA (Holland et al, 2014). In England, its alignment with the neoliberal governance of the poor family is manifestly evident. For example, the evaluation of FNP reported some programme participants' dismay at the amount of paperwork they had to complete, such as quizzes and diaries (Ball et al, 2012: 23). Mothers who desired to no longer participate in the programme but reported finding it supportive also expressed concern that the frequency of the visits made them feel they were being monitored for evidence of bad parenting, particularly in situations when the family nurse had already been in contact with child protection social work services (Ball et al, 2012: 23). Nurses keep records of fathers present during home visits and they review 'homework' completed by fathers (Barnes et al, 2008). There were also reported instances of fathers trying to give up smoking or changing their smoking habits due to family nurse input (Barnes et al, 2008: 114). Following Donzelot (1979) and Foucault (1977), such findings draw attention to the programme's productive use of professional power to incite self-governance on the part of parents and to leverage what agency they have to rise to normative middle-class standards of family life.

The Troubled Families Programme

Knepper (2007) observed that family-centred crime policies tend to fuse images of families as both troubled and troublesome. In December 2011, in the aftermath of what was to become known as the London riots in England, the Troubled Families Programme (TFP) was launched, targeting 120,000 'troubled' families (Crossley, 2018). More families were targeted in subsequent phases of the programme (15,000 by 2014) (Crossley, 2016).

'Troubled' families were identified as those involved in crime and ASB, in which the parents were unemployed and children were engaged in school truancy (DCLG, 2012). Families experiencing domestic violence, children in need of help and parents with health problems were also added to the 'Troubled Families' categorisation and at least two of the criteria had to be present to merit intervention (DCLG, 2014). McKendrick and Finch (2017) raised concern with the connections made politically between the TFP and counterterrorism, which sought to create in the public mind ideas about vulnerable persons as terrorists. They also drew attention to the implication of Birmingham City Council's criterion – 'family member believed to have been influenced by violent extremism' – as one of a list of criteria that could be used to justify including a family in the TFP (McKendrick and Finch, 2017: 318).

'Troubled' families were targeted for intervention because it was claimed they cost the state £9 billion yearly (DCLG, 2013). Local authorities agreeable to deliver the programme receive funding via a payment-by-results model based on numbers of families targeted and on family improvement indicators. The claim by the Prime Minister, David Cameron in 2015, that the programme was successful on the basis that it had 'turned around' 99 per cent of families was used to recommend its expansion into child protection and beyond (DCLG, 2015). However, not so long after, the National Institute of Economic and Social Research (Day et al, 2016) found no evidence that the programme had any significant or systematic impact on the primary outcome measures.

To avoid the cost incurred in multi-agency work with families, TFP was reportedly staffed by a new 'breed' of family workers capable of operationalising a distinctive whole family practical intervention model specifically designed to 'turn families around' by being sufficiently persistent, assertive and challenging in their approach (DCLG, 2012). The workers, who entered family homes, were required, as Prime Minister David Cameron envisaged, 'to put in place the building blocks of an orderly home and a responsible life' (Cameron, 2011a). The discourse left little doubt that a 'corrective normalisation' (McCallum, 2007: 113) of family life was required or further penalties applied. The TFP aimed to model homemaking and mothercraft so that its subjects could develop skills of organisation and discipline as well as habits of morality, austerity and workfare. The TFP's focus on domesticating families and particularly mothers in accordance with heteronormative values (Nunn and Tepe-BelFrage, 2017) has been shown to involve a remobilisation and reconfiguration of colonial logics (Turner, 2017). The targeting of 'problem' families is not new (Jordan, 1974; Macnicol, 1987) and the TFP can be justifiably viewed as a discursive and programmatic revival of the notion of an underclass (Garrett, 2017) during economic austerity. Yet its distinctive neoliberal features, such as payment by results and close attention to outcomes turning around families, show it to be a 'top-down, neoliberal, de-professionalised and politicised governance' of poor families (Lambert, 2018: 88). The explicit stigmatising and pathologising label of the 'troubled family' as distinct from the family experiencing trouble was of its time also, in terms of paving the way for English state-imposed austerity and punishing welfare reform (Shildrick et al, 2016; Lambert and Crossley, 2017).

As the universal supports for families and vital public services were retracted in England during austerity, TFP was being rolled out and extended. The programme, which was to end in 2020, was continued until 2021–2 with a further financial commitment of £165 million (Preece, 2020). Silver and Crossley (2020: 570) queried the absence of any mention of poverty and welfare reform in the TFP and its evaluation reports on the grounds that 66 per cent of the TFP families who completed a family survey reported that their household income was less than £12,500, a figure which was well below the poverty line for families with children. Families living in poverty are conveniently not identified as poor in the TFP discourse, rather they are represented as lacking the knowledge and skills to live successfully on very low incomes. For example, an evaluation of the programme undertaken for the British government by Ipsos MORI (Pereira et al, 2018), which utilised case studies and qualitative data, featured a lone parent, Catherine, and her three children, one of whom had a serious health condition and one of whom was a baby. Catherine could not find paid work she could successfully reconcile with the care of her children. It was reported that 'Meeting everyday costs of food, bills and school uniforms made daily life a struggle' for Catherine and her family. Therefore, it was determined that 'Catherine's finances are her main problem'. However, it should be noted that in 2018, nearly half of children in lone-parent families live in poverty compared to one in four in couple families in the UK (Barnard et al, 2018). The TFP worker Helen helped Catherine with her finances by offering her advice on saver deals to enable her to make her money go further, referring her for budgeting support and organising voluntary work for her as a stepping-stone to employment. Helen also made Catherine aware of employment opportunities and childcare options available to her when her child would be six months old so that she build her confidence and 'raise her ambition towards work'. With Helen's help, Catherine's outlook and confidence improved; she could manage her bills and she valued her time with her son, who had improved at school (Pereira et al, 2018: 74– 5). Unfortunately, finding ways to modify impacts of socio-economic inequalities in households further propagates notions that if only poor people were more enterprising they could make ends meet and not suffer the consequences of being poor. The no-nonsense, challenging approach, adopted by key workers and celebrated by politicians (Cameron, 2011a), and a distinctive hallmark of the programme was counted as a success as evidenced by TFP-participating parents, such as this particular father:

> I liked her [TF worker] straight away, she's got that realistic attitude where 'you do something wrong I'll tell you if you're doing something wrong, if you're doing something right I'll pat you on the back all day'. And I like that, I like the bluntness, and if I'm doing something wrong I'll fix it. (Father, in-depth interview, cited in Pereira et al, 2018: 63)

Here is the perfect exemplar of a subjectification process in a programme of government; the subject who transforms himself into a project, spurred on to work at fixing himself in line with TFP guidance and norms of conduct. It is not difficult to see why the TFP is viewed as a flagship programme at the forefront of states' political strategies aimed at regulating the poor via disciplinary social policy and practice (Tyler, 2013; Gillies, 2014; Lambert and Crossley, 2017; Nunn and Tepe-Belfrage, 2017; Sayer, 2017).

Child protection and non-consensual adoption policy

The evidence that poverty impacts child development and wellbeing is incontrovertible (Wilkinson and Pickett, 2010). The systemic links between family poverty and deprivation, child protection intervention and children being in the care of the state rather than their families of origin are stark (Bywaters et al, 2017). Children from marginal communities tend to be overrepresented in the child welfare system in countries generally. Despite failings in many countries to collect useful data on the socio-economic backgrounds of children in state care, that child protection systems bear down on the poorest and the most marginal is known. A child in the most deprived decile of neighbourhoods in England has a ten times greater chance of being placed on a child protection plan and a 12 times greater chance of being looked after by the state in comparison to a child in the most affluent decile (Bunting et al, 2018). In Scotland, children living in the poorest 10 per cent of neighbourhoods are 20 times more likely to be taken into care than those in the wealthiest 10 per cent (Bywaters et al, 2020). Across the United States, black children are 2.4 times more likely than white children to experience the termination of parental rights. In New Jersey, New York and a host of other American states, black children are at least four times more likely than white children to see their parents' rights terminated (Wildeman et al, 2020; Guggenheim,

2020). Indeed, Dorothy Roberts (2020: n.p.) has argued that the child welfare system in the USA could more accurately be called the 'Family Regulation System' given the intensity of its practices of surveillance and regulation of African American families. Agreeing with calls to defund the police in the USA, she firmly rejected proposals seeking the transfer of resources from police departments to child welfare agencies, seeing it as a shift in the operation of carceral powers from one state agency to another (Roberts, 2020). In Ireland, children from ethnic minorities, including Traveller children, are seven times more likely to be subject to care proceedings that white Irish children (Coulter, 2015). Families from Syria being accommodated in refugee reception/direct provision centres in Ireland have reported having their parenting and family practices monitored, problematised, regulated and referred by staff in the centres to statutory agents to a significant extent (Ní Raghallaigh et al, 2020). This can be considered in the context of a disproportionate presence of children from ethnic minorities in the child protection system in Ireland (Coulter, 2015). There is also emerging evidence in England of child protection social workers' surveillance of service users' lives by their own active online searching or by being made aware (by managers and colleagues) of aspects of services users' lives, as revealed on social networking sites such as Facebook (Singh Cooner et al, 2020). This raises further concerns about professional intrusion into and the monitoring of poor people's lives made possible by social networking sites.

What is manifestly evident is that over time societies have developed child protection systems that have become increasingly preoccupied with assessing risk and parenting capacity in families, and in configuring responses which sideline the damaging impact of poverty, socio-economic inequality and the negative impact of governments' policies on these families (Saar-Heiman and Gupta, 2020; Rogowski, 2021). To illustrate this further, adoption of children in state care, which dispenses with parental consent, is chosen as the focus for attention in the following section. The assumption that adoption may provide the optimum kind of timely early intervention for children to achieve positive outcomes may not be the intended policy outcome from prevention science, research on ACEs and so on, but their research findings can certainly be used to provide the underlying rationale for the pursuit of adoption without consent. British politician, Michael Gove, when Secretary of State for Education, made clear the state's favoured policy approach where looked-after children were concerned: 'Adoption transforms the lives of some of the most neglected children in our country. It is a generous act and it can achieve considerable results. ... That's why we are determined that adoption should happen more often and should happen more speedily' (Gove, 2012).

Adoption without consent

Adoption involves the permanent legal transfer of a child from one family to another, irrespective of practices of openness (Garrett, 2018). It is the highest sanction that courts can impose to punish parenting failure (Broadhurst and Mason, 2017). Permanent removal of children from their parents is not an equal opportunity practice impervious to social class, gender, race/ethnicity differentials (Lewis and Brady, 2018). Kirton (2018: 320) has argued that adoption of children in state care sits comfortably with neoliberal governance. Indeed, adoption-driven child protection and welfare practice is desirable in neoliberal capitalist countries where social problems such as poverty can be conveniently reframed as individual/familial problems and where negative views about the parenting capacities of poor people and migrants prevail. The conditions can be created so that the adoption of children in state care is done much swifter by legal requirement and justified on the basis that the delays deemed detrimental to children (derived from scientific knowledge claims) are avoided. Speeding up the adoption of the looked-after child means that money spent on foster care or residential placements is reduced, as is the cost of support and time spent with vulnerable families seeking to meet the standards of responsibilisation required for successful reunification with their children. Indeed, it is not unusual in most countries for services to reduce their investment in the family of origin as soon as a child is placed in the care of the state (Broadhurst and Mason, 2017).

Many countries have provision to permit adoption of children without parents' consent but only a few countries could be viewed as pursuing an adoption-driven 'customer service' approach (Garrett, 2018: 1250), which prioritises child rescue to a much greater extent than family support. The number of adoptions without consent is high in England and in Wales, which are outliers in this practice. Germany has the next highest rate, albeit much lower than in England and Wales (Fenton Glynn, 2015); other countries in Europe which permit adoption without consent do not come close to the prevalence of the practice in England and Wales. For instance, Palacios et al (2019) reported that while almost 50 per cent of all adoptions in England could be without parental consent, in Sweden adoption without parental consent was fairly exceptional. The scale of the adoption of children born into care (that is, children taken into state care through care proceedings taken in the first week of their life) in England and Wales has generated concern, as has the concentration of children in this specific category who are children of parents who were themselves brought up in state care (Roberts et al, 2019). Considerable variation in this practice in local authority areas has been found, as well as evidence of a growing number of parents who, up until the time of having a child born into care had not experienced having any of their other children removed from their care (Bilson and Bywaters, 2020). In Australia legislation also permits more timely removal of young children from their parents. In New South Wales in Australia where Aboriginal children and young people comprise 40 per cent of the state's looked-after children, a law was introduced in 2018 further enabling adoption from the state's foster care system without parents' consent (Allam, 2018). Critics of the legislation argued that it would lead to another 'stolen generation', adding to Australia's already shameful history of Aboriginal child abuse, ill-treatment and neglect (Allam, 2018). In the USA, the Adoption and Safe Families Act 1997 has been condemned as a racist law because of the impact it is having on African American families (Guggenheim, 2020). The legislation shifts the emphasis from family preservation to the health, safety and permanency needs of children, so that parents who are incarcerated or who have failed to show the change demanded of them within short timeframes can have their parenting rights permanently terminated (Whitt-Woosley and Sprang, 2014; Sayer, 2020).

Within four months of a child entering the state care system, local authorities in England are required by the state to decide whether adoptive care is best for the child. Very worrisome is the evidence of England and Wales setting adoption targets to be achieved. Adoption targets introduced formally by the Labour government in the UK in 2001 were officially abolished in 2008. However, evidence of adoption targets being used by local authorities and being monitored by OFSTED re-emerged as a result of freedom of information requests made by the Transparency Project in 2016 (Stevenson, 2016, Tickle, 2016). Since 2010 adoption has been actively promoted politically in England (Featherstone and Gupta, 2020) and this is set to continue. In 2020, Michelle Donelan MP wrote to all directors of children's services, informing them that adoption ' is a priority for the new government and we also wish to see a renewed focus on adoption by all local authorities' (Donelan, 2020). The UK has seen rising care proceedings involving migrant families, and the Latvian paliament challenged the House of Commons about the practice of adoption without consent, as it impacts Latvian families residing in England and Wales (Bowcott, 2015). Parents, some of whom had English-language barriers and have been impacted by adoption-driven practice have also brought their concerns to Members of the European Parliament (Kirton-Darling, 2016). Indeed, the obstacles, which potentially slowed down the adoption of black and minority ethnic children (for example, the removal of an ethnicity clause in the Children and Families Act 2014, which prior to this would have required a child's background to be considered in adoption decision-making) have been removed over time (Kirton, 2018). A Council of Europe Report in 2015 criticised England's and Wales' over-reliance on adoption by strangers and their miscarriages of justice in relation to some of the adoption practice examined as well as the lack of legal provision to reverse unjust adoption decisions (Borzova, 2015). The same report criticised the lack of systematic disaggregated anonymised data on the care population in the different member states in the EU, which would provide more insight into the categories of persons and their families most impacted by child protection and welfare decision-making.

Supporting parents and families: future directions

The poor parent, but more specifically the poor lone mother, is the pedagogical subject of the neoliberal welfare state (Crossley, 2016; Turner, 2017). In such a climate, early intervention into working-class families and the responsibilisation of parents identified as deficient is increasingly relied on as providing the optimum solution to addressing the 'reproduction' of crime and poverty. Over-optimistic claims generated by 'new' knowledges/ sciences, including ACEs, provide this kind of approach with its raison d'être, and it is one which has become increasingly normative in legislation, policy and practice in many country contexts (for example, the USA, UK, Ireland, France, New Zealand and so on). In this context, the evidence-based policy approach needs to be treated sceptically when it is more accurately a 'policy-based evidence' approach (Macvarish et al, 2015; Cairney, 2019). It is only the evidence compatible with neoliberal political preferences that is consistently being distilled for translation into policy and practice. Even if participants experience programmatic staff and their offerings as supportive and if they enhance their parenting and household organisation capacities, it does not detract from the fact that, at their very best, they only ameliorate and further obscure the ongoing damage done by poverty and socio-economic inequality. The wider context since 2010 is such that the redistributive potential of welfare states is sharply constrained at the same time as poor people are being subjected to intense monitoring and discipline in the name of 'family support'. These families are also at greater risk of experiencing the permanent removal of their children within a short timeframe via adoption, as a result of recent legislative amendments introduced in a number of country contexts (for example, England, Australia, the USA).

Poverty and inequality have increasingly become the taken-for-granted backdrops to social provision. As demonstrated, poverty is overwhelmingly framed and understood as a cultural rather than a structural phenomenon, driving policy and practices accordingly. For practitioners, it has become 'too big to tackle' (Morris et al, 2018: 370) or so familiar that it is invisible (McCartan et al, 2018). Universal services supporting families need resourcing and states need to refocus on redistributing wealth rather than seeking to make families resilient to economic adversity. While parenting and family support conjure up notions of a response driven by families' own identified needs, the reality is that policy and programmes in this field are increasingly making parents the objects of expert-led responsibilisation and social control, and their behaviours the locus of prescribed interventions (Morris and Featherstone, 2010; Daly and Bray, 2015).

Approaches that promote non-punitive, relational, strengths-based family support and child protection/welfare practice, which are not decontextualised from, but show understanding of families' resources, diversity and circumstances (Featherstone et al, 2014a; Gupta, Featherstone and White, 2016), have to offer a more promising alternative to what exists. There is renewed interest in social inequalities approaches (Bywaters et al, 2020) and anti-poverty practice frameworks for social work (McCartan et al, 2018). Saar-Heiman and Gupta (2020) have elaborated a poverty-aware framework as a practical alternative to the narrow risk-focused paradigm that pervades child protection practice in many country contexts. There is a re-envisioning of social work as a human rights and social justice profession aimed at moving societies closer to social equality and there are suggested frameworks for application in practice (Alseth, 2020). Critical and radical social work perspectives proffer an appropriate critique and the vital ideas for an interventionist social work that has the potential to expose inequality's damage and to transform practices in line with progressive social values.

7

Criminalising Justice-Involved Persons through Rehabilitation and Reintegration Policies

Introduction

The idea and practice of rehabilitation and reintegration of justice-involved persons as one of the main goals and principles of punishment have been well-established principles of modern criminal justice systems (Rotman, 1990). Rehabilitation and reintegration as a field of policy and practice and the 'enormous social struggles faced by formed prisoners to reintegrate ... has gone from essentially a non-topic in the 1980s and 1990s to being possibly *the* hot topic in recent years' (Maruna, 2020: 577). The story usually goes that those who have excluded themselves by upsetting moral, social and legal norms are expected to re-enter and re-attach themselves to the 'circuit of inclusion' (Rose, 2000: 324). Throughout this chapter it will be shown how the policy field of reintegration and rehabilitation under neoliberal rule takes on particular shapes and practices. Different configurations of neoliberal rule demand not only that 'law-breakers' become law-abiding citizens, but also that they become productive members of society who can avail themselves of opportunities in highly unequal and competitive societies. In market-oriented penal politics, citizens are re-educated 'to become self-reliant and enterprising through property ownership, minimising their demands on public welfare, adapting to more precarious labour markets and adhering to marketized norms and traditions' (Corcoran, 2020: 23). Underpinned by the modern penal welfare state's structures and practices (Garland, 2001), contemporary rehabilitation and reintegration regimes offer and sometimes also demand engagement with various services such as education and training, employment, welfare, addiction, housing or family support services. Informed by previous critiques of welfarist practices, it is posited that seemingly well-intentioned supports can equally be understood as further attempts of containing what are perceived as 'social problem' populations: 'Re-entry programs are not an antidote to but an extension of punitive containment as government technique for managing problem categories and territories in the dualising city ... re-entry must therefore be understood as an element in the redrawing of the perimeter, priorities, and modalities of action of the state as a stratifying and classifying agency and not as an "industry" geared to "reintegrating" a marginalised population that was never socially and economically integrated to start with' (Wacquant, 2010: 616). From such a critical perspective, rehabilitation and reintegration policies seek to contain marginalised populations and mould them into law-abiding and productive citizens.

Also, neoliberal modalities of rehabilitation and reintegration are not primarily concerned with changing the deeper forces at play affecting justice-involved persons' lives but are often focused on charging individuals with spearheading their personal desistance and reintegrative journeys (Gray, 2007; Carlen, 2012; de Lint and Chazal 2013; De Giorgi, 2017). As a result, reintegration and rehabilitation policies often remain 'imaginary' (Carlen, 2008) and are complicit in perpetuating 'neoliberal neglect' (De Giorgi, 2017). Ironically, the unsurprising lack of success of such rehabilitative imaginaries is responded to by endless 'recursive patterns' (Freeman, 1999: 24), with further refinements, permutations and add-ons, resulting in the intensified management of justice-involved persons. Rarely are materially tangible changes prioritised, such as reducing material inequalities, provision of guaranteed housing or strategies of decriminalisation or decarceration. In other words, the ubiquitous presence of rehabilitation and reintegration policies recognises the importance of social reintegration for justice-involved individuals but does not necessarily redistribute towards its achievement (Fraser and Honneth, 2003).

The overarching argument proposed in this chapter is that the obstacles created or tolerated by welfare states for justice-involved persons on their reintegrative journeys contribute to further stigmatisation and even re-criminalisation. This chapter will focus on three interrelated yet separate processes and contexts at play when considering contemporary approaches to rehabilitation and reintegration. First, it will show that reintegration and rehabilitation policies do not occur in ideologically neutral spaces but are implicitly built upon middle-class values. Very similar to the origins of welfare practices (Tyler, 2013, 2020), rehabilitative ideals and norms have from their very beginnings been based on classed, paternalising and stigmatising assumptions (Carlen, 2012). The failure to live up to these expressively middle-class norms can systematically exclude people from successfully accessing much-needed supports and, therefore, directly contribute to criminalisation.

Secondly, it will be considered how the provision of reintegration and rehabilitation services for justice-involved persons is strongly determined by the broader political economies in which they are situated. The connection between modes of punishment and political economies has long been established and now forms a significant field of criminological and sociological enquiry (Garland, 2001; Cavadino and Dignan, 2006; De Giorgi, 2006; Wacquant, 2009a; Melossi, 2011; Massa, 2016). Similarly, the analysis of welfare states' political economies in all their permutations is an essential element of the core social policy canon (Esping-Andersen, 1990; Streeck and Thelen, 2005; Taylor-Gooby, 2005; Wilkinson and Pickett, 2010; Hemerijck, 2013). However, these two fields rarely meet when it comes to the discussion of reintegration and rehabilitation practices for justice-involved persons. Crewe (2011: 525) observes that 'it is striking that much of the recent literature on the relationship between political-economy and penal severity stops at the gates of the prison'. By considering how different types of welfare state constellations impact reintegration and rehabilitation policies and practices, it will be highlighted how neoliberal political economies and penal regimes particularly interlink with the shape of reintegration policies and services. This is important, because as a policy and practice field, reintegration and rehabilitation for justice-involved persons transverses both criminal justice and social policy and therefore often falls through the cracks in analysis as well as systematic consideration by policymakers.

Thirdly, this chapter argues that one can't blindly idealise rehabilitation and reintegration policies in *any* socio-political context. Rights-based welfare states generally serve as buffers to offset the harsh realities of rehabilitation and reintegration for many justice-involved persons. Nevertheless, it is suggested that the neoliberal forces universally at play have shaped and permutated the 'ideal' subject of rehabilitation and reintegration at a deeper level. This ideal subject of rehabilitation and reintegration is modelled on the parameters of self-activation and entrepreneurship of the self (Kelly, 2006). 'Citizen subjects of the welfare state' have 'gradually been erased from the penal frame ... replacing them with the risk-laden techno-entities of surveillance and security fetishism' (Carlen, 2012: 5). It will be shown how these demands of self-activation and entrepreneurship of the self unduly responsibilise justice-involved persons *as if* they were entirely in charge of their rehabilitative journeys, and by doing so create obstacles and opportunities for disappointment and failure.

Finally, this chapter will consider how we can start to think about *genuinely* transformative rehabilitation and reintegration cultures and practices. It is suggested that, ultimately, a more extensive reimagining of punishment, crime, subjectivity and, as a consequence, reintegration, may be necessary.

Problematising the classed nature and effects of the rehabilitation paradigm

The terms of rehabilitation, reintegration, resettlement, re-entry or re-socialisation are often used interchangeably. Reflection on these terms' exact use would be interesting in unravelling some of their underlying assumptions, genealogical legacies, geographical/jurisdictional contexts, and how each of these descriptors balances between individual and societal responsibility. It is possible to sift through numerous typologies, classifications and models that focus on simplifying the complexities, clarifying the boundaries and defining the responsible actors involved in the rehabilitation and reintegration of justice-involved persons (Rotman, 1990; McNeill, 2005; Raynor and Robinson, 2005; Carlen, 2012; Burke et al, 2018). The policy and academic literature is also rife with discussions on which types of legal frameworks, support programmes, interventions and other social supports most effectively impact a person's 'desistance' journey and successful 'rehabilitation', 'reintegration', 're-socialisation' or 're-entry' (Raynor and Robinson, 2005; Ward and Langlands, 2009; McNeill, 2014). The interchangeability and relatively blurry use of these terms, as well as the continuous search for improvements and increased effectiveness of rehabilitation and reintegration measures, are good indicators of how rehabilitation has become a generally accepted and often unquestioned concept and ideal of penal policy as well as adjacent fields of social policy. The central argument proposed here is that the 'classed' nature of rehabilitation of justice-involved persons as a policy field, and equally its criminalising features of 'returning the poor and the powerless to their place' (Carlen, 2012: 10), are often overlooked.

Class-based critiques of rehabilitation and reintegration policy regimes are not new. In what is now considered one of the classics of rehabilitation scholarship, Rotman describes the authoritarian model of rehabilitation as 'only a subtler version of the old repressive model, seeking compliance by means of intimidation and coercion. Rehabilitation and reintegration in this sense is essentially a technical device to mould the offender and ensure conformity to a predesigned pattern of thought and behavior ...' (Rotman, 1990: 292). Other revisionist commentators, such as Cohen (1979: 611), have argued that the very idea of rehabilitation reflects an expansion of the penal state and 'entails merely more subtle calibrations of care, control, welfare, punishment and treatment'. In reality, Cohen argued that rehabilitation and other service provision in the community are intensely class-based and, rather than empowering marginalised populations, are 're-processing the same old group of deviants, with a few new ones thrown in' (Cohen, 1979: 611). Rehabilitation and other forms of more benign intervention are built upon a notion of community which 'only exists for middle-class, white, healthy, middle-aged socially powerful males. The rest have all been classified by them' (Cohen, 1979: 611).

Policymakers would probably downplay such critiques as cynical and abstract academic commentary and point to the absence of authoritarian rehabilitation models in contemporary welfare states. However, the lack of overtly authoritarian rehabilitation and reintegration regimes overlooks how they are closely intertwined with welfare politics shaped by paternalistic attitudes of well-meaning middle-class professionals and policymakers. Problematically, the failure to live up to middle-class norms on the journey of rehabilitation and reintegration can reinforce various marginalities that many justice-involved persons experience (de Lint and Chazal, 2013; De Giorgi, 2017). By shifting the primary responsibility for rehabilitation and reintegration to the individual, it also becomes easier to evade broader rights-based social reforms (Gray, 2007; Carlen, 2012).

One can get a first glimpse of this classed nature of rehabilitation and reintegration policy if we consider internationally agreed protocols that spell out universally agreed minimum definitions on reintegration and rehabilitation. What they have in common is a near universal emphasis on the importance of the pillars of housing, employment, (mental) health (including drugs and alcohol), family and social support systems for successful rehabilitation and reintegration. For example, the 'United Nations Standard Minimum Rules for the Treatment of Prisoners', the so-called Mandela rules, spell out that personal rehabilitation and social reintegration should be provided by 'prison administrations and other competent authorities' and that these should include an emphasis on 'education, vocational training, work, treatment and other forms of assistance ...' (UN General Assembly, 2016). These same pillars of rehabilitation and reintegration are also emphasised in other international instruments such as the Tokyo rules on non-custodial measures (UN General Assembly, 1990), the Bangkok rules for the social reintegration of female prisoners (UN General Assembly, 2010) and those considering reintegration of young people (UN General Assembly 1985, 1989, 1990; UN CRC/GC24, 2019).

It is difficult to argue against the importance of these elements for successful rehabilitation and reintegration policies. The question as to *who* is typically targeted by reintegration and rehabilitation regimes is not posed. It mostly goes unnoticed that they are, *by default*, focused on already marginalised, stigmatised and criminalised populations. One does not automatically think of white-collar offenders when thinking about government policies in the field of reintegration and rehabilitation (Carlen, 2012). Reintegration and rehabilitation regimes are *inherently* geared towards poor 'lawbreakers'. It is, of course, known from many different national contexts that those entering different criminal justice systems are – based on intersections of poverty, ethnicity, race and social class – nearly universally marginalised in their respective societies before they become criminalised (Rabuy and Kopf, 2015; Jewkes et al, 2016). Therefore, one might say that additional support offered to these marginalised groups of people is necessary and desirable.

However, from a more critical perspective, the rehabilitation and reintegration consensus based the main pillars of social policy indicates how closely intertwined poverty, involvement with the criminal justice system and, as a result, rehabilitation and reintegration are. One can't look at rehabilitation and reintegration efforts and their demands on justice-involved persons without considering who and why we punish in late modern societies. As such, the presence of rehabilitation and reintegration policies has to be understood not primarily as a support infrastructure for justice-involved persons, but as the result of state failures of social policy and maybe societal failure more generally, rather than a criminal justice problem. Carlen observes how the progressive consensus around rehabilitation, through its exclusion of corporate or white-collar criminals, reveals the rehabilitative paradigm's class-based assumptions. In cultures that celebrate capitalist societies' 'subterranean values, rehabilitation is not seen as being necessary for corporate and other white-collar criminals because their punishment seldom de-habilitates them in either material or status terms' (Carlen, 2012: 7).

The classed nature of the rehabilitation paradigm is also apparent when one considers another commonality across international standards on rehabilitation and reintegration, namely the repeated emphasis on the importance of public and community safety. This implicit juxtaposition of community safety versus individual rehabilitation is emblematic of conservative and paternalistic ideologies that gloss over criminal justice systems' classed nature. The subject of rehabilitation or reintegration is positioned as outside of communities, implying a judgemental and elitist notion of how such subjects are in need of rehabilitation and reintegration. Finally, these international standards also share another commonality, namely the repeated emphasis on the need for multi-agency, well-coordinated and indeed whole society support. These have also become much-rehearsed arguments across many national or state-level policies on rehabilitation and reintegration. Wendy Brown points out that these attempts to manage communication and coordination protocols between different entities are emblematic of the neoliberal state trying to 'manage' and 'shift' social problems without substantially addressing their underlying causes (Brown, 2015: 127).

One can consider some tangible examples that show how the classed nature of reintegration and rehabilitation of justice-involved persons translates into material consequences. One example is the increasingly frequent and taken-for-granted need to be IT-savvy and to have access to IT equipment, that is, computers, tablets or smartphones, to access services. The case of accessing universal credit in the UK is an excellent example to illustrate this and highly relevant for justice-involved persons who are very often dependent on accessing welfare supports.

Although its designers suggested it is more manageable than previous crisis loans (DWP, 2010), delays in universal credit payments in post-release contexts are reportedly still common (Day, 2018). Also, beneficiaries have to be computer-savvy and be able to access the Internet. This presumes a high level of digital literacy and the cultural and financial possibility of having access to digital devices. Despite proponents pointing towards available supports for formerly incarcerated persons in accessing universal credit and navigating the online system, others are more sceptical and argue that a smartphone is needed as a minimum, with enough digital literacy to respond to the frequent demands for information and meetings by bureaucrats (Cheetham et al, 2018). Also, while there seems to be a telephone number for those who can't claim online, this number is ironically set up to facilitate persons to claim online (Cheetham et al, 2018). Besides, these support services are often contracted to VSOs, which results in a highly uneven support landscape. Commentators have suggested that, ultimately, the system of universal credit remains confusing and stressful, which would significantly affect persons in post-release contexts, quickly setting up justice-involved persons for failure (Fletcher and Wright, 2018; Day, 2018).

The classed nature of reintegration policies is also highlighted in De Giorgi's (2017) ethnographic fieldwork of prisoner re-entry and reintegration in Oakland. Contrary to his initial expectations of charting intrusion and surveillance by the penal state, De Giorgi noted 'widespread public neglect, institutional indifference, and programmatic abandonment of these marginalized populations by both the social and the penal arm of the state' (De Giorgi, 2017: 92). Essentially, the extremely low standards for classification of 'successful re-entry' as non-committal of crime, results merely in 'recidivism suppression', and abandons any ideals or any 'meaningful institutional effort to improve former prisoners' socioeconomic stability, well-being, physical and mental health, and civic integration' (De Giorgi, 2017: 93).

Recent academic debates on reintegration and desistance have started to acknowledge reintegration and desistance as a two-way street, emphasising societal responsibility towards justice-involved persons (Carlen, 2012; de Lint and Chazal, 2013; Burke et al, 2018; Vanstone 2020). In contrast to some of the earlier focus in desistance research on the internal, psychological and sometimes individualising/individual decisions to desist from crime, it is now often argued that 'desistance is not only the responsibility of the desister; the state and community also have their own roles to play in this drama'. For example, a 'desister will always be impeded so long as the state and community do not recognise this transformation and take steps to reintegrate the individual into the fold of society' (Mac Pherson, 2017). Similarly, according to McNeill, 'no amount of personal change can secure desistance if change is not recognised and supported by the community (social rehabilitation), by the law and by the state (judicial rehabilitation)' (McNeill, 2015: 204). Despite this recognition, a social class-based critique that considers the profound social inequalities that justice-involved persons face on their journeys of desistance remains lacking in many instances, yet it should form the context and backdrop of every investigation of rehabilitative and reintegration policies, initiative and practices. It seems that the 'classic bifurcation that has poisoned the rehabilitative ideal from its origins: redemption for "us" (the middle and upper classes), condemnation for "them" ...' (Maruna, 2020: 579) is as valid today, as it has always been: 'Poor, urban, minority members were never included under the umbrella of the redeemable in the revivals of modern-day Calvinism' (Maruna, 2020: 579).

Extending punishment and hindering rehabilitation and reintegration: risk-managing justice-involved persons' criminal records

The classed nature of reintegration and rehabilitation policies also becomes evident when considering how many jurisdictions have institutionalised extended periods of labelling and stigmatisation by requiring justice-involved persons to disclose their criminal records when applying for training, education or employment. The need for criminal records disclosures is usually justified by emphasising community safety. Also, the avoidance of 'institutional lies', that is, the possibility of employers denying their knowledge of dangerous and risky individuals, as well as the deterrent effect of being labelled as offenders, are sometimes cited as further justifications for the necessity of criminal records disclosure (Paterson and Naylor, 2011: 941).

A plethora of research has repeatedly confirmed the link between generativity, that is, employment, education, training or engagement with other meaningful activities and reintegration, showing conclusively how amongst others, education and employment are central to justice-involved persons' desistance journeys (Uggen, 2000; Maruna, 2001). Generativity is also helpful in terms of rebuilding a 'coherent sense of self that can withstand the multiple difficulties that post-release life brings with it' (Maruna, 2001: 102). Given the many hurdles created or at least tolerated by different jurisdictions to access employment for justice-involved persons, it is quite ironic to note that work has always held a central position in the development of modern penal systems: 'Wherever you look in the development of modernist penality, you will find labour. Exhort the offenders with religious tracts, but make them work ... Educate them as citizens, but make them work. Treat their pathological features, but make them work' (Simon, 1993: 39).

It is clear that the state has a central role in facilitating, at a minimum, justice-involved persons' 'judicial reintegration', which McNeill describes as a 'kind of a passport', 'a process of formal, legal de-labelling in which the status of the (once-degraded) citizen is elevated and restored' (McNeill, 2018a: 17). However, even more than that, being given a clean slate can have powerful emotional reintegrative effects. In her analysis of French judicial rehabilitation, Herzog-Evans (2011) describes the deeply felt effects of the very formal process at court, when justice-involved persons are cleared of the duty of having to declare their serious offences on paperwork for employment and beyond. Judges and lawyers involved in the process retell the very moment of expungement of offences 'the atmosphere in the Court was poignant. Many ex-offenders have a trembling voice and cry when the ruling is voiced. The effect resembles citizenship ceremonies. There is a shared feeling of extreme satisfaction, elation even, both for the Court (which is also "making good" on such occasions) and the ex-offender. The sense of pride, of being welcomed (in this instance back) into the community (remember Braithwaite's model too) is palpable and mirrored by the Court's obvious pleasure at having thus ruled' (Herzog-Evans, 2011: 135).

However, it seems that, overall, legislators across different national contexts can struggle to resolve their discomfort with prioritising the needs of justice-involved individuals. This is indicative of a deeper lack of recognition that justice-involved persons who want to shed their 'penal tattoos' (Tyler, 2020) have already been punished by the criminal justice system, have most likely already been punished by deep social inequalities and are now again penalised. By requiring justice-involved persons to reveal their offending history, the state extends 'not only a moral judgment as to when someone is entitled to "redemption", but implicitly an assessment of how much extended punishment is needed' (Paterson and Naylor, 2011: 950). As such, justice-involved persons remain punished, even when their formal sentence has ended.

There is considerable variation in how different jurisdictions attempt to manage the tension between justice-involved persons' rights to reintegration and community safety on their path to reintegration. States usually include different gradients of disclosure requirements for employment purposes in legislation, varying with regards to the necessary time periods, offence types and frequencies until a criminal record can be expunged. In some jurisdictions, the use of 'staggered' good behaviour periods, linking disclosure requirements to sentencing lengths, are used to incentivise law-abiding behaviour (Paterson and Naylor, 2011: 954). In other instances, attempts to consider a person's rehabilitative and reintegrative needs are made by individualising and adjusting criminal record disclosure requirements through individual court applications (Herzog-Evans, 2011). Equally, the introduction of anti-discriminatory clauses in employment laws has been a significant development in acknowledging the needs and indeed rights of justice-involved persons (Paterson, 2011).

Nevertheless, even in the presence of such positive moves, justice-involved persons remain far too often unduly disadvantaged, stigmatised and further criminalised when looking for employment (Bumiller, 2015). In their genealogy of Australian criminal records disclosure policy, for example, Paterson and Naylor (2011) show how privacy considerations for individual offenders were weighted less than arguments of public protection, indicating the prioritisation of crime control over rehabilitation and reintegration. Similarly, in the UK, the Supreme Court has only recently ruled in its judgement on the UK Rehabilitation Act 1974 that amongst other things, the exclusions of persons with multiple convictions from their 'spent convictions' regime were not proportionate and therefore in breach of the ECHR, specifically the right to private and family life (UK Supreme Court, 2019). The state had, in this instance, unfairly and disproportionately disadvantaged justice-involved persons' employment opportunities. These fairly recent and contested processes of granting justice-involved persons a second chance show how powerful elites have difficulties with acknowledging justice-involved persons' deep social exclusion.

The Irish case of 'spent convictions' legislation is also reflective of this and particularly interesting, as the Republic of Ireland was the last European country to legislate in this area, in 2016 (Swirak and Forde, 2020). Despite the vast amount of research available at the time on the importance of employment and de-labelling for reintegration and rehabilitation of justice-involved persons, the approach chosen in the Criminal Justice (Spent Convictions and Certain Disclosures) Act 2016 showed an inherent scepticism towards reintegration and rehabilitation, and some would say even a clear disdain for justice-involved persons. Persons with multiple offences or longer sentences were completely excluded from the remit of the legislation. From a review of different submissions at the time, it appears that Irish legislators were more sympathetic to conservative voices such as the Irish Law Reform Commission, rather than more progressive views. Indeed, the very elitist attitude adopted by policymakers in the 2016 Act smacked of class-based arrogance.

Also the Irish Penal Reform Trust (IPRT) tried to bring legislators' attention to the social context of offending behaviour, by highlighting that 'two or more convictions for separate offences does not indicate a pattern or propensity for offending but rather a set of circumstances or factors that contribute to the offending – which might be immaturity and impulsivity, or it could be poverty, mental health, homelessness, addictions, experiences of violence or domestic abuse' (IPRT, 2019: 3). The exclusion of more serious or frequent offending histories from spent convictions legislation lacked recognition of the deeply entrenched marginalisation that people with offending behaviours often face. The IPRT also argued, concerning the same legislation, that it was so limited that it forfeited its purpose of facilitating rehabilitation and reintegration of justice-involved persons: 'it does little to address the social inequalities that underlie most crime, and that it compounds the multiple disadvantages experienced by marginalised communities' (IPRT, 2019: 2).

Ultimately, the restrictive approach adopted by Irish policymakers in 2016 showed how privileged legislators often have difficulties recognising the classed complexities of people's experiences underlying offending behaviour. At the time of writing, the Irish government is revisiting its 'spent conviction' legislation, primarily due to an initiative by a social justice-orientated independent senator and penal reform activists' lobbying. However, it remains obvious that justice-involved persons' right to a truly fresh start remains contested. States' interests to further regulate people's lives beyond the duration of actual punishment indicate the marginalised position accorded to justice-involved persons. Not only is their access to capital, employment and income limited before their involvement with the justice system, but it is further hindered through piecemeal approaches to judicial and social reintegration. In light of the recognition that 'de-labelling' is 'a duty that the punishing state owes to those citizens who have settled their debts (whether by losses or by contributions)' (McNeill, 2018a: 17), legislators' reluctance of and failure to facilitate this de-labelling process means that they contribute to the re-criminalisation of justice-involved persons.

The politics of the welfare state and its effects on reintegration

It is crucially important to consider how broader political economies shape particular reintegration and rehabilitation regimes. The analysis of different political constellations of welfare states and social policy areas such as welfare, housing, health and so on is central in social policy and welfare state studies. The classical distinction of Esping Andersen's (1990) three worlds of welfare capitalism has been tested and modified further since he developed his typology in the 1990s (see, for example, Arts and Gelissen, 2002). In his original theorisation of Western capitalist welfare states, Esping-Andersen differentiated between liberal, conservative and social democratic welfare states and how each regulates social security, welfare and labour markets in different ways. In the academic discipline of criminology, the relationship between political economies, the welfare state and punishment has also been theorised extensively in the 2000s (Garland, 2001; Cavadino and Dignan, 2006; De Giorgi, 2006; Wacquant, 2009a; Melossi, 2011; Massa, 2016).

Quite tellingly, however, the particular relationship between reintegration policies and political economies is less often the focus of academic research. This may partially be because it is considered a pastiched policy field that spans across different criminal justice and social policy areas, making its delineation as a distinct policy field difficult. Also, the fashionable preoccupation with effectiveness research, coupled with the corollary colonisation of psychologising and individualising narratives, easily sidelines more contextual types of analysis, specifically in relation to rehabilitation and reintegration research. Finally, justice-involved persons' status as outsiders may also be contributing to the political economy-rehabilitation field's 'Cinderella status'. Underlying this outsider status is arguably an expressive discomfort with the idea that 'lawbreakers' could access more resources than law-abiding persons. The principle of 'lesser eligibility' (Carlen, 2012) is firmly rooted in common-sense and popular notions of justice. Quite conveniently, neoliberal governmental rationalities benefit from this idea and govern by mobilising different groups against each other through 'liberal and conservative othering' (Young, 2011: 63), thus supporting sentiments of welfare envy, particularly when it comes to justice-involved persons.

To illustrate the relationship between welfare state provision, reintegration policies and criminalisation, three particular constellations of political economies and reintegration regimes are now discussed in turn. It is important to highlight that these classifications are, of course, 'ideal-type' simplifications of what in reality is much more complex. Nevertheless, it is useful to consider how different welfare state arrangements configure rehabilitation and regimes correspondingly. First, what Esping-Andersen has classified as 'liberal regimes' will be discussed, to show how political economies dominated by free market principles and privatisation of public goods have particular ramifications on the shape of rehabilitation and reintegration landscapes. Secondly, social democratic contexts, where rights-based approaches to rehabilitation and reintegration are underway, and at least on paper reducing the differentiation between justice-involved and law-abiding persons, will be considered. Finally, conservative contexts, where the state seems to struggle with its role of providing welfare rights to justice-involved persons, will be considered.

Privatised reintegration and rehabilitation

It will not come as a surprise that the United States of America are chosen when discussing liberal reintegration and rehabilitation regimes. The

USA is known for its notoriously high levels of inequality, high levels of lethal violence and its infamous prison industrial complex, incarcerating predominantly poor, black and brown populations (Davis, 2003; Wacquant, 2009b; Alexander, 2010). A combination of 'tough on crime policies' and a perpetual recycling of poverty and racism into carceral systems means that the United States has one of the highest incarceration rates globally (Prison Policy, 2020). The importance accorded to free markets and a strong tendency to favour privatisation of public goods have resulted in a minimalist and residual welfare state that perpetuates high levels of inequality and provides a safety net for citizens only in the most marginal ways. In tandem with this, and quite unthinkable in most European contexts, privatisation of the criminal justice system across its entire spectrum represents the norm in many US states. For example, defendants entering the criminal justice system often have to pay for the delivery of functions of the criminal justice system, such as for psychological assessment for sentencing, probation supervision and so on. Even constitutionally guaranteed rights that were previously paid for by the state, such as room and board for prison stays, access to public defendants or the use of electronic monitoring devices, have become increasingly privatised across the country (Shapiro, 2014).

Mirroring this heavy emphasis on market logics, reintegration policies and regimes are either non-existent or rudimentary, resulting in very harsh consequences for justice-involved persons. For example, in as many as 44 states across the USA, criminal justice-involved persons have to pay for their probation and parole supervision and mandatory drugs and alcohol therapy and class fees. Consequently, many justice-involved persons end up back in jail for not being able to pay their probation or parole supervision fees (Atkinson, 2016; Hampson, 2016). Therefore, quite bizarrely, the state directly contributes to high levels of inequality and violence (Wilkinson and Pickett, 2010). The state also makes poor justice-involved persons responsible for financially providing various parts of their sentence execution, management and post-release supports (Shapiro, 2014). The machinery of the prison industrial complex, facilitated and bolstered by the state, contributes directly to the criminalisation of justice-involved persons. The privatisation of punishment and the consequence of privatised rehabilitation and reintegration services are pushing poor and justice-involved persons into a cycle of poverty, containing the same 'urban outcasts' (Wacquant, 1993) in situations of further oppression and hopelessness. Justice-involved persons in fully marketised systems are often strangled by debt related to non-payment of criminal justice-related fines, that is, fines incurred for the inability to pay, for example, for parole or probation supervision (Atkinson, 2016; Hampson, 2016). This results in a dual punishment for criminal justice-involved persons: once for their original offence and then once again for their lack of financial ability to extricate themselves from the web of punishment.

Contestation by civil society organisations such as the ACLU has led to minor reforms in some states, arguably without shedding the privatisation fetish. For example, in Colorado, the governor signed a law forbidding incarceration for inability to pay fines and fees (Shapiro, 2014). In New Jersey, a state-wide amnesty for 'non-violent felons' was announced in 2014, when the situation regarding unpaid fees of formerly incarcerated persons had become untenable. Makeshift courtrooms were set up, and those who showed up to pay the debt related to their sentences received significant reductions in their payments and could clear their bill at a specially set-up counter. Indicative of a highly unequal and divided society, the move of debt relief for criminal justice-related fines was contested by some local communities, who protested against debt amnesties, arguing that they were generating income from these fees and fines (Shapiro, 2014). These local community protests not only show once again how incarcerated or justice-involved persons are considered as outcasts, but also how they are seen as profitable resources. Neoliberalism's powerful governing rationality of dividing practices is apparent here.

In adjacent policy fields, such as education, it is also clearly visible how the 'tough on crime' policy stance, coupled with a two-tier and highly privatised education system, systematically impedes justice-involved persons' rehabilitative journeys. Leverentz et al (2020: 520) show how an explicit policy change to the Higher Education Act in 1998 meant the large majority of justice-involved persons were denied access to federally funded educational Pell grants. The amendments introduced were 'specifically directed towards drug convictions ...' (Leverentz et al, 2020: 520), adding another layer of punitiveness on top of a criminal conviction for drug-related offences and excluding large numbers of persons from accessing education. The use of social policy measures to deepen the punitive effects of criminal sanctions as part of the highly unsuccessful but nevertheless vigorously pursued 'war on drugs' has a longer legacy, of course, starting from the mid-1980s onwards, legislating amongst others for different levels of benefit withdrawal for persons convicted of drug trafficking or possession (Goodman et al, 2017).

The punitive use of social policy through the sanctioning of mostly highly vulnerable populations via benefit withdrawal is intensified further by highly uneven and patchy provisions for rehabilitation and reintegration for justice-involved persons. Take the example of one of the US states, New Jersey, where the 'Successful Transition and Re-entry Series' (STARS) programme includes topics such as 'employment, housing, transportation, education, family reunification and finances', demonstrating a recognition of the importance of these elements for re-entry by legislators (Lanigan, 2016: 40). However, if one takes a closer look, the STARS programme organises access based on undefined eligibility criteria, and service provision in these areas is not always available and is regarded as a privilege rather than a secured right.

Furthermore, a heavy reliance on contracts with not-for-profit agencies, community partners and volunteers to organise re-entry services indicates a patchy reintegration and rehabilitation landscape (Lanigan, 2016: 36). Several studies conducted by the Urban Institute Policy Centre have shown how various re-entry services in the areas of education, employment and housing in the area of New Jersey were completely underfunded and reached only a small minority of incarcerated persons (Urban Institute, Policy Centre, 2003: 65–6). Very recently, the legislature of New Jersey has initiated proposal S2519, aimed at reducing sentences for prisoners and facilitating early release in a response to curb the effects of the COVID-19 pandemic on incarcerated persons. However, re-entry organisations have noted how, in addition to previous re-entry budget cuts, the funding of re-entry services has been excluded from an emergency budget in June 2020 (Nelson, 2020). From these examples, the consequences of the lack of statutory provision for rehabilitation and reintegration in the context of a liberal and minimalist welfare state can be seen. The systematic 'institutional neglect and abandonment' of reintegration services and supports fundamentally reproduces a 'surplus humanity', punished for their inability to compete in highly unequal and market-driven societies (De Giorgi, 2017: 88–9). While definitely representative of one of the extreme examples, the case of the United States demonstrates well how privatisation of punishment, as well as re-entry, directly impact the policy field of rehabilitation and reintegration (De Giorgi, 2017). The criminalisation of poverty and the privatisation of both punishment and rehabilitative supports result in an endless loop of criminalisation of the same groups of people (Shapiro, 2014).

Unsurprisingly, market-driven impulses in rehabilitation and reintegration are found in other jurisdictions as well. The 2014 English and Welsh experiment of privatising the probation service through the Transforming Rehabilitation programme into several private CRCs, was propelled primarily by the market-driven 'more for less' rationale. At the time, the English and Welsh Ministry of Justice was interested in reducing 'reoffending rates in the context of increasing efficiency' (Albertson and Fox, 2020: 81). In 2015, the originally publicly run CRCs, which in turn were set up to replace previous probation trusts, were transferred to eight private sector suppliers. The service delivery model was to be operationalised through outcomes-based commissioning but, from a purely financial perspective, the probation ventures became unprofitable after a short while: 'none of the CRCs managed to meet all their performance targets, with severe implications for income' (Albertson and Fox, 2020: 83). Despite several attempts to rectify the fledgling initiative through further public investment in the CRCs, the privatisation attempt failed not only from an efficiency perspective, but also in terms of outcomes for persons on probation (Burke et al, 2018), with more reliance on phone contact or automated check-ins and 'lower levels of human contact' (McNeill, 2018a: 111). The privatisation of probation seems to also have disproportionately affected women (Cooper and Mansfield, 2020). Recall rates to custody for women under mandatory probation supervision have risen disproportionately (131 per cent) since the privatisation of probation, which also excluded women's voluntary services from its remit (Cooper and Mansfield, 2020: 205).

Overall, the English and Welsh privatisation of probation experiment offers an empirically well-examined instance of the failure of privatised services (Albertson and Fox, 2020). It was a damning indictment that even government-commissioned research into the quality of resettlement services for both short-term and long-term offenders found that CRCs were prioritising profit margins over the reintegrative and rehabilitative needs of justice-involved persons. Instead, the official evaluation found that 'most of their efforts [were spent] on meeting their contractual targets, to produce written resettlement plans. Responding to the needs of prisoners received much less attention' (HM Inspectorate of Probation and HM Inspectorate of Prisons, 2017: 3). Ultimately, the Chief Inspector of Prisons concluded that CRCs did not contribute effectively to the reduction of reoffending. Political economies that emphasise free market reign over public goods, including the delivery of justice, unsurprisingly struggle with offering rights-based rehabilitation and reintegration services, which by default leads to harsher realities for justice-involved persons on their desistance journeys. The governing logic of neoliberal welfare states is that 'blame for recidivism, swelling prison populations and decaying management structures' can be 'apportioned to the "system", rather than a lack of resourcing or the neo-liberal ideology underpinning the system' (Cooper and Mansfield, 2020: 205).

The right to rehabilitation and reintegration

Directly juxtaposed to the residual welfare state, with its heavy emphasis on privatised rehabilitation and reintegration services, are Scandinavian jurisdictions. Much admired both in social policy and criminal justice policy commentary and visited during study trips by policymakers, 'Scandinavian exceptionalism' has since 2012 been put under more critical scrutiny. These revisions of Scandinavian exceptionalism include critiques of less progressive penal practices, for example, the duration and frequent use of pre-trial detention (Reiter et al, 2018), the use of long-term solitary confinement (Smith, 2012), the detention and criminalisation of asylum seekers (Barker, 2013; Aas, 2014) as well as more generally the harsh realities of alternative forms of incarceration (Shammas, 2014).

Nevertheless, the Scandinavian welfare state landscape and, correspondingly, provisions for rehabilitation and reintegration can be found at the diametrically opposite end to minimalist welfare states and privatised reintegration regimes. With traditionally universal welfare states that generally guarantee a high level of social rights to their citizens, it is not surprising that this is translated into rehabilitation and reintegration policies. Ugelvik (2016) describes how the Norwegian government has recently established a so-called reintegration guarantee, which states that 'all prisoners shall upon release, if relevant, be offered employment, further education, suitable housing accommodation, medical services, addiction treatment services and debt counselling'. The choice of terminology, with the term 'guarantee' signifying unconditional support, is quite a radical departure from the 'popular belief that ex-prisoners and ex-offenders should always be last in the queue for any available welfare goods whatsoever' (Carlen, 2012: 6). With a reintegration guarantee, the state takes full responsibility to provide unconditional supports for justice-involved persons across all areas of life that we know are crucial for desistance journeys and more generally for dignified livelihoods. Although the reintegration guarantee is not of legal, but of political nature, it nevertheless 'represents the intentions of all the various welfare state agencies to cooperate on the common objective that is prisoner rehabilitation and reintegration' (Ugelvik, 2016). Even in terms of abstract political commitments, such an approach would be quite unthinkable in residual and marketised welfare states with stringent exclusion and targeting criteria and a strong emphasis on individuals' responsibility for their circumstances. It is also interesting to consider how the Norwegian welfare state organises its services for incarcerated populations, namely through the so-called importation model. Under this model, and in contrast to models which outsource service delivery to non-state service providers, that is, the private or voluntary sectors, the 'correctional services import services such as health care, education and cultural and social services from the external public welfare system on the other side of the wall' (Ugelvik, 2016). As a result, incarcerated persons draw on the same resources and institutions as their fellow citizens. A by-product of this model is that, although imprisoned, it could be said that Norwegian prisoners are still included in the community outside. They are still acknowledged as citizens with fundamental social rights, even when serving a custodial sentence.

Another rights-based example of reintegration, which even goes a step further from the political to the legal, is the 2018 legislative initiative in Hamburg, Germany, where in the summer of that year the so-called Hamburgisches Resozialisierungs- und Opferhilfegesetz – HmbResOG (2018) (Hamburg Resocialisation and Victim Support Law) came into force. This statutory reintegration instrument, which sets up an extensively regulated transition management for justice-involved persons, is the first of its kind in Germany. Although Germany as a whole is usually classified as a conservative welfare state, the northern part of Germany, with its Protestant heritage, might be slightly deviating from national norms. The Hamburg resocialisation law is innovative as it obliges relevant agencies and services, on a statutory basis, to support justice-involved persons after their prison release. The resocialisation law specifies precisely which services, institutions and processes are to be provided to justice-involved persons, if it also falls short of precise financial resourcing, as had been proposed in previous draft versions (Schatz, 2020: 4). At the core of the law is a detailed system of integrated transition management for persons who are due to be released from prison, supporting them with a resocialisation case manager from a dedicated office of 'transition management', starting six months before and lasting six months post-release, with some flexibility permitted. Tailormade resocialisation plans, drawing on support from an interdisciplinary team of different public and community-based agencies and services and coordinated by the resocialisation case manager, address the different areas of housing, health, employment, resident status, family support, social services and addiction support as well as financial planning. The case manager ensures that the different interventions and supports are synchronised and she or he documents and steers the support package as well as remaining a steady and supportive contact for the justice-involved person. As the resocialisation law has been only recently put in place, no evaluations are yet available, but first reports from practitioners indicate that it has positively affected the organisation of reintegration processes (Schatz, 2020: 7). Roughly 1,400 persons have been referred to the service and, importantly, were, through its statutory character, *entitled* to avail themselves of these supports. This is particularly relevant for those justice-involved persons outside the remit of probation services, offering them individualised support previously not available. Although a detailed legal analysis would show exact differences between the Norwegian reintegration guarantee and the Hamburg resocialisation law, what unites both of these cases is a spearheading by and statutory provision of reintegration supports for justice-involved persons. In both cases, relatively strong welfare states also mean that the adjacent infrastructure is in place to materially resource the processes institutionalised in these reintegration laws.

Contentious rights in conservative welfare states

The third type of political economy-shaping rehabilitation and reintegration regimes in the Global North are conservative welfare states. These are typically characterised by early Bismarckian influences of state-centric welfare provision, meshed with conservative Catholic inflections of charity. Although they provide more robust supports for justice-involved persons' reintegration at first sight, their conservative undertone means that they remain fraught with contradictions and challenges. This becomes, for example, evident when we consider legislators' attempts in Austria to withdraw access to welfare payments for justice-involved persons. In 2018, the conservative-right government proposed legislation aimed at removing welfare supports from persons who have been convicted of a crime (Austrian Parliament, 2018). Notably, the legislative proposal was mainly aimed at addressing populist sentiments against asylum seekers and therefore focused primarily on stripping back welfare supports of 'temporary refugees' (*subsidiaer schutzberechtigte*) to the bare minimum. However, it went largely unnoticed in the public domain that the proposed legislation also included welfare support removal for justice-involved persons, including those serving suspended sentences. If passed as initially proposed by the government, the law would have effectively catapulted a large number of justice-involved individuals into a downward spiral of poverty (IRKS, n.d.) and as a consequence would have enormously increased their chances of recurring involvement with the criminal justice system.

As a consequence of lobbying by organisations such as the Institute for the Sociology of Law Criminology (IRKS), the revised and passed law (Austrian Parliament, 2019) has been somewhat softened concerning justice-involved persons, albeit notably not concerning asylum seekers. Effectively, the exclusion from welfare supports now does not affect justice-involved persons with sentences of less than six months. It also does not affect persons with suspended sentences (Austrian Parliament, 2019: § 4.4). While prisoner rights' activists welcomed this softening of the legislation, the grouping together of asylum seekers and justice-involved persons in an attempt to strip down access to social welfare payments is an indication of the perceived location of both these populations and the contentious nature of both groups' rights in the social policy landscape. Ultimately, excluding all persons with unconditional prison sentences of over six months from access to social welfare supports ('Sozialhilfe', which includes monetary and non-monetary resources to cover a person's basic needs), while incarcerated, offers a prime example of how a discrete instrument of social policy excludes, further punishes and withdraws social rights from justice-involved persons.

Similarly, impulses that seek to differentiate between law-abiding and justice-involved persons through the criminal justice system and social policy provision are visible in the context of the Republic of Ireland. Here, it was only in 2017 that the Irish Supreme Court ruled that prisoners were entitled to the state's contributory state pension while incarcerated (Supreme Court of Ireland, 2017). The Social Welfare (Consolidation) Act 2005 (Irish Statute Book, 2005) had explicitly excluded certain groups of persons, including those absent from the state and those 'undergoing penal servitude, imprisonment or detention in legal custody' (see section s.249 (1) of the Act) from receiving various social benefit payments (disability, carer's and so on), including pension benefits under various state-based contributory and non-contributory schemes. The Supreme Court ruled in 2017 that this was unconstitutional. In its judgement, the court traced the genealogy of the exclusion of justice-involved persons from social welfare payments and found that it was rooted in an overly punitive clause from the Old Age Pensions Act 1908. The Act had ruled that prisoners were to be excluded from the payment 'for a further period of 10 years after the date on which he is released from prison' (Old Age Pension Act, 1908: section s.3 (2)). While this highly punitive clause was subsequently relinquished, the ruling identified that 'the remainder of the provision continued in force for many years. Thereafter, the remaining disqualification provisions in that Act were repeated on at least four occasions post-1937' (Supreme Court of Ireland, 2017: section 14). The appellant in the final winning case argued that he could not buy basic provisions for himself such as clothes or tuck-shop goods and was disadvantaged significantly vis-à-vis prisoners with other incomes such as private or military pensions, which were not affected by the social welfare legislation. The Minister of Social Protection argued in the case at hand that, given that prisoners' needs were looked after by the state while incarcerated, 'to make payment of the State pension to him during imprisonment would constitute an unjust enrichment of the appellant' (Supreme Court of Ireland, 2017: section 15).

In its decision, the Supreme Court decided that the exclusion of prisoners from social benefit payments, in this case a public service pension, would place prisoners 'under a significant "disability", or more accurately, a detriment' (Supreme Court of Ireland, 2017: section 57). The judgement continued to state that, as a result, 'the State may not operate a disqualification regime that applies only to convicted prisoners and, thereby, constitutes an additional punishment not imposed by a court dealing with an offender' (Supreme Court of Ireland, 2017: section 65). However, the judgement also qualified this decision by pointing out that through compensation orders under criminal law, courts in the future would be able to still limit social welfare payments to prisoners 'as a source of compensation for victims of crime' (Irish Supreme Court of Ireland, 2017: section 66). The criminal law, therefore, is empowered to nevertheless limit and qualify payments to incarcerated persons. The contentious basis of social welfare rights is very clearly visible in this case.

In addition to the watered-down rights-based approach to rehabilitation and reintegration, another feature of conservative welfare states is such states' reliance on charitable organisations to deliver rehabilitation and reintegration services to justice-involved persons (Swirak, 2018). The usually patchy and short-term funded provision of these outsourced services is problematic, potentially contributing to the criminalisation of justice-involved persons. The lack of statutory duty to promote reintegration means that there is no mandatory requirement for state agencies to provide either in quantity or quality what is needed by justice-involved persons. Instead, government agencies rely on activating charitable and VSOs, who are competing for short-term funded, project-based supports for justice-involved persons (Corcoran, 2011). This 'carceral devolution' is 'best understood as a reformist shift in criminal justice and social welfare policy and practice where the state's capacities to rehabilitate prisoners have been offloaded onto community-based actors and organisations' (Miller, 2014: 321). What this means in effect is that the state abdicates itself from the responsibility for guaranteeing reintegration rights, but instead charges VSOs, through competitive bidding and the unavoidable steady race to the bottom, to provide supports and services to justice-involved persons. While this can work very well on the one hand, mainly due to the commitment by VSO staff and small organisations' capacity to adjust flexibly, it is, on the other hand, an indication of the lack of importance accorded to reintegration services. It can also result in an uneven geographical distribution of services (Hucklesby and Corcoran, 2016), where access for justice-involved persons is dependent on luck and postcodes, which does not provide equal chances of systematically addressing issues likely to lead to criminalisation. The patchy provision of welfare supports for criminal justice-involved persons in conservative welfare states, therefore, is problematic from a rights-based perspective that would guarantee rights to justice-involved persons in terms of their access to rehabilitation and reintegration services.

Reintegrating the entrepreneurial self: setting people up for failure?

Unquestionably, and as discussed above, jurisdictions criminalise justice-involved persons through reintegration and rehabilitation policies to different degrees. Nevertheless, the inescapable dominance and logic of neoliberalism extend themselves across jurisdictions. Without wanting to brush over its various permutations in different national contexts, where neoliberalism takes on 'diverse shapes … diverse content, normative details' and even 'different idioms', its governing logics remain 'globally ubiquitous' (Brown, 2015: 21). Neoliberalism is uniquely fashioned in the context of different welfare states, yet despite its particular national and regional permutations it possesses some overarching tendencies that shape how rehabilitation and reintegration policies criminalise justice-involved persons. These overarching tendencies are mutually reinforcing and make it difficult to imagine any alternatives. Transformative alternatives are often dismissed as unfeasible, utopian, too expensive and not capable of having immediate impacts on justice-involved persons' lives.

Significantly, neoliberal rehabilitation and reintegration regimes transform the 'rehabilitative subject'. Under neoliberal rule more broadly, citizens are turned into consumers (Brown, 2015: 32). Neoliberalism, through its all-encompassing culture of consumerism, 'celebrates the subject's ability to choose and construct him or herself through multiple choices, but choosing functions to preclude the subject from questioning and challenging the wider frameworks (of neoliberalism) in which those choices are located' (Salecl, 2010, cited in Delint and Chazal, 2013: 166). Translated into rehabilitation and reintegration spheres, this means that the consumer of rehabilitation and reintegration is enabled in choosing from a menu of options available to him or her, optimising how to transform their selves into socially acceptable and law-abiding entities.

Successfully rehabilitating subjects also have to render themselves amenable to continuous self-improvement and 'ethical reconstruction' (Rose, 2000). Typical of advanced liberal governing, 'ethical reconstruction' is part of the new politics of control in advanced liberal societies and is an incredibly useful term for describing neoliberal tendencies of rehabilitation and reintegration. Dubbed much earlier by Cohen as 'new behaviourism', the term offers a helpful critique of rehabilitation and reintegration policies that focus on changing and monitoring behaviour and are accompanied by a lack of consideration for broader social reform (Cohen, 1985: 148). Within the logics of this rationality, the 'perpetrator of crime … is the responsible subject of moral community – guided – or misguided – by ethical self-steering mechanisms' (Rose, 2000: 321). Exclusion is recast as a fundamentally subjective condition, 'not a psychological subjectivity with social determinants as in welfare regimes' (Rose, 2000: 335). Different from the traditional welfare state, where the welfare component and psychological intervention were combined, the emphasis is now placed on working with individuals to fit into highly competitive and supposedly meritocratic societies. The individual lawbreaker has to be reinserted and reintegrated into law-abiding communities, by considering her or his own moral and personal failures, often void of considerations of more significant systemic inequalities and challenges. This rationality then requires particular technologies to address the problem of the individual (potential) offender: 'This ethical reformulation opens up the possibility for a whole range of psychological techniques to be recycled into programmes for governing "the excluded"' (Rose, 2000: 334). The focus is on individual subjects' active contribution and choice-making to change their moral and ethical choices so as to belong to the community of inclusion. This in itself emerges as a powerful standard by which individual subjects are monitored.

Empirical research shows how these neoliberal forms of governing have a real effect on justice-involved persons' experiences of reintegration and rehabilitation. In her analysis of resettlement policies in English and Welsh youth justice for example, Gray (2007) showed how much greater attention was paid to individual, rather than social risks, and on programmes working on individual shortcomings, rather than supporting young people in changing their actual material circumstances. She concluded that across the English and Welsh youth justice system, young offenders were positioned as individuals, responsible for their failures at multiple levels, for example, in failing in education or employment, rather than 'pinpointing broader structural barriers arising from shortcomings in the actual availability and quality of educational resources or job opportunities' (Gray, 2007: 409).

Similarly, Miller's (2014) research on the experiences of former prisoners in re-entry services in a large Midwestern city in the USA issued a damning report on re-entry organisations. He claims that these 'do not seek to remove the barriers of ex-offenders ... in the labor, housing and educational markets'. In line with the neoliberal demands of producing citizen-consumers, they instead 'seek to enhance the soft skills and personal characteristics of former prisoners, transforming them into the kinds of people that will make informed, rational decisions when faced with a dilemma' (Miller, 2014: 317). Mirroring the strategies of neoliberal governmentality, Miller identified, through conversations with former prisoners and their reflections on support offered by re-entry organisations, that re-entry remains symbolic at every level. Rather than focusing on employment, individuals are supported in developing their employability skills, making them into productive and tenacious citizens: 'Rather than attempting to broker employment relationships, such initiatives seek to transform the unemployed criminal dependant into not only an employable and therefore productive member of society but also a trustworthy, dependable and tenacious one' (Miller, 2014: 317). Miller's ethnography and conversations with re-entry organisations showed that the focus of support provided was placed on cognitive reframing, 'looking inside themselves' and primarily focusing on 'brokering a qualitative change in the rationalities, mentalities and meaning-making processes of their clients' (Miller, 2014: 321).

Similarly, De Giorgi's (2017) research participants, formerly incarcerated individuals, blame themselves entirely for their past and their circumstances, 'which they systematically attribute to their own choices – never to the structural dynamics of class and racial oppression that constrained their life opportunities since childhood' (De Giorgi, 2017: 111). The emphasis on subsequent internalisation of the 'stubborn behaviorist ideology that is actively promoted at every turn of these populations' journey through the criminal legal system' upholds the status quo of deeply segregated and unequal societies: 'In this sense, the emergence of any kind of political consciousness as members of a subordinated social group targeted by structural oppression, social inequality, and racial discrimination is effectively prevented' (De Giorgi, 2017: 111). Neoliberal rehabilitation and reintegration regimes engage in 'moral re-training, where former prisoners learn to manage the triple stigma of racially coded deviance (through geography and inmate selection), criminal history and poverty by reframing their understanding of their social circumstances, managing their emotions, and maximising their choices to make good decisions' (Miller, 2014: 328). As a result, rehabilitation and reintegration act as another layer of creating docile bodies (Foucault, 1977) that do not interrupt the dominant social order. In addition, what this means is that those prisoners who do not show an interest, ability or willingness to engage in self-reflection and transform into docile bodies (Foucault, 1977) are either not chosen for these programmes or positioned as unwilling and problem clients, leading to a cycle of further stigmatisation, exclusion and ultimately criminalisation.

At the same time, one has to remember that the extent of production of docile bodies might be closely related to penal regimes. In the Canadian context, Balfour et al (2018) argue that former prisoners were very vocal in understanding the reinforcement of their precarious status through imprisonment. In their reintegration narratives, formerly incarcerated persons actively resisted the internalisation of the lack of social supports, but rather understood these as system failures.

Closely coupled with the focus on de-contextualised behaviour change, individual responsibility and ethical reconstruction, the neoliberal subject of rehabilitation and reintegration also has to live up to the ideal of self-activation. Justice-involved persons' reintegration, and rehabilitation journeys, are deemed successful if entrepreneurial selfhood is activated: 'initiative, "enterprise", "responsibility" and "activity" are narrowly imagined in relation to the performance of exchange relations in the extended order of capitalist markets – of all sorts' (Kelly 2006: 28). The larger socio-political, cultural and economic forces at play are not considered central in this quest for self-activation. In line with neoliberal meritocracy, the focus is instead on convincing justice-involved persons that their poor living conditions and life chances were not entirely deterministic and that they could better their lives if only they tried hard enough. These assemblages of justice-involved persons' subjectivities are useful to and typical of neoliberal rehabilitation and reintegration regimes, as they render the policy area open to interventions that fit and reinforce its norms and values. Self-activation, individual responsibility and participation in evidence-based interventions can be measured and documented and become main principles in neoliberal rehabilitation and reintegration landscapes. The justice-involved person has to be open and amenable to self-investment, become law-abiding, and become a productive citizen in a neoliberal political economy.

Finally, neoliberal subjects of rehabilitation and reintegration are also expected to be 'resilient' on their paths of desistance. The emergence of the resilient subject in criminal justice policy can be explained 'through the fusion of neoliberalism and militarism' (De Lint and Chazal, 2013: 172). Similar to the logic of penal imaginaries, ethical reconstruction and activation, resilience functions as a rationality that governs individuals through placing 'the onus on the individual to adapt to unproblematised conditions (of rule). Individuals are to adapt to and thrive in or finesse conditions of market, environmental, and political uncertainty' (De Lint and Chazal, 2013: 166). Quite depressingly, the resilient subject can only activate this resilience, by 'accepting the institutional or structural conditions' and by 'adapting terms of engagement within this framework' (De Lint and Chazal, 2013: 166). Interestingly, some rehabilitation and reintegration practitioners become animated when these individualising tendencies of resilience, and ultimately their work with justice-involved persons, are mentioned. The defensive response one often hears is that justice-involved persons will usually report to professionals that they feel empowered to become resilient, entrepreneurial and self-activating through their involvement in various rehabilitative programmes. Yet from a more critical perspective, this observation could also mean that the demands of neoliberal rehabilitation and reintegration regimes have successfully achieved the production of docile bodies, making it impossible for justice-involved persons to think of alternative ways of being successfully rehabilitated and reintegrated, but into the neoliberal order: 'the resilient subject is a figuration that ensures the continuation of the status quo. Resilient subjects are cast as liberal warriors, but even as such are docile bodies' (De Lint and Chazal, 2013: 166). Resonating with the observations on ethical reconstruction and moral reengineering, resilience means that 'the individual may be sectioned and reengineered according to attributes or behavioural dimensions' (De Lint and Chazal, 2013: 165). Resilience in neoliberal terms, places 'the onus of responsibility precisely where the decision-making is weakest and where the change capacity has already been neutralised, at the individual level' (De Lint and Chazal, 2013: 166). Neoliberal reintegration and rehabilitation also transfers the demands made on resilient subjects to communities. Crime-ridden communities are to become resilient by taking over community crime control and by taking 'greater responsibility for tackling urban decline, crime, violence and anti-social behaviour in their neighbourhoods' (Wilson and Kelling, 1982, cited in Corcoran, 2020: 23). 'The role of the state in supporting industry and employment and therefore facilitating people's opportunities to make the "right" choices is neglected' (Corcoran, 2020: 23).

So how does this all relate to the criminalisation through rehabilitation and reintegration policies? It is the meshing of neoliberal governmental rationalities of ethical reconstruction, self-activation and resilience that produce powerful criminalising tendencies. The overarching ideology of neoliberalism, instrumentalised through these particular governmental rationalities, unduly disadvantage those at most need of meaningful reintegration policies and practices. Formerly incarcerated and justice-involved persons more generally are significantly affected here. The neoliberal welfare state has made the demands of self-activation, entrepreneurialism and resilience into its core tenets. Failure to live up to these ideas can easily lead to criminalisation. Justice-involved persons, particularly those who have experienced incarceration, face a double disadvantage when reintegrating into mainstream society. Not only do they have to become law-abiding citizens, against the background of poverty, exclusion and lack of meaningful opportunities, but they now also have to be docile in the form of being entrepreneurial, resilient and active citizens. The ideal of the entrepreneurial self is also underpinned by a particular understanding of how we are told to think about crime and 'offending' behaviour: 'criminal culpability is interwoven with narratives about deficient self-management and inadequate compliance with labour and wage discipline' (Corcoran, 2020: 23). Coupled with the neglect of an entirely individualised understanding of social reform, that is aimed at 'returning these excluded groups, if not to prosperity, then at least to functional resilience' (Corcoran, 2020: 23), neoliberal rehabilitation and reintegration is set up as a project that can only fail.

Neoliberal rationalities of governing are nothing less than a signifier of 'imaginary penalities' (Carlen, 2012). If entrepreneurialism, activation and resilience are expected in a context empty of meaningful opportunities and working *upon* rather than collaborating *with* service users, then this can contribute to stigmatisation, lack of perceived success and ultimately also criminalisation. Importantly, rehabilitation as 'imaginary penalty' cannot answer the question: 'reintegration into what'? (Carlen, 2012). Without addressing the deep inequalities that structure justice-involved persons' avenues into criminal justice systems, rehabilitation and reintegration remain imaginary.

From transformative to mutual reintegration?

The question that then remains towards the end of this chapter is this: if reintegration and rehabilitation regimes in many contexts operate through the production of docile subjects who have to submit themselves to the requirements of self-improvement, self-activation and resilience against broader societal odds, what avenues could offer better alternatives for justice-involved persons, their families and communities, and the delivery of justice in democratic states overall? It is not within the remit of this book to provide policy recommendations here, but some broader concepts that are necessary before one starts to conceive of alternative ways of designing and implementing rehabilitation and reintegration policies are suggested here.

Increasingly, one sees the term transformative rights provision used in social policy, rehabilitation or reintegration, often used to signpost an awareness of the importance of broader social reforms. However, if one looks more closely, it is often a hollow phrase, which has become an overused catch-all phrase, stripped of relevant meaning. For example, the term 'transformative rehabilitation' is arguably in itself an oxymoron, essentially trying to repackage highly individualised practices of rehabilitation and reintegration. So under what circumstances could one speak of policies and practices in the rehabilitation and reintegration arena that are genuinely transformative?

At the most fundamental level, transformative reintegration is based on the societal and political recognition that reintegration and rehabilitation are relevant processes to all of us. Transformative reintegration would focus on removing the deep inequalities in our communities and societies and recognising that they contribute to the criminalisation of justice-involved persons. As McNeill (2017) suggests, transformative social reintegration would mean that we have to change our perspective and go further than just promoting the use of progressive concepts in transformative reintegration. Instead, we would have to 'flip the lens and apply these terms to the power-holders and the privileged – or better still, to all of us' (McNeill, 2017). Maybe uncomfortable for some and far-fetched for others, McNeill's claim for transformative reintegration is essentially radical: 'a process of reintegrative shaming might be overdue for institutions, systems, practices and people who are the perpetrators of the injustices that uneven criminalisation and penalisation and enduring exclusion exacerbates. Perhaps we all need to be confronted and shamed by our differing degrees of complicity in and responsibility for these systemic "crimes", before we can be dissociated from our offences and reintegrated' (McNeill, 2017). What this means is that we can't start to think or talk about transformative social reintegration without also questioning our assumptions about what crime is and who is responsible for crime, and how we are *all* involved in its continuous reproduction in one form or the other.

An extension of this radical claim would mean that we move from criminal justice to social justice in our assessment and design of rehabilitation and reintegration regimes (Young, 1996). If we shift the focus towards reintegration as a mutual obligation, rather than a one-way street of justice-involved persons requiring rehabilitation and reintegration, we would be doing our share in ending the symbolic domination of rehabilitation and reintegration regimes. The concept of mutual reintegration (Carlen, 2012) resembles other well-established, but seemingly forgotten ideas of 'dialogical models of justice' (Christie, 1977; Braithwaite, 1989; Young, 1996). What this would mean in practice has to be teased out in relation to different contexts, but in light of contemporary obsessions with effectiveness and psychosocial frameworks of rehabilitation and reintegration, it is refreshing to consider more radical ideas of social reform. Dialogical, rather than adversarial models of justice, emphasise 'critical views on macro-level ordering' that seek to assert dialogical relations between civilisations in which empathic dialogue 'would itself become the process of world order' (Cox, 2013, in de Lint and Chazal, 2013: 169).

In order to make this abstract idea of dialogical or mutual reintegration more tangible, it is useful to consider the concept of 'co-production' (Weaver, 2011), as maybe one of the first steps towards mutual reintegration (if it can resist co-optation). The principle and practice of co-production demand that one pays systematic and genuine attention to justice-involved persons' views and voices in the design and implementation of rehabilitation and reintegration. If genuinely implemented, co-production could move rehabilitation and reintegration towards a more rights-based policy field. Weaver (2011) argues that even in the area of penal sanctions, personalisation through drawing on user-voices in the design and delivery of services would carry transformative potential. In the context of supervision in probationary frameworks, Burke et al (2018) argue that greater involvement of formerly justice-involved persons could improve moving reintegration towards a social justice framework.

Finally, the concept of hopefulness is an interesting one to consider if we are to rethink the policy fields of rehabilitation and social reintegration. In the context of education policy, Te Riele (2010) suggests that the concept of hope, directed not only at the individual young person but at broader social hope and reform (Te Riele, 2010: 44), could replace the current thinking around risks and disadvantages. In the concrete settings of schools or youth work, she suggests that young people's hopes should become the focus of practice. Similarly, Burke et al (2018) indicate that in probation supervision practice, 'holistic and humanistic' forms of supervision should replace risk management-based forms of supervision. Resonating the idea of hope, they cite that justice-involved participants want a criminal justice system that gives people hope for their futures (Burke et al, 2018).

Of course, these are all only small pointers in what are the big issues of contemporary times, but have somewhat always been contested in human history. Who is deserving of support and inclusion and who is to be excluded and ostracised from our midst? This adversarial thinking about how to organise our societies, but also more generally about how we seek to motivate individual and social change, seem to become increasingly outdated. Amongst others, penal abolitionists (Davis, 2003; Wilson Gilmore, 2007; Scott, 2013; Ruggiero, 2018) and feminist scholars (Young, 1988; Brown, 2015; Federici, 2019) have been thinking about how we can reorganise the ways we live, the ways we organise our societies and as a consequence also how we organise justice. We also see nascent efforts to pay more attention to Indigenous forms of knowledge and practices in the field of justice (Daly and Marchetti, 2012; Cunneen and Tauri, 2016) and calls for a new social contract.

Ultimately, the challenge is to reflect on our deeply held assumptions about human nature. This includes undergoing a profound epistemological shift that reconsiders the notion of individual responsibility towards processes of mutuality and societal responsibility for those who have been excluded in our unrelenting competitive world (Corcoran, 2020). De Lint and Chazal (2013: 158), quite thought-provokingly, outline how 'a new subjectivity is needed, the dignified subject, and a higher altitude of resilience is necessary, at the species level, in order to challenge the institutions of social life and criminal justice'. They suggest that in contrast to neoliberal forms of subjectivity and resilience, we need to 'resituate resilience as a particular irruption, one that promotes the individual as having value as an end in itself' (De Lint and Chazal, 2013: 167). In combination with this, we have to situate individual action within an 'alternative alignment between agency and built structures and the ordering ideology' (De Lint and Chazal, 2014: 170). Resonating with Carlen's (2012) and McNeill's (2017) calls for mutual reintegration, they suggest that the rethinking of neoliberal subjectivity also means a rethinking of our ideological positioning on what crime is and who criminals are: 'we may perceive as civilisational criminals those actors who make more robust and add more value to the traffic of measures that for personal profit or gain up the ante of existential threat to humanity' (De

Lint and Chazal, 2014: 172). Despite all its complexity and utopianism, any serious alternatives to the contemporary dogma of individuality and 'discounted institutional' contexts (De Lint and Chazal, 2013: 157) in the field of rehabilitation and reintegration, have to be imagined and realised as part of larger processes of societal transformation.

8

Re-envisioning Alternative Futures

It is argued throughout this book that the criminalisation of social policy operates through intensified, modified and fine-tuned mechanisms in contemporary times. Our chosen mode of understanding it (based on definitions provided by Gustafson, 2009, and Bach, 2019), as elaborated in the Introduction to this book, is equipped to take account of these mechanisms. The criminalisation of social policy is not, of course, new, as, historically, social policy provision has by default operated by separating the deserving from the undeserving from amongst those worst affected by the fallout and contradictions of capitalism. The impacts of neoliberal governing have been traced and analysed by scholars and researchers across a broad range of disciplinary fields, including anthropology, history, economics, political science, geography and legal studies. This book has drawn on these extant bodies of work to illuminate and track the contours of how criminalisation of social policy is shaped in contemporary times.

From the outset, there was an awareness that poverty and poor persons who are criminalised were being written about, without direct engagement with the people in question. However, throughout each of our chapters, effort has been made to show how criminalisation of social policy across a range of themes and in a variety of national contexts has material effects on individuals, families and communities. By turning the gaze upwards towards the neoliberal state in its shifting forms and various governing technologies, the harms that welfare states can commit when designing and delivering social policy has been the focus. The intention is not to deny the benefits to be gained from various services and supports offered by neoliberal welfare states, or the good intentions of individual professionals, policymakers and organisations. However, this book shows that, at its heart, neoliberal welfarism involves dividing, individualising and responsibilising individuals for challenging circumstances, which are not of their own making, but are constructed as if they are.

Furthermore, the overall aim of our book has been to capture and illustrate how the neoliberal governmental project distracts from larger and deeper societal transformations, by continuously attaching its governing logics to new surfaces and targets; by perpetually redefining its operations and by engaging in endless loops of incremental regulation and punishment of poverty. This book has scoped how the criminalisation of social policy adheres to different themes and domains, but also how it has become ever more insidious and invisible and thus, how it has become more difficult to critique.

Despite considerable variations in how criminalisation of social policy is filtered through and shaped by different welfare state constellations and political economies, the core contention of this book has been that neoliberal governing logics produce similar types of criminalising mechanisms across geographical boundaries. Even before the imposition of the austerity politics of the 2010s, the process of 'penal differentiation' disproportionately affected 'migrants, non-nationals, ethnic minorities, young and marginalised people' (Ruggiero, 2018: 92) across the Global North. However, it is the contemporaneously growing sense of 'social, economic, and political disappointment and environmental crisis that characterizes this moment of history' (Gibson, 2019: 580), which provides welfare states with the justification to further tighten the conditions for those who cannot compete with increasingly demanding and more intensely bordered and policed exclusionary markets and welfare practices.

While it has been emphasised in different chapters that the criminalisation of social policy is not novel, that there are continuities in terms of the management of poverty and the poor, it has also been made clear that neoliberal governing rationalities are presenting themselves in sharp and more intensified forms. Importantly, they do not exclusively or primarily seek to rationalise the necessity or consequences of welfare state retrenchment, rather they operate as a framework for more tightly regulating and governing ideal citizen subjects according to ideals of Euro-centric national identity, individual responsibility, middle-class norms and late capitalism's privileging of the values of entrepreneurialism and competition.

Through the book's thematic chapters it has been highlighted that, notwithstanding geographical variations and permutations, the criminalisation of social policy, as expressed at this moment in the early twenty-first century, has several unifying features. One such feature is the deployment of thick disciplinary power, creating a feedback loop of poor people being processed back and forth between the social policy and the criminal justice apparatuses, as well as their mutual collaborations and inter-agency platforms. Through the attachment of conditionalities to most forms of welfare as well as punishment (McNeill, 2019a), we can observe slightly differentiated and subtle, yet in their combination, powerfully invasive mechanisms for the delivery of social policy and criminal justice. This results in a second feature of the criminalisation of social policy, namely the ongoing blurring of boundaries (Cohen, 1985) between criminal justice and social justice policy. Boundary blurring between welfare and control has, of course, been observed much earlier, but it is argued that under neoliberal governance the blurring and the overlaps have intensified. The concept of 'governance' is itself emblematic of antipolitical neoliberal rule, based on the dissemination of a 'depoliticizing epistemology' (Brown, 2015: 131). There is the ongoing search for efficiencies, cost savings and effectiveness. Collaboration between criminal justice and social policy institutions charged with addressing social problems is enforced from above and simultaneously enabled by increasingly diversified and specialised professional groups armed with an evidence base. Criminal justice and social policy collaborations are facilitated through the intermeshing of criminal law and administrative and civil law, a phenomenon that is discernible across all the policy themes discussed in this book. Troublingly and paradoxically, this means that criminalisation via social policy can be even more punitive, because the civil and administrative arms of the law both lack the procedural and legal safeguards more established under criminal law.

The blurring of boundaries between social policy and criminal justice policy also means that entire social fields become reconstituted. Civil society institutions, ranging from schools, third-sector organisations, community development groups, youth work organisations and family support services to social work agencies become conduits of state-moderated neoliberal governance. This operates through 'nodal' governance that depends on the active involvement of a multiplicity of sites and nodes. Small societal units are made 'responsible for themselves while binding them to the powers of the project of the whole' (Brown, 2015: 129). To avoid exclusion from the state-led governance project, civil society organisations 'drift', although with some variation in intent (Maguire et al, 2019), from their original welfare missions, redirecting their efforts to comply with state-orchestrated agendas.

Securitisation is presented as one of the central features of contemporary criminalisation of social policy. Social policy itself is designed across a wide range of social policy fields, with social order and crime control as key goals, rather than as good social provision in its own right. The securitisation of social policy means that professions and sites of governance that hitherto worked at a distance from crime control themselves become responsibilised as they centre their work around security agendas. Relatedly, crime control professionals, such as police, prison or probation officers, become involved in more benign and benevolent social control practices, which can, however, also be experienced as equally problematic.

Finally, the way in which policy subjects are imagined and moulded according to entrepreneurial ideals is considered throughout the chapters. Support is offered to individuals and families to become law–abiding citizens, good parents, responsible workers and community members, through activating their moral resilience; often, however, without addressing the fundamental issues, underlying problems and challenges being experienced. The neoliberal state operates through fictive 'penal imaginaries' (Carlen, 2008) that use individuals' failures to live up to a set of normative standards, to further refine, tweak and add to the repertoire of governing mechanisms. Policy subjects, therefore, are in constant competition not only with themselves in the name of self-betterment, but are also required to compete with others for what are presented as scarce resources. The neoliberal welfare state pitches insiders against outsiders and does this along the lines of social class, gender, ethnicity and race.

Remaining hopeful: imagining alternative futures

It is without doubt that the adoption of a deconstructive lens is an essential ingredient for imagining better alternatives. The book's application of a revisionist and critical lens and its presentation of policy examples demonstrate how the criminalisation of social policy reverberates across different themes, national contexts and institutional practices. This might incite charges of an overly pessimistic analysis being proffered.

As social scientists, we, like many others, are not convinced that large-scale revolutionary change is imminent, yet feel equally fatigued by the constant drip of incremental policy fixes that is a feature of the contemporary world order. The value of deconstructing and analysing the different ways that criminalisation of social policy operates is thought to contribute towards describing 'clearly the crux of our present day predicament' (Dorling, 2015: 39), a crucial step necessary towards imagining any alternative futures. It is hoped that by deconstructing and shining a light on the dark side of benevolent welfare and progressive penal practices, the further circulation, legitimation and popularisation of 'penal imaginaries' (Carlen, 2008), which 'restrain and disable critique' and ' inhibit the imagining of something better' (McNeill, 2020: 297), are being resisted.

In this spirit, then, inspiration is taken from writers, who claim that 'lamentations and denunciations' are not enough, and that 'affirmative energy' is also required (Sachs, 2020: n.p.). In his diaries, Kafka reflected in 1921 that when describing and 'warding off' one's despair about current circumstances, one can with the ' other hand ... jot down what [one] sees among the ruins' (Kafka, 1973: 340). Such 'affirmative energy' has been infused into each chapter, with the inclusion of positive examples and with the opening up alternative ways of thinking social policy in this concluding chapter. The policies and practices featured in this book have been selected and profiled for contouring or imagining different futures from what already exists and to consider how they might be built into our own historical, political, social and economic traditions.

Utopias offer no blueprint or handbook and neither does this book. However, it is hoped that it does provide a repository of ideas and strategies for possible futures, ones that posit alternatives to the policy choices that have been challenged throughout this book. Because the central concern of the book was with the criminalisation of social policy, it is incumbent on its authors 'to think beyond the horizon of the present arrangements' (Massey, 2014: 2039) and to critique, deconstruct and to consider the possibilities of change.

Crises as impetus for change?

Crises can prompt us to rethink what is important to us, what social policy is for and if policies need to be reappraised or recreated in light of new insights or new experiences (Hill, 2011). The crisis caused by the COVID-19 pandemic for example, at least if only temporarily, gave glimpses of what a 'welfare of the common' (Vercellone, 2015: 85) or welfare as a public good, could potentially look like. In 2020, in many countries the workfarist orientation of welfare took a back seat as states devised new schemes of income support for ill/quarantined workers, for workers providing care, for employees who lost jobs or income from self-employment, for insecure workers to stay in their homes and for businesses to stay afloat and to retain workers (Eurofound, 2020b; McGann et al, 2020; Cantillon et al, 2021; Greve et al, 2021). What was instituted showed welfare states' capacities to adapt quickly and flexibly to unprecedented events and the potential for social security provision to be better, in terms of providing unconditional and de-stigmatising financial payments, generous enough to allow people in crisis to live with dignity.

However, it is important to only be very cautiously optimistic as to the catalysing power of crises or their potential to bring any sustained change in direction. For example, the financial crisis of 2008 might have been expected to bring an end to neoliberal capitalism or at least to damage it irrevocably. Instead, as shown in the chapters of this book, it brought austerity and intensified work-first activation and criminalisation of the poor; it entrenched the marketisation and privatisation of services; and it accelerated the reorganisation of welfare states and social policy in a neoliberal capitalist way. Countries in Europe typically viewed as having more comprehensive welfare states and more enabling social policies than the UK and Ireland did not reconfigure their systems to offer significant alternatives to neoliberalism or austerity (McGann et al, 2020). The interlinked crises (financial, climate and pandemic) of our time, though unevenly experienced in diverse nation-states, can each be associated also with propagating new modes of discipline and regulation directed downwards.

Similarly, at the time of writing in 2021, there are already signs that the protective capacities of states set in motion at the start of the COVID-19 pandemic, are diminishing. The scene is set in the UK for a more repressive 'Americanised' welfare state post-Brexit (Gingrich and King, 2019), as the country sets out to distinguish its path from the European social model. However, this could also be derailed if the appetite for welfare conditionality and sanctioning becomes depleted. Chapter 3, which references developments in Scotland since 2016, proposes that distinct scalar or regional approaches to welfare policy also take hold.

Utopian visions

It may seem an unsurmountable task to disentangle welfare and social policy from their governing and criminalising orientations. A sense of despair for better futures is understandable, given the endless cycles of social reform, yet a frustration with the continuing persistence of wealth and income inequalities could also easily configure new ways of thinking and feeling (Wilkinson and Pickett, 2010; Dorling, 2019). If it is, as Zigon (2018: 2) suggests, that despair and exhaustion reflect the 'ontological grounding of our age', this makes the search for hopeful alternatives even more urgent.

Opportunities for incremental policy improvements *and* for more radical reform are all part of a project for a better world and need to be pursued simultaneously. Indeed, penal abolitionists, who have long contended with the limits of reform, have suggested that we need to work towards the 'unfinished' (Mathiesen, 1971) and towards our more radical long-term goals, 'while also providing immediate help' (Ruggiero, 2018: 105). Principles or ethical frameworks that are transformative, rather than merely upholding current conditions, are essential. Elliot Currie (2013) suggests that 'transformative intervention', diametrically opposed to 'conformist' interventions, that we see predominantly practised in contemporary welfare and penal states, has to include principles of consciousness, solidarity and hope. Taken together, these principles may work against the predatory individualism cultivated by neoliberal ideologies and create opportunities for people to 'relate differently to themselves, to those around them, and to the larger community (and the planet): to nurture alternative ways of looking at the world and their place in it that, among other things, will be less violent, less predatory and less exploitative' (Currie, 2013: 6).

A utopian turn in sociological and social policy scholarship has been evident in the last few years, as highlighted by Williams (2016) and as evidenced, amongst others, in the work of Wright (2013), McCabe (2013) and Levitas (2001, 2012, 2013). For example, Levitas (2001) has argued that any genuinely critical social policy should have a utopian dimension, which involves looking from the putative future to the present rather than allowing the present to determine and constrain the future. She advocates that this way of thinking about utopia is as a method rather than a goal (Levitas, 2013). This may enable us to start answering such questions as the one posed by Stiglitz (2018: 32): 'What kind of society do we wish to live in and what kind of individuals do we wish to be?'

Drawing on the work of French philosopher Gorz, Levitas (2012) called for an unconditional basic income (UBI) as a strategy designed to disrupt societal wage relations and to give rightful validation to non-market, voluntary work, care of others and other undervalued activities in society. She problematised the construction of the welfare state around the work ethic and identified the problems with that approach as adopted by New Labour. Contending that a basic income provision coupled with decent public services and ecologically sustainable urban generation would do much to attain a more equal society, Levitas claimed that this would be affordable if societies committed to real redistribution through corporation taxes and progressive income tax (Levitas, 2012). While there are challenges identified with instituting UBI (Greener, 2018; Artner, 2019), utopian projections as to how forms of social protection and welfare can be disconnected from labour and how power relationships between employers and workers may be altered have broader appeal. For instance, Azmanova (2020a), herself a self-proclaimed sceptic of utopian ideal theorising, has advocated for universal minimum employment to complement an UBI and regulated job-sharing as initiatives worth pursuing on the way to a post-capitalist society.

Levitas (2013) notes the restrictions imposed by the framework of the present, out of which policies for the future tended to be typically constructed but also constrained. Utopian thinking could offer a way forward in terms of thinking about criminalisation and social policy and in the ways it is envisaged by Van Parijs (2013) and Levitas (2013). Guided by Van Parijs (2013), utopian thinking can be viewed as a method or enterprise that is critically engaged, capable of mobilising ideas and putting them to the test with the help of diverse disciplines, movements and political actors and in the service of making a world committed to progressive democratic values, which are named and shared. However, the criminalisation of social policy, itself a worrisome crime and social policy intersection, cautions us that all utopian proposals merit ongoing critical interrogation and evaluation lest they reproduce or magnify inequality or repression.

In the field of criminology, utopian and alternative visions of justice also offer valuable ideas as to how societies can be reimagined, as a focus on and investment in criminal justice is replaced by a focus on social justice (Knepper, 2007). This also includes a widening of our conceptual understanding of crime, that is, always deeply imbued with the interests of the powerful. The abandonment of state-centric definitions of crime (van Swaaningen, 1999; Muncie, 2000) and the adoption of a focus on social harms (Hillyard et al, 2004; Dorling et al, 2008; Canning and Tombs, 2021), carries potential for thinking about and working towards more socially just societies. As one of many of its claims, the social harms perspective re-shifts the focus of responsibility for harms beyond the individual, towards collective social responsibility (Dorling et al, 2008), which in essence is also one of the key concerns of 'good' social policy. The social harms perspective also concurs in part with penal abolitionist claims that seek to abolish and de-centre criminal justice in favour of social policy or other less state-centric forms of justice and care. In any case, a disarticulation of crime from punishment (Ruggiero, 2018: 95) holds radical potential for rethinking social policy as well moving away from conditionalities that by definition always include punitive elements (McNeill, 2020).

Resistance, hope and respair

Throughout, this book has emphasised the central role of the state and its agents in shaping the criminalisation of social policy and thus might be accused of being overly state centric. The co-optation by state of professionals to service its agenda, as well as the part played by professionals in implementing neoliberal policy permutations have been identified, but so have discursive or material acts of resistance to the criminalisation of social policy. This is not to suggest that solace is not taken from new ideas, forms of agency and resistance inside and outside states, which are in keeping with a broad leftist vision and some of which have been referenced in the different chapters of the book. Indeed, attention is directed to forms of resistance to government-imposed criminalisation in the form of Sanctuary Cities, the Occupy movement, the Gilets Jaunes movement to name a few, and counter-discursive campaigns against poverty porn (Chapter 1). New models of communitarian care and cooperative housing, shielded from competitive market pressures, are being implemented. And there is the resurrection of Indigenous forms of justice being trialled across different national contexts. Activist scholars, indeed, claim that communities often described as marginalised or oppressed are more interested in their 'resistance being charted' rather than being represented and 'mapped' as 'another community of loss' (McElroy and Werth, 2019: 887).

Resistance infuses us with hope that alternative futures are possible. The concepts of hope and respair (Gibson, 2019) may be useful to keep in mind when considering the value of different social policy futures. In her review essay on different works on the anthropology of hope and potentiality, Gibson uses the term 'respair' 'to describe the rise of hope in social theory and its implications for anthropological thought and practice' (Gibson, 2019: 576). As a thinking tool, she refers us to Zigon's (2018) work, who suggests that critical hermeneutics, can 'open up radical ethical and political possibilities for thinking and becoming otherwise' (Gibson, 2019: 578). This would demand of us at all times to enquire if policies and interventions ultimately only engage in 'more efficient practice of state-based power' (Gibson, 2019: 578). Often, we are engaged in reshuffling rather than transforming the conditions we are hoping to address, by being limited to 'the repetition of differential sameness' (Zigon, 2018: 51).

Role of the state and democratic participation and deliberation

If anything, the chapters of this book tell us the protective and redistributive dimensions of welfare states, public service and organisations in civil society need to be reasserted. To compensate for the economic and social insecurities and precariousness wrought by global capitalism, dominant modes of governance present themselves in authoritarian populist forms; for example, and as has been shown, through measures to curb immigration, to increase public safety, to divide 'us' from 'them' and to promote self-interest rather than the common good.

It may seem paradoxical to want to harness the state for change considering the kind of state that has been unveiled in the different chapters of this book and critiqued earlier in this conclusion. It may also appear to contradict endorsement of the utopian method. Disillusionment with states is merited, as they overwhelmingly seem bent on processes of neoliberalisation via commodification, managerialism, marketisation and the imposition of discipline. In contemporary welfare states, and as elaborated in earlier chapters, there are arrangements where the same groups of persons are targeted, not for their 'actual illegitimate conduct, but their social condition that is deemed conducive to crime' (Ruggiero, 2018: 92). Those living at the margins, of our globally-speaking wealthy nations, are continuously punished for their lack of participation in markets.

Regrettably, even those political parties that we would usually have associated with the building and expansion of the welfare state, that is, social democratic parties across many different jurisdictions, have pursued strategies inherent to a neoliberal reform paradigm. This has been evident, for example, in Australia, the UK and the USA where social democratic administrations (those of Hawke, Keating; Blair and Brown; Clinton and Obama) have all been active agents instituting neoliberal reform (Hogg, 2016; Barns, 2018). Social democratic parties continue to struggle to find purpose and stay relevant (Hogg, 2016). As shown in diverse chapters of this book, so much has been imbued with neoliberal values and imbibed in projects of governmentality by political parties on the right and left when in government. As noted by Newman and Clarke (2009: 169): 'Developments as diverse as human rights legislation, community, audit, good governance, NGOs have all been viewed as the tools, sites or practices of neoliberalism: as smokescreen, as programme or as governmentality.' However, as they also point out, the political practice of scoping out the potential in each of these sites for alternative meanings, affinities and alliances to take hold should not be abandoned.

Progressive forms of social and political engagement that happen outside the state and that challenge the state are very welcome, yet, as Newman and Clarke (2015) contend, the state still matters and a politics of the state is necessary. Rolling back the state is not what is needed; rather, states need to do better for the public and not just the market (Greener, 2018). Any renewal of the state has to involve an 'expression of publicness' (Newman and Clarke, 2014: 154), one which reasserts its role in public governance, public dialogue and solidarity. If, as Stiglitz (2013) recommends, economic regulation has to be strengthened to better serve public and not market interests, states are best positioned to institute the modes of progressive taxation required as well as the regulation of the financial sector. In this context, calls for greater attention to be given to taxation in social policy and to the recognition of taxation as a tool for social change have validity (Ruane et al, 2020). Markers for change that come from a left tradition (for example, Hall, Massey and Rustin, 2015; Williams, 2016; Patrick, 2018a; Jensen et al, 2019) do exist and give us hope for the future.

A critical approach to state interventions has been sustained in this book, be they punitive or welfarist or both, yet a withdrawal of interventions is not always desirable or possible. Throughout the book, the negative implications of the hollowing out of democratic processes and institutions, the marketisation and coarsening of public discourses and their manipulation in capitalist interests have been exposed. Weariness with conventional politics, lack of trust in institutions, disaffection, inequality and exclusion lead to disenchantment with our current modes of representation and call for new thicker forms of democratic participation or deliberation (Greener, 2018; Brown, 2020). Yet, as pointed out by Wendy Brown (2020: 539) somewhat ambivalently, large-scale political democracy, notwithstanding its own limits, seems to 'be both necessary and impossible in realizing a politically free, socially just and ecologically sustainable future'. She presents it 'as something harder to achieve and sustain than anything history has ever revealed humans capable of' (Brown, 2020: 545). Her two minimal requirements for democracy are worth keeping in mind: political equality and political culture. Political equality refers to universal enfranchisement underpinned by social and economic wellbeing, information, education and participation, not controlled by the few. Political culture entails accountable and transparent institutions, protected against influence of control by concentrated interests, a commitment to the non-manipulation of the masses and an orientation to the public good (Brown, 2020).

By way of illustration and as highlighted in Chapter 3, the development of the digital welfare state presents challenges for our democracies. Some states are deploying technologies in the social security and other welfare fields at a rate in which the risks presented are not adequately configured and where the democratic oversight and governance they require are not fit for purpose (Madianou, 2020). There is an urgent need to critically debate what kind of data governance is needed in the field of digital welfare and how this governance will be shared with those who are most directly impacted by the information being gathered. In this context, the instituting of principles of data sovereignty, which would give meaningful participation rights to people in decisions affecting the collection, dissemination and stewardship of all data collected about them, should be a priority, particularly for minorities and ethnic groups (Kukutai and Taylor, 2016; Staines et al, 2020).

A progressive project of transformation, with potential to halt the criminalisation of social policy, is also contingent on a widening and deepening of democracy. Such a project is mapped out by Walby (2018). It contains a set of proposals for inclusive economic growth in which there is no gender equality trade-off. It extends beyond fiscal concerns, taxation and welfare decisions to also include measures needed in the fields of finance, employment, industry, violence prevention and democracy. The latter includes increased financial regulation and social investment, which achieves the correct balance between taxation and expenditure, an industrial policy, which prioritises only those sectors of the economy where growth is needed, and an employment policy, which has as its focus the reduction of discrimination and inequality. In Walby's (2018) blueprint, addressing inequality is embedded in the wider project of the prevention of violence, which blights lives.

Concluding note

The COVID-19 pandemic presents something of a double-edged sword for the criminalisation of social policy, some elements of which have been touched on in different chapters of this book, although its overall impact is yet unknown. Common to all states is a ratcheting-up of diverse measures to police the pandemic and to enforce public health measures. These generate questions about their proportionality and their discriminatory impact on the young, the poor, the marginal, and the risk that some of them may be sustained post-pandemic. In states generally, there are diverse combinations of legal orders, expanded police powers, fine increases, enhanced AI surveillance measures, more intensive regulation of public spaces, new penalties and sanctions, and an intensification of processes of scapegoating and stigmatisation as captured by terms such as 'covidiots' (Monaghan et al, 2020; Mykhalovskiy and French, 2020) and 'rat-lickers'. At the same time as small businesses struggled to survive due to COVID-19 restrictions, profits for large technological companies soared. The pandemic has laid bare and focused minds on the negative implications of the disinvestment in, marketisation and privatisation of public services. Societies have been directly confronted with deficits in market provision in care and have looked to the state to no longer be a provider of last resort but to better support our relational lives and our care needs. People and governments have been forced to reckon with states' unwillingness over time to address the inequalities that have been made more visible through the COVID-19 crisis (Blundell et al, 2020). Hearing birdsong in towns and cities and appreciating what public spaces offered for exercise during lockdowns enhanced awareness of how our economic ways of life are not compatible with biodiversity or our wellbeing. Governments started to do what they said was impossible to do before the pandemic, providing wage subsidies, to enable job keeping rather than job seeking (McGann et al, 2020; Wilson, 2020), to bolster our health and public services, to reverse bans on welfare benefits and to redistribute in favour of mitigating the worst effects of socio-economic inequality in our societies. However, it remains to be seen what potential exists for a significant shift towards the welfare state and public policy to be built on and sustained post-pandemic.

References

Aas, K. F. (2014) 'Bordered penality: precarious membership and abnormal justice', *Punishment & Society*, 16(5): 520–41.

Aas, K. F. and Bosworth M. (2013) 'Preface', in K. Aas and M. Bosworth (eds) *The Borders of Punishment Migration, Citizenship, and Social Exclusion*, Oxford: Oxford University Press, pp vii–xii.

ACLUPA (2014) 'Prohibiting anti-immigrant housing ordinances in Hazleton, PA and Farmers Branch, TX', March 2014, Available from: https://aclupa.org/en/press-releases/us-supreme-court-lets-stand-lower-court-rulings-prohibiting-anti-immigrant-housing [Accessed 7 April 2021].

Adler, M. (2016) 'A new Leviathan: benefit sanctions in the twenty-first century', *Journal of Law and Society*, 43(2): 195–227.

Ahmed, Z. A. (2020) 'Globalization versus securitization: borders and migration, a case study of Hungarian policy towards migration 2015–2018', *Eurasian Journal of Social Sciences*, 8(1): 1–12.

Alarm Phone (2019) 'Aegean regional analysis', 28 June, Available from https://alarmphone.org/en/2019/06/28/alarm-phone-aegean-report/ [Accessed 8 April 2021].

Albertson, K. and Fox, C. (2020) 'The progress of marketisation: the prison and probation experience', in K. Albertson, M. Corcoran and J. Phillips (eds) *Marketisation and Privatisation in Criminal Justice*, Bristol: Policy Press, pp 75–90.

Alexander, M. (2010) *The New Jim Crow: Mass Incarceration in the Age of Colorblindness*, New York: The New Press.

Aliverti, A., Milivojevic, S. and Weber, L. (2019) 'Tracing imprints of the border in the territorial, justice and welfare domains: a multi-site ethnography', *The Howard Journal of Criminal Justice*, 58(2): 240–59.

Allam, L. (2018) 'Fears of "another stolen generation" after New South Wales' move on foster care', *The Guardian*, 26 October, Available from: https://www.theguardian.com/australia-news/2018/oct/27/fears-of-another-stolen-generation-after-new-south-wales-move-on-foster-care [Accessed 7 April 2021].

Allen, K., Mendick, H., Harvey, L. and Ahmad, A. (2015) 'Welfare queens, thrifty housewives, and do-it-all mums: celebrity motherhood and the cultural politics of austerity', *Feminist Media Studies*, 15(6): 907–25.

Alseth, A. K. (2020) 'Human rights as an opportunity and challenge for social work in a changing Norwegian welfare state', *European Journal of Social Work*, 23(6): 920–32.

Alston, P. (2019) 'Report of the special rapporteur on extreme poverty and human rights on his visit to the United Kingdom of Great Britain and Northern Ireland', Available from: https://undocs.org/A/HRC/41/39/Add.1 [Accessed 7 April 2021].

Amjad, M. (2020) 'The ending of Operation Sophia: the EU sway from its human security approach', *Modern Diplomacy*, 20 February, Available from: https://moderndiplomacy.eu/2020/02/20/the-ending-of-operation-sophia-the-eu-sway-from-its-human-security-approach/ [Accessed 7 April 2021].

Amnesty International (2017) 'Criminalizing pregnancy, policing pregnant women who use drugs in the USA', Available from: https://www.amnesty.org/download/Documents/AMR5162032017ENGLISH.pdf [Accessed 7 April 2021].

AMS (2016) Ausländische Staatsangehörige am österreichischen Arbeitsmarkt, Available from: https://www.ams.at/content/dam/dokumente/berichte/001_spezialthema_0216.pdf [Accessed 8 April 2021].

Anda, R. F., Porter, L. E. and Brown, D. W. (2020) 'Inside the adverse childhood experience score: strengths, limitations and misapplications', *American Journal of Preventive Medicine*, 59(2): 293–5.

Andersen J. G. and Bjørklund T. (1990) 'Structural changes and new cleavages: the progress parties in Denmark and Norway', *Acta Sociologica*, 33(3): 195–217.

Anderson, B. (1983) *Imagined Communities, Imagined Communities: Reflections on the Origin and Spread of Nationalism*, London: Verso.

Aradau, C. and van Munster, R. (2007) 'Governing terrorism through risk: taking precautions, (un)knowing the future', *European Journal of International Relations*, 13(1): 89–115.

Arthur, R. (2010) *Young Offenders and the Law: How the Law Responds to Young Offending*, London: Routledge, Taylor & Francis.

Artner, A. (2019) 'Is unconditional basic income feasible in capitalism?', *Critique*, 47(4): 531–50.

Arts, W. and Gelissen, J. (2002) 'Three worlds of welfare capitalism or more? A state-of-the-art report', *Journal of European Social Policy*, 12(2): 137–58.

Ashworth, A. and Zedner, L. (2014) *Preventive Justice*, Oxford: Oxford University Press.

Atkinson, T. (2016) 'A fine scheme: how municipal fines become crushing debt in the shadow of the new debtors' prison', *Harvard Civil Rights–Civil Liberties Law Review*, 51(1):189–238.

Austrian Parliament (2018) 104/ME XXVI. GP – Ministerialentwurf – Gesetzestext Sozialhilfe-Grundsatzgesetz, Sozialhilfe-Statistikgesetz, Available from: https://www.parlament.gv.at/PAKT/VHG/XXVI/ME/ME_00104/index.shtml [Accessed 7 April 2021].

Austrian Parliament (2019) GP XXVI RV 512 Sozialhilfe-Grundsatzgesetz und Sozialhilfe-Statistikgesetz sowie Änderung des Integrationsgesetzes-IntG BGBl. I Nr. 41, Available from: https://www.parlament.gv.at/PAKT/VHG/XXVI/I/I_00514/index.shtml [Accessed 7 April 2021].

Azmanova, A. (2020a) *Capitalism on Edge: How Fighting Precarity Can Achieve Real Change Without Crisis or Utopia* (New Directions in Critical Theory), New York: Columbia University Press.

Azmanova, A. (2020b) 'Anti-capital for the XXIst century (on the metacrisis of capitalism and the prospects for radical politics', *Philosophy & Social Criticism*, 46(5):601–12.

Azmanova, A. (2020c) 'Precarity, not inequality is what ails the 99%', 26 April, Available from: https://www.ft.com/content/0a566844-83e7-11ea-b6e9-a94cffd1d9bf [Accessed 28 May 2021].

Bach, W. A. (2019) 'Prosecuting poverty, criminalizing care', *William & Mary Law Review*, 60(3):809–90.

Bader, A. (2020) 'Hostile architecture: our past, present, & future?' *Crit*, 86: 48–51.

Bailey, L., Harinam, V. and Ariel, B. (2020) 'Victims, offenders and victim-offender overlaps of knife crime: a social network analysis approach using police records', PloS ONE, 15(12): e0242621–e0242621, https://doi.org/10.1371/journal.pone.0242621.

Balfour, G., Hannah-Moffat, K. and Turnbull, S. (2018) 'Planning for precarity? Experiencing the carceral continuum of imprisonment and reentry', *After Imprisonment: Studies in Law, Politics, and Society*, 77: 31–48.

Ball, M., Barnes, J. and Meadows, P. (2012) 'Issues emerging form the first 10 pilot sites implementing the nurse–family partnership home-visiting programme in England'. Department of Health. Available from: http://www.iscfsi.bbk.ac.uk/projects/files/Issues%20arising%20from%20FNP%20-Evaluation-July-2012.pdf [Accessed 28 May 2021].

Ball, E., Batty, E. and Flint, J. (2016) 'Intensive family intervention and the problem figuration of "troubled families"', *Social Policy and Society*, 15(2):263–74.

Ballymun Local Drugs Taskforce (2000) 'Revised action plan', Available from: http://www.drugsandalcohol.ie/5027/1/230-1016Ballymun_Local_Drugs_Task_Force__Action_Plan_2000.pdf [Accessed 28 May 2021].

Bandura, A. (1977) 'Self-efficacy: toward a unifying theory of behavioural change', *Psychological Review*, 84(2):191–215.

Bardon, S. (2017) 'Varadkar wants to lead party for "people who get up early in the morning"', *Irish Times*, 20 May, Available from: https://www.irishtimes.com/news/politics/varadkar-wants-to-lead-party-for-people-who-get-up-early-in-the-morning-1.3090753 [Accessed 8 April 2021].

Barker, V. (2013) 'Nordic exceptionalism revisited: explaining the paradox of a Janus-faced penal regime', *Theoretical Criminology*, 17(1): 5–25.

Barker, V. (2017) 'Nordic vagabonds: the Roma and the logic of benevolent violence in the Swedish welfare state', *European Journal of Criminology*, 14(1): 120–39.

Barker, V. (2018) *Nordic Nationalism and Penal Order: Walling the Welfare State*, London and New York: Routledge.

Barnard, H., Collingwood, A., Wenham, A., Smith, E., Drake, B., Leese, D. and Kumar, A. (2018) *UK Poverty 2018: A Comprehensive Analysis of Poverty Trends and Figures.* York: Joseph Rowntree Foundation Analysis Unit.

Barnes, J. Ball, M., Meadows, P., McLeish, J., Belsky, J. and the Family–Nurse Partnership Implementation Research Team (2008) 'Nurse–family partnership programme: first year pilot sites implementation in England'. London: DCSF, Available from: http://www.iscfsi.bbk.ac.uk/projects/files/Year-1-report-Barnes-et-al.pdf [Accessed 8 April 2021].

Barnes, J. and Henderson, J. (2012) *Summary of the Formative Evaluation of the First Phase of the Group-based Family Nurse Partnership Programme*, London: Birkbeck University of London.

Barns, I. (2018) 'Can we reimagine a good society after neoliberalism?', *Arena Journal*, 49/50: 122–68.

Barton, A. and Davis, H. (2018) 'From empowering the shameful to shaming the empowered: shifting depictions of the poor in "reality TV"', *Crime, Media, Culture*, 14(2): 191–211.

Bauboeck, R. (2014) 'Demokratische Grenzen als Membranen Zeitschrift für Menschenrechte', *Journal for Human Rights*, 8(2):66–82.

Bauman, Z. (1998) *Globalization: The Human Consequences*, New York: Columbia University Press.

Bayley, D. H. (1994) *Police for the Future*, Oxford: Oxford University Press.

Beckett, K. and Western, B. (2001) 'Governing social marginality', in D. Garland (ed) *Mass Imprisonment: Social Causes and Consequences*, London: Sage, pp 35–50.

Beddoe, L. and Joy, E. (2017) 'Questioning the uncritical acceptance of neuroscience in child and family policy and practice: a review of challenges to the current doxa', *Aotearoa New Zealand Social Work*, 29(1): 65–76.

Beddoe, L. (2014) 'Feral families, troubled families: the spectre of the underclass in New Zealand', *New Zealand Sociology*, 29(3): 51–68.

Bellis, M., Lowey, H., Leckenby, N., Hughes, K. and Harrison, D. (2014) 'Adverse childhood experiences: retrospective study to determine their impact on adult health behaviours and health outcomes in a UK population', *Journal of Public Health*, 36(1): 81–91.

Bergamaschi, M., Castrignanò, M. and Rubertis, P. (2014) 'The homeless and public space: urban policy and exclusion in Bologna', *Revue Interventions Économiques*, 51: 1–20, Available from: https://journals.openedition.org/interventionseconomiques/2441 [Accessed 5 July 2021].

Beyond gentrification (2016) 'Rudolfsheim-Fünfhaus: A normal yet gentrifying district in Vienna?', Available from: http://www.beyondgentrification.com/vienna/ [Accessed 8 April 2021].

Bhatia, M. (2020) 'Crimmigration, imprisonment and racist violence: narratives of people seeking asylum in Great Britain', *Journal of Sociology*, 56(1): 36–52.

Bigo, D. (2006) 'Security, exception, ban and surveillance', in D. Lyon (ed) *Theorizing Surveillance: The Panopticon and Beyond*, Cullompton: Willan Publishing, pp 46–68.

Bilson, A. and Bywaters, P. (2020) 'Born into care evidence of a failed state', *Children and Youth Services Review*, 116, Available from: https://doi.org/10.1016/j.childyouth.2020.105164 [Accessed 14 July 2021].

Birk, R. H. and Fallov, M. A. (2020) 'Between a rock and a hard place: state-led territorial stigmatization, informal care practices and the interstitiality of local community workers in Denmark', *Community Development Journal* 56(2): 1–17.

Blasi, G. (2007) 'Policing our way out of homelessness? The first year of the safer cities initiative on Skid Row', Available from: http://www.ced.berkeley.edu/downloads/pubs/faculty/wolch_2007_report-card-policing-homelessness.pdf [Accessed 8 April 2021].

Blauberger, M., Heindlmaier, A. and Kobler, C. (2020) 'Free movement of workers under challenge: the indexation of family benefits', *Comparative European Politics*, 18: 925–43.

Bloch, S. and Meyer, D. (2019) 'Implicit revanchism: gang injunctions and the security politics of white liberalism', *Environment and Planning D: Society and Space*, 37(6): 1100–18.

Bloch, A. and Schuster, L. (2005) 'At the extremes of exclusion: deportation, detention and dispersal', *Ethnic and Racial Studies*, 28(3): 491–512.

Blundell, R., Costa Dias, M., Joyce, R. and Xiaowei, X. (2020) 'COVID-19 and inequalities', *Fiscal Studies*, 41(2): 291–319.

BMEIA (2017) Bundesministerium für Europa, Integration und Äußeres BGBl. I Nr. 68/2017. Integrationsgesetz und Anti-Gesichtsverhüllungsgesetz sowie Änderung des Niederlassungs- und Aufenthaltsgesetzes, des Asylgesetzes 2005, des Fremdenpolizeigesetzes 2005, des Staatsbürgerschaftsgesetzes 1985 und der Straßenverkehrsordnung 1960, Available at: https://www.ris.bka.gv.at/eli/bgbl/I/2017/68 [Accessed 14 July 2021].

Body, J., Statham, J., Danielsen, I., Guerts, E., Join-Lambert H. and Euillet, S. (2014) 'Beyond contact: policy approaches to work with families of looked after children in four European countries', *Children and Society*, 28(2): 152–61.

Boland, T. and Griffin, R. (2015) 'The death of unemployment and the birth of job-seeking in welfare policy: governing a liminal experience', *Irish Journal of Sociology*, 23(2): 29–48.

Bommes, M. and Geddes, A. (2000) *Immigration and Welfare: Challenging the Borders of the Welfare State*, London: Routledge.

Borzova, O. (2015) *Social Services in Europe: Legislation and Practice of the Removal of Children from their Families in Council of Europe Member States*, Strasbourg: Council of Europe.

Bosworth, M. (2013) 'Can Immigration Detention Centres be Legitimate? Understanding Confinement in a Global World', in K. F. Aas and M. Bosworth (eds) *The Borders of Punishment Migration, Citizenship, and Social Exclusion*, Oxford: Oxford University Press, pp 40–57.

Bosworth, M. (2019) 'Immigration detention, punishment and the transformation of justice', *Social & Legal Studies*, 28(1): 81–99.

Bosworth, M., Franko, K. and Pickering, S. (2018) 'Punishment, globalization and migration control: "get them the hell out of here"', *Punishment & Society*, 20(1): 34–53.

Bowling, B. (2013) 'Epilogue: the borders of punishment: towards a criminology of mobility', in K. F. Aas and M. Bosworth (eds) *The Borders of Punishment Migration, Citizenship, and Social Exclusion*, Oxford: Oxford University Press, pp 291–306.

Boushey, H. (2019) *Unbound: How Inequality Constricts Our Economy and What We Can Do about It*, Cambridge, MA: Harvard University Press.

Bowcott, O. (2015) 'Latvia complains to UK parliament over forced adoptions', *The Guardian*, 9 March, Available from: https://www.theguardian.com/uk-news/2015/mar/09/latvia-complains-to-uk-parliament-over-forced-adoptions [Accessed 8 April 2021].

Bowlby, J. (1969) *Attachment and Loss. Volume 1 Attachment*, London: The Hogarth Press and Institute of Psychoanalysis.

Bradshaw, J. and Bennett, F. (2018) 'Scotland moves away from the UK in social security policy', European Social Policy Network (ESPN) Flash Report, 2018/72. European Commission.

Braithwaite, J. (1989) *Crime, Shame and Reintegration*, Cambridge: Cambridge University Press.

Braithwaite, V. (2020) 'Beyond the bubble that is robodebt: how governments that lose integrity threaten democracy', *Australian Journal of Social Issues*, 55(3): 242–59.

Bramall, R. (2013) *The Cultural Politics of Austerity: Past and Present in Austere Times*, Basingstoke: Palgrave Macmillan.

Bramall, R. (2016) 'Introduction: the future of austerity', *New Formations*, 87: 1–10.

Brannen, J. (2020) 'The study of childhood, thoughts from a family life researcher', *Families, Relationships and Societies*, 9(1): 161–7.

Bray, J. (2020) 'Plan to review 700,000 welfare claims by end of year to make savings of €520M', *The Irish Times*, 29 July, Available from: https://www.irishtimes.com/news/politics/plan-to-review-700-000-welfare-claims-by-end-of-year-to-make-savings-of-520m-1.4316087 [Accessed 8 April 2021].

Bray, R. J. (2016) 'Several Years of evaluating income management – what have we learnt? Placing the findings of the new income management in the Northern Territory evaluation in context', *Australian Journal of Social Issues*, 51(4): 449–68.

Brent, J. J. (2016) 'Placing the criminalization of school discipline in economic context', *Punishment & Society*, 18(5): 521–43.

Bristow, J. (2013) 'Reporting the riots: parenting culture and the problem of authority in media analysis of August 2011', *Sociological Research Online*, 18(4):100–10.

Bristow, J. (2009) *Standing Up to Supernanny*, Exeter: Imprint Academic.

Broadhurst, K. and Mason, C. (2017) 'Birth parents and the collateral consequences of court-ordered child removal: towards a comprehensive framework', *International Journal of Law, Policy and the Family*, 31(1): 41–59.

Brodkin, E. Z. and Larson, F. (2013) 'Changing boundaries: the policies of workfare in the U.S. and Europe', *Poverty and Public Policy*, 5(1): 37–47.

Bronfenbrenner, U. (1979) *The Ecology Of Human Development: Experiments by Nature and Design*, Cambridge, MA: Harvard University Press.

Brooker, P., Vines, J., Sutton, S., Banett, J., Feltwell, T. and Larson, S. (2015) 'Debating poverty porn on Twitter: social media as a place for everyday socio-political talk', *CHI'15 Proceedings of the 33rd Annual ACM Conference on Human Factors in Communication Systems*, pp 3177–86.

Brown, K. J. (2017) 'The hyper-regulation of public space: the use and abuse of public spaces protection orders in England and Wales', *Legal Studies*, 37(3): 543–68.

Brown, W. (2015) *Undoing the Demos – Neoliberalism's Stealth Revolution*, New York: Zone Books.

Brown, W. (2020) 'Why is democracy so hard? University of California, Berkeley memorial lecture for Eric Olin Wright', *Politics & Society*, 48(4): 539–52.

Brubaker, R. (1992) *Citizenship and Nationhood in France and Germany*, Cambridge, MA: Harvard University Press.

Bumiller, K. (2015) 'Bad jobs and good workers: the hiring of ex-prisoners in a segmented economy', *Theoretical Criminology*, 19(3): 336–54.

Bunting, L., McCartan, C., McGhee, J., Bywaters, P., Daniel, B., Featherstone, B. and Slater, T. (2018) 'Trends in child protection across the UK: a comparative analysis', *The British Journal of Social Work*, 48(5): 1154–5.

Burke, L., Collett, S. and McNeill, F. (2018) *Reimagining Rehabilitation: Beyond the Individual*, London: Routledge.

Burnett, J. (2017) 'Racial violence and the Brexit state', *Race & Class*, 58(4): 85–97.

Butler, P. cited in Fayyad, A. (2017) 'The criminalisation of gentrifying neighborhoods', *The Atlantic*, 20 December, https://www.theatlantic.com/politics/archive/2017/12/the-criminalization-of-gentrifying-neighborhoods/548837/ [Accessed 8 April 2021].

Butterworth, P., Fairweather, K. A., Anstey, K. J. and Windsor, T. D. (2006) 'Hopelessness, demoralization and suicidal behaviour: the backdrop to welfare reform in Australia', *Australiasian Psychiatry*, 40(8): 648–56.

Bywaters, P., Kwhali, J., Brady, G., Sparks, T. and Bos, E. (2017) 'Out of sight, out of mind: ethnic inequalities in child protection and out-of-home care intervention rates', *The British Journal of Social Work*, 47(7): 1884–902.

Bywaters, P. and the Child Welfare Inequalites Project Team (2020) 'The child welfare inequalities project: final report', Nuffield Foundation, Available from: https://mk0nuffieldfounpg9ee.kinstacdn.com/wp-content/uploads/2019/11/CWIP-Overview-Final-V4.pdf [Accessed 7 April 2021].

Cairney, P. (2019) 'The UK government's imaginative use of evidence to make policy', *British Politics*, 14(1): 1–22.

Camack, P. (2010) 'The shape of capitalism to come', *Antipode*, 41(1): 262–80.

Camp, J. T. and Heatherton, C. (2016) 'Asset stripping and broken windows policing on LA's Skid Row: an interview with Becky Dennison and Pete White', in J. T. Camp and C. Heatherton (eds) *Policing the Planet: Why the Policing Crisis Led to Black Lives Matter*, London: Verso Books, n.p.

Campbell, M., Thomson, H., Fenton, C. and Gibson, M. (2016) 'Lone parents, health, wellbeing and welfare to work: a systematic review of qualitative studies', *BMC Public Health*, 16(1), https://doi.org/10.1186/s12889-016-2880-9.

Campbell, T. L. (2020) 'Screening for adverse childhood experiences in primary care, a cautionary note', *Journal of the American Medical Association*, 323(23): 2379–80.

Cameron, D. (2011a) 'Troubled families speech', 15 December, Available from: https://www.gov.uk/government/speeches/troubled-families-speech [Accessed 8 April 2021].

Cameron, D. (2011b) 'PM's speech on welfare reform bill', Available from: https://www.gov.uk/government/speeches/pms-speech-on-welfare-reform-bill [Accessed 8 April 2021].

Cammett, A. (2016) 'Welfare queens redux: criminalizing black mothers in the age of neoliberalism', *Southern California Interdisciplinary Law Journal*, 25(2): 363–94.

Canning, V. (2017) 'The multiple forms of violence in the asylum system', in V. Cooper and D. Whyte (eds) *The Violence of Austerity*, London: Pluto Press, pp 67–74.

Canning, V. and Tombs, S. (2021) *From Social Harm to Zemiology: A Critical Introduction*, London: Routledge.

Cannings-John, R., Lugg-Widger, F., Robling, M., Paranjothy, S., White, J., Pell, J. and Sanders, J. (2018) 'Evaluating the family–nurse partnership programme in Scotland: a natural experiment approach', *International Journal of Population Data Science*, 3(4), doi: 10.23889/ijpds.v3i4.994.

Cantillon, B., Seeleib-Kaiser, M. and Veen, R. (2021) 'The COVID-19 crisis and policy responses by continental European welfare states', *Social Policy & Administration*, 55(2): 326–38.

Carey, M. and Bell, S. (2020) 'Universal credit, lone mothers and poverty: some context and challenges for social work with children and families', *Critical and Radical Social Work*, 8(2): 189–203.

Carlen, P. (2008) 'Imaginary Penalities and Risk-Crazed Governance', in P. Carlen (ed) *Imaginary Penalities*, Cullompton: Willan, pp 1–25.

Carlen, P. (2012) 'Against rehabilitation: for reparative justice', speech, Available from: https://www.crimeandjustice.org.uk/resources/against-rehabilitation-reparative-justice [Accessed 8 April 2021].

Carvalho, H., Chamberlen, A. and Lewis, R. (2020) 'Punitiveness beyond criminal justice: punishable and punitive subjects in an era of prevention, anti-migration and austerity', *British Journal of Criminology*, 60(2): 265–84.

Case, A. and Deaton, A. (2020) *Deaths of Despair and the Future of Capitalism*. Princeton, NJ: Princeton University Press.

Casey, J. P. (2010) 'Open borders: absurd chimera or inevitable future policy?', *International Migration*, 48(5): 14–62.

Cassee, A. (2016) *Globale Bewegungsfreiheit – Ein philosophisches Plaedoyer fuer offene Grenzen*, Berlin: Suhrkamp Verlag/ Universitaet Zuerich.

Castells, M. (2000) 'The rise of the fourth world', in D. Held and A. McGrew (eds) *The Global Transformation Reader: An Introduction to the Globalisation Debate*, Cambridge: Polity Press, pp 348–54.

Castles, S., de Haas, H. and Miller, J. (2013) *'Age of Migration' International Population Movements in the Modern World* (5th edn), New York and London: Guilford Press.

Cavadino, M. and Dignan, J. (2006) 'Penal policy and political economy', *Criminology & Criminal Justice*, 6(4): 435–56.

Chacón, J. M. (2009) 'Managing migration through crime', *Columbia Law Review Sidebar*, 109: 138–48.

Chacón, J. M. (2013) 'Overcriminalizing immigration', Legal Studies Research Paper Series No. 2013–91.

Chan, W. (2011) 'Canada: punishing the undeserving poor', *Open Democracy*, Available from: https://www.opendemocracy.net/en/5050/canada-punishing-undeserving-poor/ [Accessed 8 April 2021].

Cheetham, M., Moffatt, S. and Addison, M. (2018) ' "It's hitting people that can least afford it the hardest", the impact of the roll-out of Universal Credit in two north east England localities: a qualitative study', final report, Available from: https://www.gateshead.gov.uk/media/10665/The-impact-of-the-roll-out-of-Universal-Credit-in-two-North-East-England-localities-a-qualitative-study-November-2018/pdf/Universal_Credit_Report_2018pdf.pdf?m=636778831081630000 [Accessed 7 April 2021].

Cheliotis, L. K. (2017) 'Punitive inclusion: the political economy of irregular migration in the margins of Europe', *European Journal of Criminology*, 14(1): 78–99.

Chisholm, T., Coulter, A. and Kantar Public (2017) 'Safeguarding and radicalisation', research report, Available from: https://assets.publishing.service.gov.uk/government/uploads/system/uploads/attachment_data/file/635262/Safeguarding_and_Radicalisation.pdf [Accessed 7 April 2021].

Christie, N. (1977) 'Conflicts as property', *British Journal of Criminology*, 17(1): 1–5. Reprinted in Gerry Johnstone (ed) *A Restorative Justice Reader*, 2003, Cullompton: Willan Publishing.

Churchin, K. (2019) 'The Illiberalism of behavioural conditionality: a critique of Australia's "no jab no pay" policy', *Journal of Social Policy*, 48(4): 789–805.

Clancey, G. (2015) 'Local crime prevention: breathing life (back) in to social democratic and penal welfare concerns', *International Journal for Crime, Justice and Social Democracy*, 4(4): 40–57.

Clarke, A., Parsell, C. and Vorsina, M. (2019) 'The role of housing policy in perpetuating conditional forms of homelessness support in the era of housing first: evidence from Australia', *Housing Studies*, 35(5): 954–75.

Clarke, A., Parsell, C. and Lata, L. N. (2020) 'Surveilling the marginalised: how manual, embodied and territorialised surveillance persists in the age of "dataveillance"', *The Sociological Review*, 69(2): 396–413.

Clarke, A., Watts, B. and Parsell, C. (2020) 'Conditionality in the context of housing-led homelessness policy: comparing Australia's housing first agenda to Scotland's rights based approach', *Australian Journal of Social Issues*, 55(1): 88–100.

Clarke, R. V. G. and Hough, J. M. (1984) 'Crime and police effectiveness', Home Office Research Study No. 79. London: HMSO.

Clarke, R. V. G. and Mayhew, P. M. (eds) (1980) *Designing Out Crime*, London: HMSO.

Clegg, D. (2017) 'Unemployment benefit and labour market policies in Europe', *Handbook of European Social Policy*, https://doi.org/10.4337/9781783476466.00026.

Cohen, S. (1972) *Folk Devils and Moral Panics: The Creation of the Mods and Rockers*, London: Macgibbon & Kee.

Cohen, S. (1979) 'The punitive city: notes on the dispersal of social control', *Crime, Law and Social Change*, 3(4): 341–63.

Cohen, S. (1985) *Visions of Social Control: Crime, Punishment and Classification*, Cambridge: Polity Press.

Coleman, R. and McCahill, M. (2011) *Surveillance and Crime*, Thousand Oaks, CA: Sage.

Collins, M. and Murphy, M. (2016) 'Activation: solving unemployment or supporting a low-pay economy', in F. Dukelow and M. Murphy (eds) *The Irish Welfare State in the Twenty First Century, Challenges and Change*, London: Palgrave Macmillan, pp 67–92.

Community Practitioner (2017–2018) 'Family nurse partnership to expand in Scotland', *Community Practitioner*, 90(12), Dec–Jan: 8–18.

Compound Security (2021) Available from: https://www.compoundsecurity.co.uk/ [Accessed 7 April 2021].

Conlon, D. and Gill, N. (2013) 'Gagging orders: asylum seekers and paradoxes of freedom and protest in liberal society', *Citizenship Studies*, 17(2): 241–59.

Connor, S. (2007) 'We're onto you: a critical examination of the department for work and pensions' "targeting benefit fraud" campaign', *Critical Social Policy*, 27(2): 231–52.

Considine, M., Lewis, J. M., O'Sullivan, S. and Sol. E. (2015) *Getting Welfare to Work: Street Level Governance in Australia, the UK and the Netherlands*, Oxford: Oxford University Press.

Cooper, V. and Mansfield, M. (2020) 'Marketisation of women's organisations in the criminal justice sector', in K. Albertson, M. Corcoran, and J. Phillips (eds) *Marketisation and Privatisation in Criminal Justice*, Bristol: Policy Press, pp 203–20.

Cook, D. (2006) *Criminal and Social Justice*, London: Sage.

Corbacho, B., Bell, K., Stamuli, E., Richardson, G., Ronaldson, S. Hood, K., Sanders, J., Robling, M. and Torgerson, D., on behalf of the Building Blocks Trial Group (2017) 'Cost-effectiveness of the family nurse partnership (FNP) programme in England: evidence from the building blocks trial', *Journal of Evaluation in Clinical Practice*, 23(6): 1367–74.

Corcoran, M. S. (2011) 'Dilemmas of institutionalization in the penal voluntary sector', *Critical Social Policy*, 31(1): 30–52.

Corcoran, M. (2020) 'Market society utopianism in penal politics', in K. Albertson, M. Corcoran, and J. Phillips (eds) *Marketisation and Privatisation in Criminal Justice*, Bristol: Policy Press, pp 15–29.

Corcoran, M. S., Williams, K., Prince, K. and Maguire, M. (2018) 'The penal voluntary sector in England and Wales: adaptation to unsettlement and austerity', *The Political Quarterly*, 89(2): 187–96.

Cox, R. (2013) 'Consciousness and civilisation: the inside story', in M. Mahdavi and W. A. Knight (eds) *Towards the Dignity of Difference? Neither 'End of History' nor 'Clash of Civilisations'*, Aldershot: Ashgate.

COST Action (2017) 'TU1203'207, Available from: http://www.costtu1203.eu/wp-content/uploads/2017/12/Case-Study-Report-Belgrade.pdf [Accessed 8 April 2021].

Coulter, (2015) 'Final report, child care law reporting project', Dublin, Ireland. Available from: https://www.childlawproject.ie/wp-content/uploads/2015/11/CCLRP-Full-final-report_FINAL2.pdf [Accessed 8 April 2021].

Cousins, M. (2019) 'Welfare conditionality in the Republic of Ireland after the great recession', *Journal of Social Security Law*, 26(1): 30–41.

Cprek, S. E., Williamson, L. H., McDaniel, H., Brase, R. and Williams, C. M. (2020) 'Adverse childhood experiences (ACEs) and risk of childhood delays in children ages 1–5', *Child and Adolescent Social Work Journal*, 37: 15–24.

Craig, A., McEwen, S. F. and Gregerson, B. A. (2019) 'A critical assessment of the adverse childhood experiences study at 20 years', *American Journal of Preventive Medicine*, 56(6): 790–4.

Cranmer, F. (2019) 'Koblenz, the burkini ban and constitutional rights', *Law & Religion UK*, 19 June, Available from: https://lawandreligionuk.com/2019/06/19/koblenz-the-burkini-ban-and-constitutional-rights/ [Accessed 8 April 2021].

Crawford, A. (1994) 'The partnership approach to community crime prevention: Corporatism at the local level?', *Social & Legal Studies*, 3(4): 497–519.

Crawford, A. (1998) *Crime Prevention and Community Safety: Politics, Policies and Practices*, London and New York: Harlow Longman.

Creswell, T. (2001) *The Tramp in America*, London: Reaktion Books.

Crewe B. (2011) 'Depth, weight, tightness: revisiting the pains of imprisonment', *Punishment & Society*, 13(5): 509–29.

Crossley, S. (2016) 'Realising the (troubled) family, crafting the neoliberal state', *Families, Relationships and Societies*, 5(2): 263–79.

Crossley, S. (2018) 'The UK government's troubled families programme: delivering social justice?', *Social Inclusion*, 6(3): 301–9.

CSO (2019) *Survey on Income and Living Conditions (SILC) 2018*. Ireland: CSO Statistical Publication. Online ISSN: 2009- 5937, Available from: https://www.cso.ie/en/releasesandpublications/ep/p-silc/surveyonincomeandlivingconditionssilc2018/ [Accessed 12 July 2021].

Cummins, I. (2018) *Poverty, Inequality & Social Work: The Impact of Neoliberalism and Austerity Politics of Welfare Provision*, Bristol: Policy Press.

Cunneen, C. and Tauri, J. M. (2016) *Indigenous Criminology*, Bristol: Policy Press.

Currie, E. (2010) 'Plain left realism: an appreciation, and some thoughts for the future', *Crime, Law, and Social Change*, 54(2): 111–24.

Currie, E. (2013) 'Consciousness, solidarity and hope as prevention and rehabilitation', *International Journal for Crime, Justice and Social Democracy*, 2(2): 3–11.

Curtice, J. (2020) 'Will Covid-19 change attitudes towards the welfare state?', *IPPR Progressive Review*, 27(1): 93–104.

Czischke, D. and Huisman, C. J. (2018) 'Integration through collaborative housing? Dutch starters and refugees forming self-managing communities in Amsterdam', *Urban Planning*, 3(4): 165–64.

Dadusc, D. and Mudu, P. (2020) 'Care without control: the humanitarian industrial complex and the criminalisation of solidarity', *Geopolitics*, doi: 10.1080/14650045.2020.1749839.

Daly, M. (2020) 'Children and their rights and entitlements in EU welfare states', *Journal of Social Policy*, 49(2): 343–60.

Daly, M. and Bray, R. (2015) 'Parenting Support in England: the Bedding Down of a New Policy', *Social Policy and Society*, 14(4): 633–44.

Daly, K. and Marchetti, E. (2012) 'Innovative justice processes: restorative justice, indigenous justice, and therapeutic jurisprudence', in M. Marmo, W. de Lint and D. Palmer (eds) *Crime and Justice: A Guide to Criminology* (4th edn), Sydney: Lawbook, pp 455–81.

Dannesboe, K. I., Bach, D., Kjaer, B. and Palludan, C. (2018) 'Parents of the welfare state: pedagogues as parenting guides', *Social Policy and Society*, 17(3): 467–80.

Davis, A. (2003) *Are Prisons Obsolete?*, New York: Seven Stories Press.

Day, A. (2018) 'Universal Credit: prisoners 'lured back into crime' by benefit delays', *Huffington Post* 12 November, Available from: https://www.huffingtonpost.co.uk/entry/universal-credit-prisoners-being-set-up-to-fail-and-lured-back-into-crime-by-benefit-delays_uk_5be595aae4b0dbe871aa26f2?guccounter=1 [Accessed 8 April 2021].

Day, L., Bryson, C., White, C., Purdon, S., Bewley, H., Kirchener Sala, L. and Portes, J. (2016) *National Evaluation of the Troubled Families Programme, Final Synthesis Report*, London: Department for Communities and Local Government.

DCLG (2012) 'The first Troubled Families Programme 2012 to 2015: an overview', London: Department for Communities and Local Government, Available from: https://assets.publishing.service.gov.uk/government/uploads/system/uploads/attachment_data/file/560776/The_first_Troubled_Families_Programme_an_overview.pdf [Accessed 8 April 2021].

DCLG (2013) *Delivery Agreement: Putting Troubled Families on the Path to Work*, London: Department for Communities and Local Government.

DCLG (2014) *Understanding Troubled Families*. London: Her Majesty's Stationery Office.

DCLG (2015) 'PM praises Troubled Families programme success', press release, 22 June, Available from: https://www.gov.uk/government/news/pm-praises-troubled-families-programme-success [Accessed 8 April 2021].

Dean, H. (2012) 'The ethical deficit of the United Kingdom's proposed Universal Credit: pimping the precariat?', *The Political Quarterly*, 83(2): 353–9.

De Benedictis, S., Allen, K. and Jensen, T. (2017) 'Portraying poverty: the economics and ethics of factual welfare television', *Cultural Sociology*, 11(3): 337–58.

Deeming, C. (2018) 'The politics of fractured solidarity: a cross-national analysis of the class bases of the welfare state', *Social Policy & Administration*, 52(5): 1106–25.

De Giorgi, A. (2006) *Rethinking the Political Economy of Punishment Perspectives on Post-Fordism and Penal Politics*, London: Routledge.

De Giorgi, A. (2010) 'Immigration control, post-Fordism, and less eligibility: a materialist Critique of the criminalization of immigration across Europe', *Punishment & Society*, 12(2): 147–67.

De Giorgi, A. (2017) 'Back to nothing: prisoner reentry and neoliberal neglect', *Social Justice*, 44(1): 83–120.

De Lint, W. and Chazal, N. (2013) 'Resilience and criminal justice: unsafe at low altitude', *Critical Criminology*, 21: 157–76.

Delgado, R. and Stefancic, J. (2016) 'Critical perspectives on police, policing, and mass incarceration', *The Georgetown Law Journal*, 104(6):1531–57.

Demetriou, S. (2020) 'Crime and anti-social behaviour in England and Wales: an empirical evaluation of the ASBO's successor', *Legal Studies*, 40(3): 458–76.

Department of Social Protection (2016) *Pathways to Work 2016-2020*, Dublin: Government of Ireland.

Deuchar, R., Crichlow, V. J. and Fallik, S. W. (2019) 'Cops in crisis?: ethnographic insights on a new era of politicization, activism, accountability, and change in transatlantic policing', *Policing & Society*, 30(1): 47–64.

Devereux, E. and Power, M. (2019) 'Fake news? A critical analysis of the "welfare cheats cheat us all" campaign in Ireland', *Critical Discourse Studies*, 16(3): 347–62.

DeVerteuil, G. (2019) 'Post-revanchist cities?', *Urban Geography*, 40(7): 1055–61.

Dixon, B. (2006) 'Development, crime prevention and social policy in post-apartheid South Africa', *Critical Social Policy*, 26(1):169–91.

Dodge, K. A. and Mandel, A. D. (2012) 'Building evidence for evidence-based policy making', *Criminology & Public Policy*, 11(3): 525–34.

Doherty, R., Poulsen, T. L. and Stoeger, A. (2017) 'Indexation of child benefits for children living in other EU member states', Available from: https://www.ft.dk/samling/20161/almdel/BEU/bilag/299/1781050/index.htm [Accessed 8 April 2021].

Dolowitz, D. and Marsh, D. (2000) 'Learning from abroad: the role of policy transfer in contemporary policy-making', *Governance*, 13(1): 5–24.

Domínguez-Mujica, J., Guerra-Talavera, R. and Parreño-Castelleno, J. M. (2014) 'Migration at a time of global economic crisis: the situation in Spain', *International Migration*, 53(6): 113–27.

Donelan, M. (2020) 'Adoption as permanence letter', 16 January, Available from: https://assets.publishing.service.gov.uk/government/uploads/system/uploads/attachment_data/file/859403/Adoption_letter_final.pdf [Accessed 8 April 2021].

Donzelot, J. (1979) *The Policing of Families* (R. Hurley, Trans.) New York: Pantheon.

Dorling, D. (2015) *Injustice: Why Social Inequality Still Persists* (rev. edn), Bristol: Policy Press.

Dorling, D. (2019) *Inequality and the 1%*, London: Verso:.

Dorling, D., Gordon, D., Hillyard, P., Pantazis, C., Pemberton, S. and Tombs, S. (2008) *Criminal Obsessions: Why Harm Matters More Than Crime* (Harm and Society, 2nd edn), London: Centre for Crime and Justice Studies.

Dowling, E. (2016) 'In the wake of austerity: social impact bonds and the wake of the financialisation of the welfare state in Britain', *New Political Economy*, 22(3): 294–310.

Downes, D. and Hansen, K. (2006) 'Welfare and punishment in comparative perspective' in S. Armstrong and L. McAra (eds) *Perspectives on Punishment, The Contours of Control*, Oxford: Oxford University Press. pp 133–54.

DSFA (2006) *Government Discussion Paper: Proposals for Supporting Lone Parents.* Dublin: Department of Social and Family Affairs, Available from: http://www.solo.ie/downloads/Proposals%20for%20Supporting%20Lone%20Parents.pdf [Accessed 8 April 2021].

Dukelow, F. and Considine, M. (2017) *Irish Social Policy, A Critical Introduction* (2nd edn), Bristol: Policy Press.

Dukelow, F., Whelan, J. and Boland, T. (2020) ' "Tossed to the wind"? The pandemic unemployment payment and the reshaping of the welfare state', Dublin: TASC, Available from: https://www.tasc.ie/blog/2020/07/27/tossed-to-the-wind/ [Accessed 8 April 2021].

Dullum, J. and Ugelvik, T. (2012) 'Introduction: exceptional prisons, exceptional societies?', in T. Ugelvik and J. Dullum (eds) *Penal Exceptionalism? Nordic Prison Policy and Practice*, London: Routledge, pp 1–10.

DWP UK Department of Work and Pensions (2010) 'Universal Credit: welfare that works', Available from: www.dwp.gov.uk/universal-credit [Accessed 5 July 2021].

Dwyer, P., Jones, K., McNeill, J., Scullion, L. and Stewart, A. (2018) *Final Findings: Disabled People, Research Briefing for the Welfare Conditionality: Sanctions, Support and Behaviour Change Project*, York: University of York.

Edwards, R., Gilllies, V. and Horsley, N. (2016) 'Early intervention and evidence-based policy and practice: framing and taming', *Social Policy and Society*, 15(1): 1–10.

EFE News Service Madrid (2019) 'NGO boat SeaWatch enters Italian waters flouting Salvini's ban', 26 June 2019, Available from: https://www.efe.com/efe/english/portada/ngo-boat-seawatch-enters-italian-waters-flouting-salvini-s-ban/50000260-4009833 [Accessed 8 April 2021].

Ennser-Jenastik, L. (2018) 'Welfare chauvinism in populist radical right platforms: the role of redistributive justice principles', *Social Policy & Administration*, 52(1): 293–314.

Ericson, M. (2018) ' "Sweden has been naïve": nationalism, protectionism and securitisation in response to the refugee crisis of 2015', *Social Inclusion*, 6(4): 95–102.

Esping-Andersen, G. (1990) *The Three Worlds of Welfare Capitalism*, Princeton, NJ: Princeton University Press.

Esping-Andersen, G. (1996) *Welfare States in Transition*, London: Sage.

Etzioni A. (1997) *The New Golden Rule*, London: Profile Books.

Eubanks, V. (2018) *Automating Inequality: How High Tech Tools Profile, Police and Punish the Poor*, New York: St. Martin's Press.

Eurofound (2020a) *New Forms of Employment 2020 Update. New Forms of Employment Series*, Luxembourg: Publications Office of the EU.

Eurofound (2020b) *COVID-19: Policy Responses across Europe*, Luxembourg: Publications Office of the EU.

Evolvi, G. (2019) 'The veil and its materiality: Muslim women's digital narratives about the burkini ban', *Journal of Contemporary Religion*, 34 (3): 469–87.

Faircloth, C. (2013) *Militant Activism? Attachment Parenting and Intensive Motherhood in the UK and France*, Oxford and New York: Berghahn Books.

Faircloth, C. (2020) 'When equal partners become unequal parents: couple relationships and intensive parenting culture', *Families, Relationships and Societies*, https://doi.org/10.1332/204674319X15761552010506.

Faircloth, C. and Lee, E. (2010) 'Introduction: changing parenting culture', *Sociological Research Online*, 15(4): 1–4.

Farnsworth, K. (2013) 'Bringing corporate welfare in', *Journal of Social Policy*, 42(1): 1–22.

Farrington, D. P., Ohlin, L.E. and Wilson, J. Q. (1986) *Understanding and Controlling Crime: Toward a New Research Strategy*, New York: Springer.

Fatsis, L. (2019) 'Grime: criminal subculture or public counterculture? A critical investigation into the criminalization of black musical subcultures in the UK', *Crime, Media, Culture*, 15(3): 447–61.

Featherstone, B. (2006) 'Rethinking family support in the current policy context', *British Journal of Social Work*, 36(1): 5–19.

Featherstone, B. and Gupta, A. (2020) 'Social workers' reflections on ethics in relation to adoption in the UK: everywhere but nowhere', *The British Journal of Social Work*, 50(3): 833–49.

Featherstone, B., Morris, K. and White, S. (2014a) 'A marriage made in hell: early intervention meets child protection', *The British Journal of Social Work*, 44(7): 1735–49.

Featherstone, B., Morris, K. and White, S. (2014b) *Re-imagining Child Protection: Towards Humane Social Work with Families*, Bristol: Policy Press.

Federici, S. (2019) *Re-Enchanting the World Feminist and the Politics of the Commons*, Oakland, CA: PM Press.

Feeley, M. and Simon, J. (1992) 'The new penology: notes on the emerging strategy of corrections and its implications', *Criminology*, 30(4), 449–74.

Fekete, L (2004) 'Anti-Muslim racism and the European security state', *Race & Class*, 46(1): 3–29.

Fekete, L. (2009) 'Europe: crimes of solidarity', *Race & Class*, 50(4): 83–97.

Felitti, V. J., Anda, R. F., Nordenberg, D., Williamson, D. F., Spitz, A. M., Edwards, V., Koss, M. P. and Marks, J. S. (1998) 'Relationships of childhood abuse and household dysfunction to many of the leading causes of deaths in adults: the adverse childhood experiences study', *American Journal of Preventative Medicine*, 14: 245–58.

Felson, M. and Clarke, R. (1997) 'The ethics of situational crime prevention' in G. Newman, R. Clarke and S. Soham (eds) *Rational Choice and Situational Crime Prevention: Theoretical Foundations*, Aldershot: Ashgate. pp 197–218.

Feltwell, T., Vines, J., Salt, K., Blythe, M., Kirnan, B., Barnett, J., Brooker, P. and Lawson, S. (2017) 'Counter-discourse activism on social media: the case of challenging "poverty porn" television', *Computer-Supported Cooperative Work (CSCW)*, 26: 345–85.

Fenton Glynn, C. (2015) 'Adoption without consent', study for the PETI Committee. European Parliament, Available from: https://www.europarl.europa.eu/RegData/etudes/STUD/2015/519236/IPOL_STU(2015)519236_EN.pdf [Accessed 8 April 2021].

Ferguson, I. (2008) *Reclaiming Social Work: Challenging Neo-liberalism and Promoting Social Justice*, Los Angeles: Sage.

Finch, L. (1993) *The Classing Gaze, Sexuality, Class and Surveillance*, Sydney: Allen & Unwin.

Finkelhor, D. (2018) 'Screening for adverse childhood experiences (ACEs): cautions and suggestions', *Child Abuse and Neglect*, 85: 174–9.

Finkelhor, D., Shattuck, A., Turner, H. and Hamby, S. (2015) 'A revised inventory of adverse childhood experiences', *Child Abuse & Neglect*, 48: 13–21.

Fletcher, D. R. (2019) 'British public employment service reform. Activating and civilizing the precariat?', *Journal of Poverty and Social Justice*, 27(3): 407–21.

Fletcher, D. R. and Wright, S. (2018) 'A Hand up or a slap down? Criminalising benefit claimants in britain via strategies of surveillance', *Critical Social Policy*, 38(2): 323–44.

Flint, J. (2019) 'Encounters with the centaur state: advanced urban marginality and the practices and ethics of welfare', *Urban Studies*, 56(1): 249–65.

Ford, K., Hughes, K., Hardcastle, K., Di Lemma, L. C. G., Davies, R., Edwards, S. and Bellis, M. A. (2019) 'The evidence base for routine enquiry into adverse childhood experiences: a scoping review', *Child Abuse & Neglect*, 91: 131–46.

Foucault, M. (1977) *Discipline and Punish: The Birth of the Prison*, New York: Pantheon Books.

Foucault, M. (1982) 'The subject and power', in H. L Dreyfus and P. Rabinow (eds) *Michel Foucault: Beyond Structuralism and Hermeneutics*, Chicago: University of Chicago Press, pp 208–26.

Foucault, M. (1984) 'The subject and power', in B. Wallis (ed) *Art and Modernism: Rethinking Representation*, New York: The Museum of Contemporary Art, pp 417–42.

Foucault, M. (2009) *Security, territory, population: Lectures at the Collège de France (1977–1978)*. Basingstoke, England: Palgrave.

Fowkes, L. (2019) 'Seeing people in the computer: the role of information technology in remote employment services', *The Australian Journal of Social Issues*, 55(1): 13–26.

Fox O'Mahony, L., O'Mahony, D. and Hickey, R. (2015) 'Criminalising squatting: setting an agenda', in L. Fox O'Mahony, D. O'Mahony and R. Hickey (eds) *Moral Rhetoric and the Criminalisation of Squatting: Vulnerable Demons?* Abingdon: Routledge, pp 1–10.

Fox Piven, F. F. and Cloward, R. (1971) *Regulating the Poor: The Functions of Public Welfare*, New York: Pantheon Books.

Franko, K. (2019) *The Crimmigrant Other: Migration and Penal Power*, Abingdon: Routledge.

Fraser, N. and Honneth, A. (2003) *Redistribution or Recognition: A Political–Philosophical Exchange*, London: Verso.

Freeman, R. (1999) 'Recursive politics: prevention, modernity and social systems', *Children & Society*, 13(4): 232–41.

Frontex (2017) *Risk analysis for 2017*, Warsaw: Frontex.

Furedi, F. (2001) *Paranoid Parenting: Why Ignoring the Experts May Be Best for Your Child*, London: Allen Lane.

Gaffney, S. and Millar, M. (2020) 'Rational skivers or desperate strivers? The problematisation of fraud in the Irish social protection system', *Critical Social Policy*, 40(1): 69–88.

Galantino M. G. (2020) 'The migration–terrorism nexus: an analysis of German and Italian press coverage of the "refugee crisis"', *European Journal of Criminology*, January: 1–23.

Gallo, C. and Kim. M. E. (2016) *Crime Policy and Welfare Policy*, Oxford: Oxford Handbooks Online.

Gantchev, V. (2019) 'Data protection in the age of welfare conditionality: respect for basic rights or a race to the bottom', *European Journal of Social Security*, 21(1): 3–22.

Garland, D. (2001) *The Culture of Control: Crime and Social Order in Contemporary Society*, Oxford: Oxford University Press.

Garrett, P. M. (2015) 'Words matter: deconstructing welfare dependency in the UK', *Critical and Radical Social Work*, 3(3): 389–406.

Garrett, P. M. (2016) '"Unmarried mothers" in the Republic of Ireland', *Journal of Social Work*, 16(6): 708–25.

Garrett, P. M. (2017) '"Castaway categories": examining the re-emergence of the "underclass" in the UK', *Journal of Progressive Human Services*, 30(1): 25–45.

Garrett, P. M. (2018) 'Ending the "cruel rationing of human love"? Adoption politics and neo-liberal rationality', *The British Journal of Social Work*, 48(5): 1239–56.

Geiger, B. B. (2017) 'Benefits conditionality for disabled people: stylised facts from a review of international evidence and practice', *Journal of Poverty and Social Justice*, 25(2): 107–28.

Geiger, B. B. (2018) 'Benefit "Myths"? The accuracy and inaccuracy of public beliefs about the benefits system', *Social Policy & Administration*, 52(5): 998–1018.

Gibb, K. (2015) 'The multiple policy failures of the UK bedroom tax', *International Journal of Housing Policy*, 15(2): 148–66.

Gibney, M. J. (2013) 'Deportation, crime and the changing character of membership in the United Kingdom', in K. F. Aas and M. Bosworth (eds) *The Borders of Punishment Migration, Citizenship, and Social Exclusion*, Oxford: Oxford University Press, pp 28–236.

Gibson, L. (2019) 'Anthropology as respair: anthropological engagements with hope and its others', *Anthropological Quarterly*, 92: 575–85.

Gillies, V. (2005a) 'Meeting parents' needs? Discourses of "support" and "inclusion" in family policy', *Critical Social Policy*, 25(1): 70–90.

Gillies, V. (2005b) 'Raising the "meritocracy": parenting and the individualisation of social class', *Sociology*, 39: 835–53.

Gillies, V. (2008) 'Childrearing, class and the new politics of parenting', *Sociology Compass*, 2(3): 1079–95.

Gillies, V. (2014) 'Troubling families: parenting and the politics of early intervention' in S. Wagg and J. Pilcher (eds) *Thatcher's Grandchildren? Politics and Childhood in the 21st Century*, Basingstoke: Palgrave Macmillan, pp 204–24.

Gillies, V. (2020) 'Parallels and ruptures in the neoliberal intensive parenting regime', *Families, Relationships and Societies*, 9(1): 169–72.

Gillies, V., Edwards, R. and Horsley, N. (2017) *Challenging the Politics of Early Intervention: Who's Saving Children and Why?*, Bristol: Policy Press.

Gilling, D. (1997) *Crime Prevention, Theory, Policy and Politics*, London: UCL Press.

Gilling, D. and Barton, A. (1997) 'Crime prevention and community safety: a new home for social policy?', *Critical Social Policy*, 17(52): 63–83.

Gilmore, J. (2019) 'Lessons from Orgreave: police power and the criminalization of protest', *Journal of Law and Society*, 46(4): 612–39.

Gilmore, R. W. (2007) *Golden Gulag: Prisons, Surplus, Crisis, and Opposition in Globalizing California*, Berkeley: University of California Press.

Gingrich, J. and King, D. (2019) 'Americanising Brexit Britain's welfare state', *The Political Quarterly*, 90(1): 89–98.

Giroux, H. (2012) 'Criminalizing dissent and punishing the occupy movement protesters', in H. Giroux (ed) *Youth in Revolt: Reclaiming a Democratic Future*, New York: Routledge, Taylor & Francis Group, pp 12–35.

Goldson, B. and Jamieson, J. (2002) 'Youth crime, the "Parenting deficit" and state intervention: a contextual critique', *Youth Justice*, 2(2): 82–99.

Gonzales, R. G. and Sigona, N. (eds) (2017) *Within and Beyond Citizenship Borders, Membership and Belonging*, London and New York: Routledge, Taylor & Francis Group.

González-Sánchez, I. and Maroto-Calatayud, M. (2018) 'The penalization of protest under neoliberalism: managing resistance through punishment', *Crime, Law, and Social Change*, 70(4): 443–60.

Goodman, P., Page, J. and Phelps, M. (2017) *Breaking the Pendulum: The Long Struggle over Criminal Justice*, New York: Oxford University Press.

Goodwin, M. (2017) 'How the criminalization of pregnancy robs women of reproductive autonomy', *The Hastings Center Report*, 47(S3): S19–S27.

Gough, I. (1979) *The Political Economy of the Welfare State*, London: Macmillan.

Gove, M. (2012) Speech on adoption, 23 February, Available from: http://www.ukpol.co.uk/michael-gove-2012-speech-on-adoption/ [Accessed 8 April 2021].

Gray, C. (2019) 'The implementation and impact of national's welfare conditionality in an international context', *New Zealand Sociology*, 34(2): 71–92.

Gray, P. (2007) 'Youth Justice, social exclusion and the demise of social justice', *Howard Journal of Criminal Justice*, 46(4): 401–16.

Gray, P. (2011) 'Youth custody, resettlement and the right to social justice', *Youth Justice: An International Journal*, 11(3): 235–49.

Gray, P. and Smith, R. (2019) 'Shifting sands: the reconfiguration of neoliberal youth penality', *Theoretical Criminology*, 25(2): 304–24.

Greener, I. (2018) *Social Policy after the Financial Crisis: A Progressive Response*, Cheltenham: Edward Elgar.

Greve, B., Blomquist, P., Hvinden, B. and van Gerven, M. (2021) 'Nordic welfare states—still standing or changed by the COVID-19 crisis?', *Social Policy & Administration*, 55(2): 295–311.

Grover, C. (2010) 'Crime and social policy', in S. G. Shoham, P. Knepper and M. Kett (eds) *International Handbook of Criminology*, New York: CRC Group Taylor & Francis, pp 425–54.

Guggenheim, M. (2020) 'Let's root out racism in child welfare too', *The Imprint* (formerly *The Chronicle of Social Change*), Available from: https://imprintnews.org/child-welfare-2/lets-root-out-racism-child-welfare-too/44327 [Accessed 8 April 2021].

Gulis G. and Safi, M. (2020) 'Rapid health impact assessment of a Danish policy document: one Denmark without parallel societies: no ghettos in 2030', *Journal of Public Health*, e-pub ahead of print, doi: 10.1007/s10389-020-01375-z.

Gupta, A. (2018) 'Punishing the poor? Child welfare and protection under neoliberalism', *Social Work & Society*, 16(2): 1.

Gupta, A., Featherstone, B. and White, S. (2016) 'Reclaiming humanity: from capacities to capabilities in understanding parenting in adversity', *The British Journal of Social Work*, 46(2): 339–54.

Gustafson, K. (2009) 'The criminalization of poverty', *The Journal of Criminal Law & Criminology*, 99(3): 643–716.

Gustafson, K. (2011) *Cheating Welfare: Public Assistance and the Criminalization of Poverty*, New York: New York University Press.

Gustafson, K. (2013) 'Degradation ceremonies and the criminalization of low-income women', *UC Irvine Law Review*, 3(2): 297–358.

Hall, S., Massey, D. and Rustin, M. (2015) *After Neoliberalism? The Kilburn Manifesto*, London: Lawrence and Wishart.

Hall, T. and Hubbard, P. (1996) 'The entrepreneurial city: new urban politics, new urban geographies?', *Progress in Human Geography*, 20(2): 153–74.

Hampson, C. (2016) 'State bans on debtors' prisons and criminal justice', *Harvard Law Review*, 129(4): 1024–45.

Hancock, L. and Mooney, G. (2012) '"Welfare ghettos" and the "broken society": territorial stigmatization in the contemporary UK', *Housing Theory and Society*, 30(1): 46–64.

Hancock, L. and Mooney, G. (2013) 'Beyond the penal state: advanced marginality, social policy and anti-welfarism', in P. Squires and J. Lea (eds) *Criminalisation and Advanced Marginality: Critically Exploring the Work of Loïc Wacquant*, Bristol: Policy Press, pp 107–28.

Haney, L. (2004) 'Introduction: gender, welfare and states of punishment', *Social Politics*, 11(3): 333–62.

Hansen, M. P. (2019) *The Moral Economy of Activation: Ideas, Politics and Policies*, Bristol: Policy Press.

Hansen, P. (2015) Undermining free movement: migration in an age of austerity, Available from: https://www.eurozine.com/undermining-free-movement/ [Accessed 8 April 2021].

Hartas, D. (2019) 'Assessing the foundational studies on adverse childhood experiences', *Social Policy and Society*, 18(3): 435–43.

Harvey, D. (1989) 'From managerialism to entrepreneurialism: the transformation in urban governance in late capitalism', *Geografiska Annaler: Series B, Human Geography*, 71(1): 3–17.

Hasselberg, I. (2014) 'Whose security? The deportation of foreign-national offenders from the UK', in M. Maguire, N. Zurawski and C. Frois (eds) *The Anthropology of Security: Perspectives from the Frontline of Policing, Counter-Terrorism and Border Control*, London: Pluto Press, pp 139–57.

Hays, S. (1996) *The Cultural Contradictions of Motherhood*, New Haven, CT: Yale University Press.

Headworth, S. (2019) 'Getting to know you welfare fraud investigation and the appropriation of social ties', *American Sociological Review*, 84(1): 171–96.

Hearne, R. and Murphy, M. (2017) 'Investing in the Right to a Home: Housing, HAPS and Hubs', Maynooth: National University of Ireland Maynooth. Available from: https://www.maynoothuniversity.ie/sites/default/files/assets/document/Investing%20in%20the%20Right%20to%20a%20Home%20Full_1.pdf [Accessed 8 April 2021].

Heber, A. (2014) 'Good versus bad? Victims, offenders and victim-offenders in Swedish crime policy', *European Journal of Criminology*, 11(4): 410–28.

Hemerijck, A. (2011) 'Crisis aftershocks and European welfare state futures', *Georgetown Journal of International Affairs*, 12(2): 89–97.

Hemerijck, A. (2013) *Changing Welfare States*, Oxford: Oxford University Press.

Henley, J. and Booth, R. (2020) 'Welfare surveillance system violates human rights, Dutch court rules', *The Guardian*, 5 February, Available from: https://www.theguardian.com/technology/2020/feb/05/welfare-surveillance-system-violates-human-rights-dutch-court-rules [Accessed 8 April 2021].

Henriques-Gomes, L. (2020) 'Cashless welfare card: how does it work and what changes is the government proposing?', *The Guardian*, 5 February, Available from: https://www.theguardian.com/australia-news/2020/feb/06/cashless-welfare-card-how-does-it-work-and-what-changes-is-the-government-proposing [Accessed 8 April 2021].

Herring C. (2019) 'Complaint-oriented policing: regulating homelessness in public space', *American Sociological Review*, 84(5): 769–800.

Herzog-Evans, M. (2011) 'Judicial rehabilitation in France: helping with the desisting process and acknowledging achieved desistance', *European Journal of Probation*, 3(1): 4–19.

Heuer, J. O. and Zimmermann, K. (2020) 'Unravelling deservingness: which criteria do people use to judge the relative deservingness of welfare target groups? A vignette-based focus group study', *Journal of European Social Policy*, 30(4): 389–403.

Hewson, D. (2020) ' "All the time watched": an analysis of disciplinary power within the Irish direct provision system', *Journal of Ethnic and Migration Studies*.

Hick, R. (2018) 'Enter the troika: the politics of social security during Ireland's bailout', *Journal of Social Policy*, 47(1): 1–20.

Hicks, A. and Kenworthy, L. (2003) 'Varieties of welfare capitalism', *Socio-Economic Review*, 1(1): 27–61.

Hill, M. (2011) 'The economic crisis and paradigm change', in K. Farnsworth and Z. Irving (eds) *Social Policy in Challenging Times Economic Crisis and Welfare Systems*, Bristol: Policy Press, pp 31–48.

Hillyard, P. and Percy-Smith, J. (1988) *The Coercive State*, London: Fontana.

Hillyard, P., Pantazis, C., Tombs, S. and Gordon, D. (2004) *Beyond Criminology: Taking Harm Seriously*, London: Pluto Press.

Hillyard, P., Sim, J., Tombs, S. and White, D. (2004) 'Leaving "a stain beyond the silence": contemporary criminology and the politics of dissent', *British Journal of Criminology*, 44(3): 369–90.

Hillyard, P. and Tombs, S. (2017) 'Social Harm and Zemiology', in A. Liebling, S. Maruna, S. and McAra, L. (eds) *Oxford Handbook of Criminology* (6th edn), Oxford: Oxford University Press, pp 284–305.

Hirdman, A. (2015) 'The passion of mediated shame: affective reactivity and classed otherness in reality TV', *European Journal of Cultural Studies*, 19(3): 283–96.

Hirschfield, P. J. (2008) 'Preparing for prison? The criminalization of school discipline in the USA', *Theoretical Criminology*, 12(1): 79–101.

Hirschi, T. (1993) 'Administrative criminology', *Contemporary Sociology*, 22(3): 348–50.

HmbResOG (Hamburgisches Resozialierungs- und Opferhilfegesetze-HmbResOGGesetz zur station ä ren und ambulanten Resozialisierung und zur Opferhilfe) Vom 31. August 2018; HmbGVBl. 2018, S. 265.

HM Inspectorate of Probation and HM Inspectorate of Prisons (2017) 'An Inspection of through the gate resettlement services for prisoners serving 12 months or more: a joint inspection by HM Inspectorate of Probation and HM Inspectorate of Prisons', June, Available from: https://www.justiceinspectorates.gov.uk/cjji/wp-content/uploads/sites/2/2017/06/Through-the-Gate-phase-2-report.pdf [Accessed 7 April 2021].

Hodgkinson, S. and Tilley, N. (2011) 'Tackling anti-social behaviour, lessons from New Labour for the coalition government', *Criminology and Criminal Justice*, 11(4): 283–305.

Hogg, R. (2016) 'Left realism and social democratic renewal', *International Journal for Crime, Justice and Social Democracy*, 5(3): 66–79.

Holland, M. L., Xia, Y., Kitzman, H. J., Dozier, A. M. and Olds, D. L. (2014) 'Patterns of visit attendance in the nurse–family partnership program', *American Journal of Public Health*, 104: e58–e65.

Home Office (2009) Guidance on Designated Public Place Orders (DPPOs): For local authorities in England and Wales.

Horgan-Jones, J. (2020) 'More than 2,500 pandemic payments stopped, says minister', *Irish Times*, Available from: https://www.irishtimes.com/news/ireland/irish-news/more-than-2-500-pandemic-payments-stopped-says-minister-1.4316118 [Accessed 8 April 2021].

HRW (2019) 'Italy: revoke abusive anti-asylum decrees – draconian migration measures put lives, rights at risk', Available from: https://www.hrw.org/news/2020/01/31/italy-revoke-abusive-anti-asylum-decrees [Accessed 8 April 2021].

Hucklesby, A. and Corcoran, M. (2016) *The Voluntary Sector and Criminal Justice*, London: Springer.

Hudson, J., Lunt, N., Hamilton, C., Mackinder, S., Swift, C. and Meers, J. (2016) 'Nostalgia narratives? Pejorative attitudes to welfare in historical perspective: survey evidence from Beveridge to the British social attitudes survey', *The Journal of Poverty and Social Justice: Research, Policy, Practice*, 24(3): 227–43.

Hudson, J., Patrick, R. and Wincup, E. (2016) 'Introduction to themed special issue: exploring "welfare" attitudes and experiences', *Journal of Poverty and Social Justice*, 24(3): 215–26.

Hughes, K., Bellis, M. A., Hardcastle, K. A., Sethi, D., Butchart, A. Mikton, C., Jones, L. and Dunne, M. P. (2017) 'The effect of multiple adverse childhood experiences on health: a systematic review and meta-analysis', *The Lancet Public Health*, 2(8): 356–66.

Hughes Miller, M. (2020) 'Introduction to special issue: criminalizing motherhood and reproduction', *Women & Criminal Justice*, 30(5): 310–15.

Humphreys, H. (2020) 'Statement by Minister Humphreys on Pandemic Unemployment Payment', Dublin: Department of Social Protection, 29 July, Available from: https://www.gov.ie/en/speech/0c19b-statement-by-minister-humphreys-on-pandemic-unemployment-payment/ [Accessed 8 April 2021].

ILO (2020) 'The COVID-19 crisis: a wake-up call to strengthen social protection systems', 24 April, Available from: https://www.ilo.org/global/about-the-ilo/newsroom/news/WCMS_742676/lang–en/index.htm [Accessed 8 April 2021].

Indecon (2017) *Indecon Independent Review of the Amendments to the One Parent Family Payment Since 2012*, Dublin: Indecon.

IOM (2019) *Glossary on Migration*, Available from: https://publications.iom.int/system/files/pdf/iml_34_glossary.pdf [Accessed 7 April 2021].

IRKS (n.d.) *Stellungnahme zum Entwurf eines Sozialhilfe-Grundsatzgesetzes (104/ME XXVI. GP)*, Available from: https://www.irks.at/assets/irks/Stellungnahme_IRKS.pdf [Accessed 7 April 2021].

IPRT (2019) Opening Statement to Oireachtas Joint Committee on Justice and Equality Spent Convictions, July , available from: https://www.iprt.ie/site/assets/files/6503/iprt_openingstatement_10july2019.pdf [Accessed 8 April 2021].

Irish Statute Book (2005) 'Social Welfare (Consolidation) Act 2005', number 26 of 2005, Available from: http://www.irishstatutebook.ie/eli/2005/act/26/enacted/en/html [Accessed 8 April 2021].

Irish Times (2020) 'Plan to review 700,000 welfare claims this year to make €520m in "savings"', 29 July, *Irish Times*, Available from: https://www.irishtimes.com/news/politics/plan-to-review-700-000-welfare-claims-by-end-of-year-to-make-savings-of-520m-1.4316087 [Accessed 8 April 2021].

Isin, Engin F. (2000) 'Introduction: democracy, citizenship, sovereignty, politics', in Engin F. Isin, (ed) *Democracy, Citizenship, and the Global City*, London: Routledge, pp 1–21.

Jack, S. M., Busser, L. D., Sheehan, D., Gonzalez, A., Zwiggers, E. J. and MacMillan, H. L. (2012) 'Adaptation and Implementation of the nurse–family partnership in Canada', *Canadian Journal of Public Health*, 103: S42–S48.

Jaehrling, K., Kalina, T. and Mesaros, L. (2014) 'A paradox of activation strategies why increasing labour market participation among single mothers failed to bring down poverty', *Social Politics: International Studies in Gender, State and Society*, 22(1): 85–110.

Jamieson, J. (2012) 'Bleak times for children? The anti-social behaviour agenda and the criminalization of social policy', *Social Policy & Administration*, 46(4): 448–64.

Jarrín Morán, A. J., Rodríguez García, D. and de Lucas, J. (2012) 'Los centros de internamiento para extranjeros en España: Una evaluación crítica' ['Centres of internment for foreigners in Spain: A critical evaluation'], *Revista CIDOB d'afers internacionales*, 99: 201–20.

Javier, J. R., Hoffman, L. R. and Shah, S. I. on behalf of the Pediatric Policy Council (2019) 'Making the case of ACEs: adverse childhood experiences, obesity and long-term health', *Pediatric Research*, 86: 420–2.

Jeffreys, E., Matthews, K. and Thomas, A. (2010) 'HIV criminalisation and sex work in Australia', *Reproductive Health Matters*, 18(35): 129–36.

Jensen, T. (2013) 'Austerity parenting', *Soundings*, 55: 60–70.

Jensen, T. (2014) 'Welfare commonsense, poverty porn and doxosophy', *Sociological Research Online*, 19(3): 1–7.

Jensen, T. (2018) *Parenting the Crisis: The Cultural Politics of Parent Blame*, Bristol: Policy Press.

Jensen, T., Allen, K., de Benedictis, S., Garthwaite, K. and Patrick, R. (2019) 'Welfare imaginaries at the interregnum', *Soundings*, 72: 79–89.

Jensen, T. and Tyler, I. (2015) '"Benefits broods": the cultural and political crafting of anti-welfare common sense', *Critical Social Policy*, 35(4): 470–91.

Jessop, B. (2002) *The Future of the Capitalist State*, Cambridge: Polity Press.

Jewkes, Y., Crewe, B. and Bennett, J. (eds) (2016) *Handbook on Prisons* (2nd edn), London: Routledge.

Johansen, N. B. (2013) 'Governing the funnel of expulsion: Agamben, the dynamics of force, and minimalist biopolitics', in K. F. Aas and M. Bosworth (eds) (*The Borders of Punishment Migration, Citizenship and Social Exclusion*, Oxford: Oxford University Press, pp 257–72.

Johnstone, C. (2016) 'After the ASBO: extending control over young people's use of public space in England and Wales', *Critical Social Policy*, 36(4): 716–26.

Join-Lambert, H. (2016) 'Parental involvement and multi-agency support services for high need families in France', *Social Policy and Society*, 15(2): 317–29.

Jones, C. and Novak, T. (1999) *Poverty, Welfare and the Disciplinary State*, London: Routledge.

Joppke, C. (2010) *Citizenship and Immigration*, Cambridge and Malden, MA: Polity.

Jordan, B. (1974) *Poor Parents*, London: Routledge.

Jordan, B. and Drakeford, M. (2012) *Social Work and Social Policy under Austerity*, Basingstoke: Palgrave Macmillan.

Jørgensen, M. B. (2018) 'Dependent, deprived or deviant? The case of single mothers in Denmark', *Politics and Governance*, 6(3): 170–9.

Joy, E. and Beddoe, L. (2019) 'ACEs, cultural considerations and "common sense" in Aotearoa New Zealand', *Social Policy and Society*, 18(3): 491–7.

Joy, M. and Shields, J. (2018) 'Austerity in the making: reconfiguring social policy through social impact bonds', *Policy and Politics*, 46(4):681–95.

Joy, M. and Shields, J. (2020) 'Debate: how do social impact bonds economize social policy?', *Public Money & Management*, 40(3): 190–2.

Kaakinen, J. (2018) 'The government is trying to reduce chronic homelessness ... Here's how Finland ended it', *The Journal*, Available from: https://www.thejournal.ie/finland-homeless-housing-first-ireland-4303419-Oct2018/ [Accessed 8 April 2021]

Kabir, N. (2005) 'Muslims in Australia: immigration, race relations and cultural history', *Sydney Papers*, 17(2): 62–72.

Kafka. F. (1921) *Tagebuecher 1910–1923*, Frankfurt am Main: S. Fischer Verlag, 1973, 34.

Kalhan, A. (2010) 'Rethinking immigration detention', *Columbia Law Review*, Sidebar 110: 24.

Kaufman, E. and Bosworth, M. (2013) 'Prison and national identity: citizenship, punishment and the sovereign state', in D. Scott (ed) *Why Prison?* Cambridge: Cambridge University Press, pp 170–88.

Keele, J. (2020) 'City of Winnipeg to discontinue controversial noise project, in: CTV News Winnipeg', Available from: https://winnipeg.ctvnews.ca/city-of-winnipeg-to-discontinue-controversial-noise-project-1.4998289#_gus&_gucid=&_gup=twitter&_gsc=WBrg46I [Accessed 8 April 2021].

Kelly-Irving, M. and Delpierre, C. (2019) 'A critique of the adverse childhood experiences framework in epidemiology and public health: uses and misuses' *Social Policy and Society*, 18(3): 445–56.

Kelly, P. (2006) 'The entrepreneurial self and youth at-risk: exploring the horizons of identity in the 21st century', *Journal of Youth Studies*, 9(1): 17–32.

Keskinen, S. (2016) 'From welfare nationalism to welfare chauvinism: economic rhetoric, the welfare state and changing asylum policies in Finland', *Critical Social Policy*, 36 (3): 352–70.

Khan, M. (ed) (2020) *Its Not all about the Burqa: Women on Faith, Feminism, Sexuality and Race*, London: Pan Macmillan.

Khoshravi, S. (2009) 'Sweden: detention and deportation of asylum seekers', *Race & Class*, 50(4): 38–56.

Kiely, E. and Leane, M. (2012) *Irish Women at Work: 1930–1960, An Oral History*, Dublin: Irish Academic Press.

Kiely, E. and Meade, R. (2018) 'Contemporary Irish youth work policy and practice: a governmental analysis', *Child & Youth Services*, 39(1):17–42.

Kirton, D. (2018) 'Neoliberalism, "Race" and Child Welfare', *Critical and Radical Social Work*, 6(3): 311–27.

Kirton-Darling, J. (2016) 'Adoptions without consent, children's rights are paramount', The Blog, *Huffington Post*, 8 November.

Kliem, S., Sandner, M., Lohmann, A., Sierau, S., Dähne, V., Klein, A. M. and Jungmann, T. (2018) 'Follow-up study regarding the medium-term effectiveness of the home-visiting program "pro kind" at age 7 years: study protocol for a randomized controlled trial', *Trials*, 19(323), https://doi.org/10.1186/s.13063-018-2707-3 [Accessed 8 April 2021].

Knepper, P. (2007) *Criminology and Social Policy*, London: Sage.

Knepper, P. (2013) 'An international crime decline: lessons for social welfare crime policy?' in H. Kemshall (ed.) *Crime and Social Policy*, Chichester: John Wiley & Sons, pp 5–21.

Knijn, T. and van Wel, F. (2001) 'Careful or lenient? welfare reform for lone mothers in the Netherlands', *Journal of European Social Policy*, 11(3): 235–52.

Kronen Zeitung (2018) 'Familienbeihilfe ins Ausland: Kürzung beschlossen', Available from: https://www.krone.at/1701953 [Accessed 8 April 2021].

Koch, I. (2018) *Personalizing the State: An Anthropology of Law, Politics and Welfare in Austerity Britain*, Oxford: Oxford University Press.

Koch, I. and James, D. (2020) 'The state of the welfare state: advice, governance and care in settings of austerity', *Ethnos*, doi: 10.1080/00141844.2019.1688371.

Kohler-Hausmann, J. (2007) '"The crime of survival": fraud prosecutions, community surveillance and the original "welfare queen"', *Journal of Social History*, 41(2): 329–54.

Kukutai, T. and Taylor, J. (2016) 'Data sovereignty for indigenous peoples: current practice and future needs', in T. Kukutai and John Taylor (eds) *Indigenous Data Sovereignty: Toward an Agenda*, Canberra: ANU Press, pp 1–24.

Kupchik, A. (2009) 'Things are tough all over: race, ethnicity, class and school discipline', *Punishment & Society*, 11(3): 291–317.

Kupchik, A. (2010) 'Editor's introduction: crime, crime prevention, and punishment in schools', *Journal of Contemporary Criminal Justice*, 26(3): 252–3.

Kvist, J. and Greve, B. (2011) 'Has the Nordic welfare model been transformed?', *Social Policy & Administration*, 45(2): 146–60.

Lacey, N. (2009) 'Historicising criminalisation: conceptual and empirical issues', *Modern Law Review*, 72(6): 936–60.

Lacey, N. (2010) 'Differentiating among penal states', *The British Journal of Sociology*, 61(4): 778–94.

Lacey, N. (2018) 'Theorising criminalities through the modalities approach, a critical appreciation', *International Journal for Crime, Justice and Social Democracy*, 7(3): 122–7.

Lacey, R. E. and Minnis, H. (2019) 'Practitioner review: twenty years of research with ACE scores – advantages, disadvantages and applications to practice', *The Journal of Child Psychology and Psychiatry*, 61(2): 116–30.

Lambert, M. (2018) 'Between "families in trouble" and "children at risk": historicising "troubled family" policy in England since 1945', *Children & Society*, 33(1): 82–91.

Lambert, M. and Crossley, S. (2017) 'Getting with the (troubled families) programme: a review', *Social Policy & Society*, 16(1): 87–97.

Lanigan, G. (2016) *State of New Jersey Department of Corrections Annual Report 2016*. New Jersey Department of Corrections, Available from: https://www.state.nj.us/corrections/pdf/NJDOCNewsletter/2016_Annual_Report.pdf [Accessed 8 April 2021].

Laniyonu, A. (2018) 'Coffee shops and street stops: policing practices in gentrifying neighborhoods', *Urban Affairs Review*, 54(5): 898–930.

Lappi-Seppälä, T. (2008) 'Trust, welfare, and political culture: explaining differences in national penal policies', *Crime and Justice: A Review of Research* 37: 313–88.

Lareau, A. (2011) *Unequal Childhoods: Class, Race and Family Life*, Berkeley: University of California Press.

Larkin, P. M. (2007) 'The "criminalization" of social security law: towards a punitive welfare state', *Journal of Law and Society*, 34(3): 295–320.

Larsen, C. A., Frederiksen, M. and Nielsen, M. H. (2018) 'European welfare nationalism: a democratic forum study in five countries', in P. Taylor-Gooby and B. Leruth (eds) *Attitudes, Aspirations and Welfare*, Cham: Palgrave Macmillan, pp 63–91.

Lawler, S. (2005) 'Disgusted subjects: the making of middle-class identities', *The Sociological Review*, 53(3): 429–46.

Lea, J. and Hallsworth, S. (2013) 'Bringing the state back in: understanding neoliberal security', in P. Squires and J. Lea (eds) *Criminalisation and Advanced Marginality: Critically Exploring the Work of Loïc Wacquant*, Bristol: Policy Press, pp 19–40.

Leane, M. and Kiely, E. (1997) 'Single lone motherhood: rhetoric versus reality', in A. Byrne and M. Leonard (eds) *Women and Irish Society, A Sociological Reader*, Belfast: Beyond the Pale Publications, pp 296–310.

Lechuga, M. (2014) 'Affective boundaries in a landscape of shame: writing HB 56', *Journal of Argumentation in Context*, 3(1): 83–101.

Lee, E., Bristow, J., Faircloth, C. and Macvarish, J. (2014) *Parenting Culture Studies*, Basingstoke: Palgrave Macmillan.

Lees, L. (2012) 'The geography of gentrification: thinking through comparative urbanism', *Progress in Human Geography*, 36(2): 155–71.

Lefebvre, H. (1970) *La revolution urbaine*, Paris: Editions Gallimard.

Letourneau, N., Dewey, D., Kaplan, B. J., Ntanda, H., Novick, J., Thomas, J. C., the APrON Study Team (2019) 'Intergenerational transmission of ACEs via maternal depression and anxiety and moderation by child sex', *Journal of Developmental Origins of Health and Disease*, 10(1): 88–99.

Letter to Mr Alan Shatter, President of the European Council for Justice and Home Affairs, 15 April 2013, Available from: docs.dpaq.de/3604-130415_letter_to_presidency_final_1_2.pdf [Accessed 8 April 2021].

Leverentz, A., Chen, E. Y. and Christian, J. (2020) *Beyond Recidivism: New Approaches to Research on Prisoner Reentry and Reintegration*, New York: New York University Press.

Levitas, R. (2001) 'Against work, a utopian incursion into social policy', *Critical Social Policy*, 21(4): 449–65.

Levitas, R. (2012) 'The just's umbrella: austerity and the big society in coalition policy and beyond', *Critical Social Policy*, 32(3): 320–42.

Levitas, R. (2013) 'Some varieties of utopian method', *Irish Journal of Sociology*, 21(2): 41–50.

Lewis, S. and Brady, G. (2018) 'Parenting under adversity: birth parents' accounts of inequality and adoption', *Social Sciences*, 7(12): 257–71.

Little, C. (2015) 'The "Mosquito" and the transformation of British public space', *Journal of Youth Studies*, 18(2): 167–82.

London Borough of Hammersmith and Fulham, Community Trigger, Available from: https://www.lbhf.gov.uk/crime/anti-social-behaviour/community-trigger [Accessed 8 April 2021].

Loopstra, R., Reeves, A., Taylor-Robinson, D., Barr, B., McKee, M. and Stuckler, D. (2015) 'Austerity, sanctions and the rise of food banks in the UK', *British Medical Journal*, 350, doi: 10.1136/bmj.h1775.

Loopstra, R., Fledderjohann, J., Reeves, A. and Struckker, D. (2018) 'Impact of welfare sanctioning on food insecurity: a dynamic cross-area study of food bank usage in the UK', *Journal of Social Policy*, 47(3): 437–57.

Luddy, M. (2011) 'Unmarried Mothers in Ireland, 1930–1973', *Women's History Review*, 20(1): 109–26.

Lundqvist, Å. (2015) 'Parenting support in Sweden: new policies in old settings', *Social Policy and Society*, 14(4): 657–68.

Lynch, K., Cantillon, S. and Crean, M., 'Inequality', in W. K. Roche, P. J. O'Connell, and A. Prothero (eds) *Austerity and the Recovery in Ireland: Europe's Poster Child and the Great Recession*, Oxford: Oxford University Press, pp 252–71.

Macanico, Y., Hayes, B., Kenny, S. and Barat, F. (2018) 'The shrinking space for solidarity with migrants and refugees: how the European Union and member states target and criminalize defenders of the rights of people on the move', Available from: https://www.tni.org/files/publication-downloads/web_theshrinkingspace.pdf [Accessed 8 April 2021].

Machin, R. (2020) 'Regressive and precarious: analysing the UK social security system in the light of the findings of the UN special rapporteur on poverty and human rights', *Social Work and Social Sciences Review*, 21(3): 70–85.

MacLeod, G. (2002) 'From urban entrepreneurialism to a "revanchist city"? On the spatial injustices of Glasgow's Renaissance', *Antipode*, 34(3): 602–24.

MacPherson, K. (2017) 'Governmentalities, tertiary desistance and the responsibilisation deficit' [Blog entry online], Available from: https://discoveringdesistance.home.blog/2017/09/15/governmentalities-tertiary-desistance-and-the-responsibilisation-deficit/ [Accessed 7 April 2021].

Macnicol, J. (1987) 'In pursuit of the underclass', *Journal of Social Policy*, 16(3): 293–318.

Macnicol, J. (2017) 'Reconstructing the underclass', *Social Policy and Society*, 16(1): 99–108.

Macvarish, J., Lee, E. and Lowe, P. (2015) 'Neuroscience and Family policy, what becomes of the parent?' *Critical Social Policy*, 35(2): 248–69.

Macvarish, J. and Lee, E. (2019) 'Constructions of parents in adverse childhood experiences discourse' *Social Policy and Society*, 18(3): 467–77.

Madden, L. (2014) 'Opinion: austerity cuts that directly affect women and children have been piled on by this government' thejournal.ie, 16 December, Available from: https://www.thejournal.ie/readme/lone-parents-feminisation-of-poverty-1835949-Dec2014/ [Accessed 8 April 2021].

Madianou, M. (2020) 'A second order disaster? Digital technologies during the Covid-19 pandemic', *Social Media and Society*, July–September: 1–5.

Madigan, S., Wade, M., Plamondon, A., Maguire, J. L. and Jenkins, J. M. (2017) 'Maternal adverse childhood experience and infant health: biomedical and psychosocial risk as intermediary mechanisms', *The Journal of Pediatrics*, 187: 282–9.

Maguire, M. (2014) 'Counter-terrorism in European airports', in M. Maguire, C. Frois and N. Zurawski (eds) *The Anthropology of Security: Perspectives from the Frontline of Policing, Counter-Terrorism and Border Control*, London: Pluto Press, pp 86–104.

Maguire, M., Williams, K. and Corcoran, M. (2019) 'Penal drift and the voluntary sector', *Howard Journal of Crime and Justice*, 58(3): 430–49.

Malmberg-Heimenon, I. and Tøge, A. G. (2020) 'Comparing the effects of governmental and local family intervention projects on social work practices in Norway: a cluster randomised study', *The British Journal of Social Work*, 50(5): 1475–94.

Manjikian, M. (2013) *Securitization of Property Squatting in Europe*, New York: Routledge, Taylor & Francis.

Marhold, F. and Ludvik, C. P. (2020) 'Thoughts about indexing family benefits: are authorities permitted to apply the Austrian indexation of family benefits? The primacy of EU law and the right/obligation to request a ruling from the Court of Justice of the European Union', *European Journal of Social Security*, 22(3): 273–86.

Maritime Executive (2020) 'Italy's highest court rejects charges against rescue ship captain', Available from: https://www.maritime-executive.com/article/sea-rescue-captain-cleared-of-charges-for-unauthorized-port-entry [Accessed 8 April 2021].

Martin, D. and Wilcox, P. (2013) 'Women, welfare and the carceral state', in P. Squires and J. Lea (eds) *Criminalisation and Advanced Marginality: Critically Exploring the Work of Loïc Wacquant*, Bristol: Policy Press, pp 151–72.

Martin, J. P. (2015) 'Activation and active labour market policies in OECD countries: stylised facts and evidence on their effectiveness', *IZA Journal of Labour Policy*, 4(4), doi: 10.1186/s40173-015-0032-y.

Maruna, S. (2001) *Making Good: How Ex-convicts Reform and Rebuild Their Lives*, Washington DC: American Psychological Association.

Maruna, S. (2020) 'Afterword: can the rehabilitative ideal survive the age of Trump?', in A. Leverentz, E. Y. Chen and J. Christian (eds) *Beyond Recidivism: New Approaches to Research on Prisoner Reentry and Reintegration*, New York: NYU Press, pp 315–20.

Massa, E. (2016) 'Punishment and political economy', in Y. Jewkes, B. Crewe and J. Bennett (eds) *Handbook on Prisons* (2nd edn), London: Routledge, pp 309–23.

Massey, D. (2014) 'The Kilburn manifesto: after neoliberalism', *Environment and Planning A.*, 46: 2034–41.

Mathiesen, T. (1971) *Det uferdige. Bidrag til politisk aksjonsteori* [The Unfinished. Contributions to the Theory of Political Action], Oslo: Pax Forlag.

McCabe, C. (2013) 'Transforming capitalism through real utopias: a critical engagement', *Irish Journal of Sociology*, 21(2): 51–61.

McCallum, D. (2007) 'Coercive normalization and family policing: the limits of the "Psy" complex in Australian penal systems', *Social & Legal Studies*, 16(1): 113–29.

McCarthy, D. J. (2011) 'Classing early intervention social class, occupational moralities and criminalisation', *Critical Social Policy*, 31(4): 495–516.

McCartan, C., Morrison, A., Bunting, L., Davidson, G. and McIlroy, J. (2018) 'Stripping the wallpaper of practice: empowering social workers to tackle poverty', *Social Sciences*, 7(10), https://doi.org/10.3390/socsci7100193.

McCashin, A. (2019) *Continuity and Change in the Welfare State: Social Security in the Republic of Ireland*, Basingstoke: Palgrave.

McDonald, C. and Marston, G. (2006) 'Room to move?: professional discretion at the frontline of welfare-to-work', *The Australian Journal of Social Issues*, 41(2): 171–82.

McElroy, E. and Werth, A. (2019) 'Deracinated dispossessions: on the foreclosures of "gentrification" in Oakland, CA', *Antipode*, 51(3):878–98.

McEwen, C. A. and Gregerson, S. F. (2019) 'A critical assessment of the adverse childhood experiences study at 20 years', *American Journal of Preventive Medicine*, 56(6): 790–4.

McFadden, J. J. (2014) 'Disciplining the "Frankenstein of pauperism"": the early years of charity organization case recording, 1877–1907', *The Social Service Review (Chicago)*, 88(3): 469–92.

McGann, M., Murphy, M. and Whelan, N. (2020) 'Workfare redux? Pandemic unemployment, labour activation and the lessons of post-crisis welfare reform in Ireland', *International Journal of Sociology and Social Policy*, 40(9/10): 963–78.

McGimpsey, I. (2017) 'Late neoliberalism: delineating a policy regime', *Critical Social Policy*, 37(1): 64–84.

McGuire, P. (2019) 'The ghost in the nursery: how adversity can harm children', *Irish Times*, 11 May, Available from: https://www.irishtimes.com/news/social-affairs/the-ghost-in-the-nursery-how-adversity-can-harm-children-1.3886361 [Accessed 8 April 2021].

McInnes, C. and Rushton, S. (2004) 'HIV/AIDS and securitization theory', *European Journal of International Relations*, 18(4): 1–24.

McKendrick, D. and Finch, J. (2017) ' "Under heavy manners?": social work, radicalisation, troubled families and non-linear war', *The British Journal of Social Work*, 47(2): 308–24.

McLennan, J. D., Macmillan, H. L. and Afifi, T. O. (2020) 'Questioning the use of adverse childhood experiences (ACEs) questionnaires', *Child Abuse and Neglect*, 101. https://doi.org/10.1016/j.chiabu.2019.104331.

McNamara, L., Quilter, J., Hogg, R., Douglas, H., Loughnan, A. and Brown, D. (2018) 'Theorising criminalisation: the value of a modalities approach', *International Journal for Crime, Justice and Social Democracy*, 7(3): 91–121.

McNeill, F. (2005) 'Remembering probation in Scotland', *Probation Journal*, 52(1): 23–38.

McNeill, F. (2012) 'Four forms of supervision: towards an interdisciplinary perspective', *Legal and Criminological Psychology*, 17(1): 18–36.

McNeill, F. (2014) 'Punishment as rehabilitation', *Encyclopedia of Criminology and Criminal Justice*, New York: Springer, pp 4195–206.

McNeill, F. (2015) 'Desistance and criminal justice in Scotland', in H. Croall, G. Mooney and M. Munro (eds) *Crime, Justice and Society in Scotland*, London: Routledge.

McNeill, F. (2017) 'Punishment, rehabilitation and reintegration: closing plenary address at the British criminology conference at Sheffield Hallam University', 8 July, Available from: https://discoveringdesistance.home.blog/2017/08/29/punishment-rehabilitation-and-reintegration/ [Accessed 8 April 2021].

McNeill, F. (2018a) 'Rehabilitation, corrections and society', *Advancing Corrections Journal*, Available from: http://eprints.gla.ac.uk/159625/7/159625.pdf [Accessed 12 July 2021].

McNeill, F. (2018b) *Pervasive Punishment: Making Sense of Mass Supervision*, Bingley: Emerald Publishing Limited.

McNeill, F. (2019a) 'Penal and welfare conditionality: discipline or degradation?', *Social Policy Administration*, 54(2): 295–310.

McNeill, F. (2019b) 'Mass supervision, misrecognition and the "Malopticon"', *Punishment & Society*, 21(2): 207–30.

McNeill, F. (2020) 'Penal and welfare conditionality: Discipline or degradation?', *Social Policy & Administration*, 54(2): 295–310.

Mead, L. M. (1989) 'The logic of workfare: the underclass and work policy', *The Annals of the American Academy of Political and Social Science*, 501(1): 156–69.

Meade, R. R. and Kiely, E. (2020) '(Neo)liberal populism and Ireland's "squeezed middle"', *Race & Class*, 61(4):29–49.

Measor, L. (2013) 'Loïc Wacquant, gender and cultures of resistance', in P. Squires and J. Lea (eds) *Criminalisation and Advanced Marginality: Critically Exploring the Work of Loïc Wacquant*, Bristol: Policy Press, pp 129–50.

Meese, H., Baker, T. and Sisson, A. (2020) 'We are beneficiaries, contesting poverty stigma through social media', *Antipode*, 52(4): 1152–74.

Mehta, J., Taggart, D., Clifford, E. and Speed, E. (2020) ' "They say jump, we say how high?" Conditionality, sanctioning and incentivising disabled people into the UK labour market', *Disability & Society*, 36(5): 681–701.

Meingast, L. V. (2014) EUGH-Urteil: EU-Buerger ohne Anspruch auf Hartz IV, Available from: https://www.treffpunkteuropa.de/eugh-urteil-eu-burger-ohne-anspruch-auf-hartz-iv?lang=fr [Accessed 8 April 2021].

Mejdoubi, J. van den Heijkant, SCCM., van Leerdam, F. J. M., Heymans, M. W., Crijnen, A. and Hirasing, R. A. (2015) 'The effect of VoorZorg, the Dutch nurse-family partnership on child maltreatment and development: a randomized controlled trial', *PLoS One*, 10(4) e0120182, doi: 10.1371/journal. pone.0120182.

Melossi, D. (1998) 'Introduction', in D. Melossi (ed) *The Sodology of Punishment: Sodo-Structural Perspectives*, Aldershot: Ashgate, pp xi–xxx.

Melossi, D. (2011) 'Neoliberalism's "elective affinities": penality, political economy and international relations', in D. Melossi, M. Sozzo and R. Sparks (eds) *Travels of the Criminal Question: Cultural Embeddedness and Diffusion*, London: Hart Publishing, pp 45–64.

Melossi, D. (2013) 'People on the move: from the countryside to the factory/prison', in K. F. Aas and M. Bosworth (eds) *The Borders of Punishment: Migration, Citizenship, and Social Exclusion*, Oxford: Oxford University Press, pp 273–90.

Metzler, M. and Merrick, M. T., Klevens, J., Ports, K. A. and Ford, D. C. (2017) 'Adverse childhood experiences and life opportunities: shifting the narrative', *Child and Youth Services Review*, 72: 141–9.

Millar, M., Crosse, R. and Canavan, J. (2019) 'Understanding, negotiating and navigating the politicisation of evidence based policy research: the case of Irish research on lone parent labour market activation policy', *Evidence & Policy*, 15(4): 559–77.

Millar, M. and Crosse, R. (2016) *Lone Parents Activation, what works and why: a review of the international evidence in the Irish context*, Galway: UNESCO Child and Family Research Centre Galway.

Millar, M. and Crosse, R. (2018) 'Lone parent activation in Ireland: putting the cart before the horses', *Social Policy and Administration*, 52(1): 111–29.

Millar, J. and Ridge, T. (2020) 'No margin for error: fifteen years in the working lives of lone mothers and their children', *Journal of Social Policy*, 49(1): 1–17.

Miller, P. and Rose, N. (1990) 'Governing economic life', *Economy and Society* 19(1): 1–31.

Miller, R. J. (2014) 'Devolving the carceral state: race, prisoner reentry, and the micro-politics of urban poverty management', *Punishment and Society*, 16(3): 305–35.

Minichiello, V., Scott, J. and Cox, C. (2018) 'Commentary: reversing the agenda of sex work stigmatization and criminalization: signs of a progressive society', *Sexualities*, 21(5–6): 730–5.

Minister for Employment Affairs and Social Protection (2019) Social Welfare Benefits Data, Dáil Éireann Debate, 10 July, Available from: https://www.oireachtas.ie/en/debates/question/2019-07-10/405/ [Accessed 8 April 2021].

Mink, G. (1995) *The Wages of Motherhood: Inequality in the Welfare State, 1917–1942*, Ithaca, NY: Cornell University Press.

Mireanu, M. (2014) 'The criminalisation of environmental activism in Europe', *Studia Universitatis Babes-Bolyai. Sociologia*, 59(2): 87–103.

Misetics, B. (2013) 'The criminalisation of homelessness in Hungary', in S. Jones (ed) *Mean Streets. A Report on Criminalisation of Homelessness in Europe*, Belgium: l'Imprimerie Chauveheid, pp 10–12.

Mitha, S. (2020) 'UK Covid-19 diary: policy and impacts', *National Tax Journal*, 73(3): 847–78.

Mocca, E., Friesenecker, M. and Kazepo, Y. (2020) 'Greening Vienna. The multi-level interplay of urban environmental policy-making', *Sustainability*, 12(4): 1577.

Mohl, R. A. (2016) 'The politics of expulsion: a short history of Alabama's anti-immigrant law HB 56', *Journal of American Ethnic History*, 35(3): 42–67.

Monaghan, L. (2020) 'Corona Virus (Covid-19), Pandemic Psychology and the Fractured Society: A Sociological Case for Critique, Foresight and Action', *Sociology of Health and Illness*, 42(8): 1982–95.

Monahan, T. (2017) 'Regulating belonging: surveillance, inequality and the cultural production of abjection', *Journal of Cultural Economy*, 12(2): 191–206.

Mooney, G. (2009) 'The "broken society" election: class hatred and the politics of poverty and place in Glasgow East', *Social Policy and Society*, 8(4): 437–50.

Morris, K. and Featherstone, B. (2010) 'Investing in children, regulating parents, thinking family: a decade of tensions and contradictions', *Social Policy and Society*, 9(1): 557–66.

Morris, K., Mason, W., Bywaters, P. Featherstone, B., Daniel, B., Brady, G., Bunting, L., Hooper, J. Mirza, N., Scourfield, J. and Webb, C. (2018) 'Social work, poverty and child welfare interventions', *Child and Family Social Work*, 23(3): 364–72.

Muehlebach, A. (2016) 'Anthropologies of austerity', *History and Anthropology*, 27(3): 359–72.

Müller, M. M. (2013) 'The universal and the particular in Latin American penal state formation' in P. Squires and J. Lea (eds) *Criminalisation and Advanced Marginality: Critically Exploring the Work of Loïc Wacquant*, Bristol: Policy Press, pp 195–216.

Mulvey, G. (2018) 'Social policy, social citizenship and refugee integration: a case of policy divergence in Scotland', *Journal of Social Policy*, 47(1): 161–78.

Muncie. J. (2000) 'Decriminalising criminology', in G. Lewis, S. Gewitz and J. Clarke (eds) *Rethinking Social Policy*, Buckingham: Open University Press, pp 217–28.

Murphy, C., Keilithy, P. and Caffrey, L. (2008) *Lone Parents and Employment: What are the Real Issues? Key Findings, Conclusions and Recommendations*, Dublin: One Family & the Combat Poverty Agency.

Murphy, F. (2017) 'The austerity myth: parenting and the new thrift culture in contemporary Ireland', in E. Heffernan, J. McHale and N. Moore-Cherry (eds), *Debating Austerity in Ireland: Crisis, Experience and Recovery,*) Dublin: Royal Irish Academy, pp 204–18.

Murphy, M. (2012) 'Interests, institutions and ideas: explaining Irish social security policy', *Policy and Politics*, 40(3): 347–65.

Murphy, M. (2020) 'Dual conditionality in welfare and housing for lone parents in Ireland: change and continuity', *Social Policy & Administration*, 54(2): 250–64.

Murray, C. (1990) 'The British underclass', *The Public Interest*, 99: 4–28.

Mykhalovskiy, E. and French, M. (2020) 'COVID-19, public health, and the politics of prevention', *Sociology of Health & Illness*, 42(8): e4–e15.

Mythen, G., Walklate, S. and Peatfield, E. J. (2017) 'Assembling and deconstructing radicalisation in PREVENT: a case of policy based evidence making?', *Critical Social Policy*, 37(2): 180–201.

Nail, T. (2016) *Theory of the Border*, Oxford: Oxford University Press.

NCLHP (2019) 'Housing not handcuffs: ending the criminalisation of homelessness in U.S. cities', Available from: http://nlchp.org/wp-content/uploads/2019/12/HOUSING-NOT-HANDCUFFS-2019-FINAL.pdf [Accessed 8 April 2021].

Nelson, B. (2020) 'Thousands of N.J. inmates could be released soon. But funding to keep them from returning to prison has been cut', Available from: https://www.njreentry.org/news_blog/thousands-nj-inmates-could-be-released-soon-funding-keep-them-returning-prison-has-been-cut [Accessed 8 April 2021].

Nethery, A. and Holman, R. (2016) 'Secrecy and human rights abuse in Australia's offshore immigration detention centres', *The International Journal of Human Rights*, 20(7): 1018–38.

Newburn, T. (2007) '"Tough on crime": penal policy in England and Wales', *Crime and Justice*, 36(1): 425–70.

Newcastle City Council (2016) 'Newcastle upon Tyne: public spaces protection order: consultation document', Newcastle upon Tyne City Council, available from: https://letstalknewcastle.co.uk/files/2016_PSPO_consultation.pdf [Accessed 8 April 2021].

Newman, J. and Clarke, J. (2009) *Publics, Politics and Power: Remaking the Public in Public Services*, London: Sage.

Newman, J. and Clarke, J. (2014) 'States of imagination: the state remains crucial for a left politics, but needs radical rethinking' *Soundings*, 57: 153–69.

Newman, J. and Clarke, J. (2015) 'States of reimagination' in S. Hall, D. Massey and M. Rustin (eds) *After Neoliberalism: The Kilburn Manifesto*, London: Lawrence and Wishart, pp 99–115.

Newman, O. (1972) *Defensible Space: Crime Prevention Through Urban Design*, New York: Macmillan.

Nguyen, N. (2018) 'Educating force multipliers: constructing terrorism in a US public high school', *Discourse: Studies in the Cultural Politics of Education*, 39(6): 841–55.

Nguyen, N. (2019) '"The eyes and ears on our frontlines": policing without police to counter violent extremism', *Surveillance & Society*, 17(3/4): 322–37.

Ní Raghallaigh, M., Smith, K. and Scholtz, J. (2020) 'Problematizing parenting: the regulation of parenting practices within reception centres for Syrian refugees in Ireland', *Journal of Refugee Studies*, doi: 10.1093/jrs/fez110.

Novak, N. L., Geronimus, A. T. and Martinez-Cardoso, A. M. (2017) 'Change in birth outcomes among infants born to Latina mothers after a major immigration raid', *International Journal of Epidemiology*, 46(3): 839–49.

Nugent, C., Pembroke, S. and Taft, M. (2019) 'Precarious work in the Republic of Ireland', NERI WP2019/No.64. Available from: https://www.nerinstitute.net/sites/default/files/research/2019/precarious_work_in_the_republic_of_ireland_july_19_final.pdf [Accessed 8 April 2021].

Nunn, A. and Tepe-Belfrage, D. (2017) 'Disciplinary social policy and the falling promise of the new middle classes: the Troubled Families Programme', *Social Policy and Society*, 16(1): 119–29.

Nurse–Family Partnership (2020) 'The David Olds story', Available from: https://www.nursefamilypartnership.org/about/program-history/ [Accessed 8 April 2021].

Nygård, M., Nyby, J. and Kuisma, M. (2019) 'Discarding social investment and redistribution in the name of austerity? The case of Finnish family policy reforms 2007–2015', *Policy & Society*, 38(3): 519–36.

Obinger, H., Schmitt, C. and Starke, P. (2013) 'Policy diffusion and policy transfer in comparative welfare state research', *Social Policy and Administration*, 47(1): 111–29.

O'Brien, C. (2016) 'Irish prison service and HSE confirm that all ex-convicts will automatically receive a medical card once they are released from prison', *The Liberal*, 16 September, Available from: https://theliberal.ie/irish-prison-service-and-hse-confirm-that-all-ex-convicts-will-automatically-receive-a-medical-card-once-they-are-released-from-prison/ [Accessed 8 April 2021].

O'Brien, M. and Penna, S. (1998) *Theorising Welfare: Enlightenment and Modern Society*, London: Sage.

Ocampo, J. A. and Stiglitz, J. E. (2018) 'Preface', in J. A. Ocampo and J.E. Stiglitz (eds) *The Welfare State Revisited*, New York: Columbia University Press, pp xi–xxiii.

OCHCR (2019) Joint Communication from Special Procedures Ref AL ITA 4/2019.

OCHCR (2020) 'UN human rights experts urge Denmark to halt contentious sale of "ghetto" buildings', Available from: https://www.ohchr.org/EN/HRBodies/HRC/Pages/NewsDetail.aspx?NewsID=26414&LangID=E [Accessed 8 April 2021].

O'Flynn, M., Monaghan, L. F. and Power, M. (2014) 'Scapegoating during a time of crisis: a critique of post-celtic tiger Ireland', *Sociology*, 48(5): 921–37.

Offe, C. (1984) *Contradictions of the Welfare State* (edited by John Keane), London: Hutchinson.

Olds, D. L. (2007) 'Preventing crime with prenatal and infancy support of parents; the nurse family partnership', *Victims and Offenders*, 2(2): 205–25.

Olds, D. L., Eckenrode, J., Henderson C. R. Jr., Kitzman, H., Powers, J., Cole, R., Sidora, K., Morris, P., Pettit, L. M. and Luckey, D. (1997) 'Long-term effects of home visitation on maternal life course and child abuse and neglect. Fifteen-year follow-up of a randomized trial', *Journal of the American Medical Association,* 278: 637–43.

Olds, D. L., Henderson C. R. Jr., Chamberlin, R. and Tatelbaum, R. (1986) 'Preventing child abuse and neglect: a randomized trial of nurse home visitation', *Pediatrics*, 78: 65–78.

Olds, D. L., Kitzman, E., Anson, E., Smith, J. A., Knudtson, M. D., Miller, T., Cole, R., Hopfer, C. and Conti, G. (2019) 'Prenatal and infancy nurse home visiting effects on mothers: 18-year follow up of a randomized trial', *Paediatrics*, 144(6): e20183889.

Olds, D. L., Robinson, J., O'Brien, R., Luckey, D. W., Pettitt, L. M., Henderson, C. R. and Talmi, A. (2002) 'Home visiting by nurses and by paraprofessionals: a randomized controlled trial', *Pediatrics*, 110(3): 486–96.

Oliveira e Costa, S. and Tunström, M. (2020) 'Urban planning policy in the Danish "ghetto" – overcoming or creating barriers to inclusion?', in M. Stjernberg, H. R. Sigurjónsdóttir, S. Oliveira e Costa and M. Tunström, Nordregio Report 2020:9, Overcoming barriers to social inclusion in Nordic cities through policy and planning, Available from: https://www.diva-portal.org/smash/get/diva2:1472442/FULLTEXT01.pdf#page=47 [Accessed 8 April 2021].

Ombudsman for Children's Office (2019) *No Place Like Home, Children's Views and Experiences of Living in Family Hubs*, Dublin: Ombudsman for Children's Office.

O'Neill, M. and Loftus, B. (2013) 'Policing and the surveillance of the marginal: everyday contexts of social control', *Theoretical Criminology*, 17(4): 437–54.

ORF (2020) 'Mann gequält: StA ermittelt gegen drei Polizisten', 2 August, Available from: https://wien.orf.at/stories/3060438 [Accessed 8 April 2021].

Ostner, I. and Stolberg, C. (2015) 'Investing in children, monitoring parents: parenting support in the changing German welfare state', *Social Policy & Society*, 14(4): 621–32.

O'Sullivan, E. (2012) 'Varieties of punitiveness in Europe: homelessness and urban marginality', *European Journal of Homelessness*, 6(2): 69–97.

Overgaard, S. (2020) 'Facing eviction, residents of Denmark's "ghettos" are suing the government', Available from: https://www.npr.org/2020/08/15/900874510/facing-eviction-residents-of-denmarks-ghettos-are-suing-the-government?t=1608073670947 [Accessed 8 April 2021].

Pakes, F. and Holt, K. (2017) 'Crimmigration and the prison: comparing trends in prison policy and practice in England & Wales and Norway', *European Journal of Criminology*, 14(1):63–77.

Palacios, J., Adroher, S., Brodzinsky, D. M., Grotevant, H. D., Johnson, D. E., Juffer, F., Martínez-Mora, L., Muhamedrahimov, R. J., Selwyn, J., Simmonds, J. and Tarren-Sweeney, M. (2019) 'Adoption in the service of child protection an international, interdisciplinary perspective', *Psychology, Public Policy and Law*, 25(2): 57–72.

Pantazis, C. (2016) 'Policies and discourses of poverty during a time of recession and austerity', *Critical Social Policy*, 36(1): 3–20.

Parliament of Australia (2015) 'Income management: a quick guide', Available from: https://www.aph.gov.au/About_Parliament/Parliamentary_Departments/Parliamentary_Library/pubs/rp/rp1516/Quick_Guides/IncomeManagement [Accessed 8 April 2021].

Parsell, C., Vincent, E., Klein, E., Clarke, A. and Walsh, T. (2020) 'Introduction to the special issue on welfare conditionality in Australia', *Australian Journal of Social Issues*, 55(1): 4–12.

Patel, G. T. (2017) 'It's not about security, it's about racism: counter-terror strategies, civilizing processes and the post-race fiction', *Palgrave Communications*, 3(17031), doi: 10.1057/palcomms.2017.31.

Paterson, M. (2011) 'Criminal records, spent convictions and privacy: a trans-Tasman comparison', *New Zealand Law Review*, (1): 69–89.

Paterson, M. and Naylor, B. (2011) 'Australian spent convictions reform: a contextual analysis', *University of New South Wales Law Journal*, 34(3): 938–63.

Patrick, R. (2018a) 'Welfare futures', *Progressive Review*, 25(3): 320–9.

Patrick, R. (2018b) 'What we learn from Scotland's approach to social security', No. 38, UK Social Policy Association, 15 October, Available from: http://www.social-policy.org.uk/50-for-50/scotland-social-security/ [Accessed 8 April 2021].

Pavolini, E., León, M., Guillén, A. M. and Ascoli, U. (2015) 'From austerity to permanent strain? The EU and welfare state reform in Italy and Spain', *Comparative European Politics*, 13(1): 56–76.

Peck, J. and Theodore, N. (2010) 'Recombinant workfare, across the Americas: transnationalizing "fast" social policy', *Geoforum*, 41(2): 195–208.

Penna, S. (2005) 'The Children Act 2004: child protection and social surveillance', *The Journal of Social Welfare & Family Law*, 27(2): 143–57.

Pennings, F. (2015) *European Social Security Law* (6th edn), Cambridge: Intersentia.

Pereira, I., Mollidor, C. and Maguire, K. (2018) *Troubled Families, Qualitative Case Study Research, Phase 2: Wave 1*, England: Ipsos MORI.

Persak, N. (ed) (2016) *Regulation and Social Control of Incivilities*, London: Routledge.

Phoenix, J. (2008) 'ASBOs and working women: a new revolving door?', in P. Squires (ed) *ASBO Nation: The Criminalisation of Nuisance*, Bristol: Policy Press, pp 297–311.

Pickering, S. and Weber, L. (2006) (eds) *Borders, Mobility and Technologies of Control*, Dordrecht: Springer.

Pilkington, E. (2011) 'Alabama red-faced as second foreign car boss held under immigration law', *The Guardian*, 2 December, Available from: www.theguardian.com/world/2011/dec/02/alabama-car-boss-immigration-law [Accessed 7 April 2021].

Pitts, J. (2013) 'The third time as farce: whatever happened to the penal state?', in P. Squires and J. Lea (eds) *Criminalisation and Advanced Marginality: Critically Exploring the Work of Loïc Wacquant*, Bristol: Policy Press, pp 61–86.

Podesta, J. (2017) 'Children's agency, getting by, getting back, getting out and getting organised under welfare to work in Australia', *Children & Society*, 31(5): 353–64.

Podoletz, L. (2016) 'Tackling homelessness through criminalisation: the case of Hungary', in N. Persak (ed) *Regulation and Social Control of Incivilities*, London: Routledge, pp 75–92.

Povey, L. (2017) 'Where welfare and criminal justice meet: applying Wacquant to the experiences of marginalised women in austerity Britain', *Social Policy and Society*, 16(2): 271–81.

Powell, F. W. (1992) *The Politics of Irish Social Policy 1600–1900*, New York: Edwin Mellen Press.

Power, M., Haynes, A. and Devereux, E. (2020) 'Indelible stain: territorial stigmatization and the limits of resistance', *Community Development Journal*, 56(2): 1–22.

Pratt, J. (2008) 'Scandinavian exceptionalism in an era of penal excess. Part 1: the nature and roots of Scandinavian exceptionalism', *British Journal of Criminology*, 48(2): 119–37.

Pratt, J. and McLean, T. (2015) 'Inspector Wallander's angst, social change and the reconfiguration of Swedish exceptionalism', *Punishment and Society*, 17(3): 322–44.

Preece, S. (2020) 'Government announce £165 million new funding for "troubled families" scheme', *Welfare Weekly*, 5 January, Available from: https://welfareweekly.com/government-announce-165-million-new-funding-for-troubled-families-scheme/ [Accessed 7 April 2021].

Prentice, S. (2009) 'The "investable" child and the economic reframing of childcare', *Signs*, 34: 687–710.

Prison Policy (2020) Available from: https://www.prisonpolicy.org/profiles/US.html [Accessed 7 April 2021].

Prosinger, J. and Thomma, M. (2017) 'Schleuser sind für viele die einzige Rettung', 15 August, Available from: https://www.tagesspiegel.de/gesellschaft/fluechtlingsanwaeltin-berenice-boehlo-schleuser-sind-fuer-viele-die-einzige-rettung/11145528.html [Accessed 7 April 2021].

Public Finance (2020) 'Troubled families programme extended', *Public Finance*, p 49.

Rabuy, B. and Kopf, D. (2015) 'Prisons of poverty: uncovering the pre-incarceration incomes of the imprisoned', Prison Policy Initiative, Available from: https://www.prisonpolicy.org/reports/income.html [Accessed 7 April 2021].

Ragazzi, F. (2017) 'Countering terrorism and radicalisation: securitising social policy', *Critical Social Policy*, 37(2): 163–79.

Raisborough, J. and Adams, M. (2008) 'Mockery and morality in popular cultural representations of the white working class', *Sociological Research Online*, 13(6): 1–13.

Ranchordás, S. and Schuurmans, Y. (2020) 'Outsourcing the welfare state: the role of private actors in welfare fraud investigations', *European Journal of Comparative Law and Governance*, 7(1): 5–42.

Raynor, P. and Robinson, G. (2005) *Rehabilitation, Crime, and Justice*, New York: Palgrave Macmillan.

Rea, A., Martiniello, M., Mazzola, A. and Meuleman, B. (eds) (2019) *The Refugee Reception Crisis in Europe: Polarized Opinions and Mobilizations*, Brussels: Éditions de l'Université de Bruxelles.

Redman, J. (2020) 'The benefit sanction: a correctional device or a weapon of disgust?', *Sociological Research Online*, 25(1): 84–100.

Reeskens, T. and van Oorschot, W. (2012) 'Disentangling the "New Liberal Dilemma": on the relation between general welfare redistribution preferences and welfare chauvinism', *International Journal of Comparative Sociology*, 53: 120–39.

Reeves, A. and Loopstra, R. (2017) ' "Set up to fail?" How welfare conditionality undermines citizenship for vulnerable groups', *Social Policy & Society*, 16(2): 327–38.

Regan, M. Keane, C. and Walsh, J. R. (2018) 'Lone-Parent Income and Work Incentives', Budget Perspectives 2019, Paper 1. Dublin: Economic and Social Research Institute.

Rehm, P. (2020) 'The future of welfare state politics', *Political Science Research and Methods*, 8(2): 386–90.

Reiner, R. (2007) *Law and Order: An Honest Citizen's Guide to Crime and Control*, Cambridge: Polity Press.

Reiter, K., Sexton, L. and Sumner, J. (2018) 'Theoretical and empirical limits of Scandinavian exceptionalism: isolation and normalization in Danish prisons', *Punishment & Society*, 20(1): 92–112.

Resoma (2020) 'Criminalisation of solidarity in Europe', Available from: https://www.migpolgroup.com/wp-content/uploads/2020/03/ReSoma-criminalisation-.pdf [Accessed 8 April 2021].

Reyhani, A. N. (2020) 'Refugees', in Binder, Nowak, Hofbauer, Janig (eds) *Elgar Encyclopedia of Human Rights*, Available from: https://papers.ssrn.com/sol3/Data_Integrity_Notice.cfm?abid=3731541 [Accessed 7 April 2021].

Ridge, T. and Millar, J. (2011) 'Following families: working lone-mother families and their children', *Social Policy and Administration*, 45(1): 85–97.

Roberts, A. (2017) *Gendered States of Punishment and Welfare: Feminist Political Economy, Privileged Accumulation and the Law*, Abingdon: Routledge.

Roberts, D. (2020) 'Abolishing Police also means Abolishing Family Regulation' *Abolition*, Available from: https://abolitionjournal.org/abolishing-policing-also-means-abolishing-family-regulation/ [Accessed 3 March 2021].

Roberts, L., Maxwell, N. and Elliott, M. (2019) 'When young people in and leaving state care become parents: what happens and why?', *Children and Youth Services Review*, 104, https://doi.org/10.1016/j.childyouth.2019.104387.

Robling, M., Bekkers, M., Bell, K., Butler, C. C., Cannings-John, R., Channon, S., Corbacho, B. M., Gregory, J. W., Hood, K., Kemp, A., Kenkre, J., Montgomery, A. A., Moody, G., Owen-Jones, E., Pickett, K., Richardson, G., Roberts, Z. E. S., Ronaldson, S. and Torgerson, D. (2016) 'Effectiveness of a nurse-led intensive home-visitation programme for first-time teenage mothers (building blocks): a pragmatic randomised controlled trial', *The Lancet*, 387(10014): 146–55.

Rodger, J. (2008) *Criminalising Social Policy: Anti-Social Behaviour and Welfare in a De-Civilised Society*, London: Willan.

Rodger, J. (2013) 'Loic wacquant and norbert elias: advanced marginality and the theory of the de-civilising process', in P. Squires and J. Lea (eds), *Criminalization and Advanced Marginality: Critically Exploring the Work of loic wacquant*, London: Routledge, 87–106.

Rogowski, S. (2021) 'Neoliberalism, austerity and social work with children and families: challenges and critical/radical possibilities', *Critical and Radical Social Work*, 1–16, https://doi.org/10.1332/204986021X16109919707738.

Roosma, W. and Van Oorschot F. (2017) 'The social legitimacy of welfare states in Europe: regions and countries: balancing between popular preferences and evaluations', in P. Kennett and N. Lendvai-Bainton (eds) *Handboook of European Social Policy*, Cheltenham: Edward Elgar, pp 415–31.

Rose, N. (1990) *Governing the Soul: The Shaping of the Private Self*, London: Routledge.

Rose, N. (1999) *Powers of Freedom: Reframing Political Thought*, Cambridge: Cambridge University Press.

Rose, N. (2000) 'Government and control', *British Journal of Criminology*, 40(2): 321–39.

Rose, N. (2016) 'Governing the soul – a quarter of a century on', *Self and Society*, 44(4): 431–3.

Rose, N. (2017) 'Still Like "Birds on the wire"? Freedom after neoliberalism', *Economy and Society*, 46(3–4): 303–23.

Rose, N. and Miller, P. (2010) 'Political power beyond the state: problematics of government', *The British Journal of Sociology*, 61(1): 271–303.

Rosen, R. (2018) 'Poverty and family troubles: mothers, children and neoliberal "anti-poverty" initiatives', *Journal of Family Issues*, 40(16): 2330–53.

Rosen, R. and Faircloth, C. (2020) 'Adult–child relations in neoliberal times: insights from a dialogue across childhood and parenting culture studies', *Families, Relationships and Societies*, 9(1): 7–22.

Rotman, E. (1990) *Beyond Punishment: A New View of the Rehabilitation of Offenders*, Westport, CT: Greenwood Press.

Ruane, S., Collins, M. L. and Sinfield, A. (2020) 'The centrality of taxation to social policy', *Social Policy & Society*, 19(3): 437–53.

Ruggiero, V. (2013) 'Illicit economies and the carceral social zone', in P. Squires and J. Lea (eds) *Criminalisation and Advanced marginality: Critically Exploring the Work of Loic Wacquant*, Bristol: Policy Press, pp 173–94.

Ruggiero, V. (2015) The Legacy of Abolitionism, *Penal Field*, XII, https://doi.org/10.4000/champpenal.9080.

Ruggiero, V. (2018) 'No prison: old and new challenges', in M. Pavarini and L. Ferraro (eds) *No Prison*, Capel Dewi: EG Press Limited, pp 91–110.

Saar-Heiman, Y. and Gupta, A. (2020) 'The poverty-aware paradigm for child protection: a critical framework for policy and practice', *The British Journal of Social Work*, 50(4): 1167–84.

Sabir, R. (2017) 'Policing anti-austerity through the "war on terror"', in V. Cooper and D. Whyte (eds) *The Violence of Austerity*, London: Pluto Press, pp 211–16.

Sachs, A. (2020) 'Human rights: the battle between concept and understanding', Available from: https://www.transformingsociety.co.uk/2020/06/10/human-rights-the-battle-between-concept-and-understanding/ [Accessed 8 April 2021].

Salecl, R. (2010) *Choice*, London: Profile Books.

Savage, M., Callan, T., Nolan, B. and Colgan, B. (2015) 'The great recession, austerity and inequality: evidence from Ireland' (Working Paper No. 499), Dublin: The Economic and Social Research Institute, Available from: https://www.econstor.eu/bitstream/10419/129395/1/823265064.pdf [Accessed 8 April 2021].

Sassen S. (2002) 'Locating cities on global circuits', *Environment and Urbanization*, 14(1): 13–30.

Sayer, A. (2017) '"Responding to the troubled families programme": framing the injuries of inequality', *Social Policy and Society*, 16(1): 155–164.

Sayer, R. (2020) 'Incarcerated Parents and child welfare in Washington', *Washington Law Review*, 95(1): 531–54.

Schack, L. and Witcher, A. (2021) 'Hostile hospitality and the criminalization of civil society actors aiding border crossers in Greece', *Society and Space*, 39(3): 477–95.

Schatz, H. (2020) 'Evolution des Wiedereingliederungsprozesses – Das Hamburgische Resozialisierungs- und Opferhilfegesetz Ein Beitrag zum 80. Geburtstag von Bernd-Rüdeger Sonnen', *NK Neue Kriminalpolitik*, 32(4): 403–14.

Scharff Smith, P. S. (2012) 'A critical look at Scandinavian exceptionalism: welfare state theories, penal populism and prison conditions in Denmark and Scandinavia', in T. Ugelvik and J. Dullum (eds) *Penal Exceptionalism? Nordic Prison Policy and Practice*, Abingdon: Routledge, pp 38–57.

Schlichtman, J., Patch, J. and Hill, M. L. (2017) *Gentrifier*, Toronto: University of Toronto Press.

Schou, J. and Svejgaard Pors, A. (2018) 'Digital by default? A qualitative study of exclusion in digitalised welfare', *Social Policy and Administration*, 53(3): 464–77.

Schram, S. F., Soss, J., Houser, L. and Fording, R. C. (2010) 'The third level of US welfare reform: governmentality under neoliberal paternalism', *Citizenship Studies*, 14(6): 739–54.

Schroeder, M. (2009) 'Integrating welfare and production typologies: how refinements of the varieties of capitalism approach call for a combination of welfare typologies', *Journal of Social Policy*, 38(1): 19–43.

Scott, D. (2013) 'Visualising and abolitionist real utopia', in M. Malloch and B. Munro (eds) *Crime, Critique and Utopia*, London: Palgrave Macmillan, pp 90–113.

Seemann A. (2020) 'The Danish "ghetto initiatives" and the changing nature of social citizenship 2004–2018', *Critical Social Policy*, December, doi: 10.1177/0261018320978504.

Selbourne, D. (1994) *The Principle of Duty: An Essay on the Foundations of Civic Order*, London: Sinclair-Stevenson.

Shah, S. (2020) *The Next Great Migration: The Beauty and Terror of Life on the Move*, New York: Bloomsbury.

Shammas V. L. (2014) 'The pains of freedom: asssessing the ambiguity of Scandinavian penal exceptionalism on Norway's prison island', *Punishment & Society*, 16(1): 104–23.

Shanahan, C. (2016) 'Prisoners to get medical card when they leave jail', *Irish Examiner*, 16 September, Available from: https://www.irishexaminer.com/news/arid-20421351.html [Accessed 8 April 2021].

Shapiro, J. (2014) 'As court fees rise, the poor are paying the price', Available from: https://www.npr.org/2014/05/19/312158516/increasing-court-fees-punish-the-poor?t=1572819955948 [Accessed 8 April 2021].

Shapland, J. (2008) 'Contested ideas of community and justice', in J. Shapland (ed) *Justice, Community and Civil Society*, pp 1–29.

Shenker, J. (2017) 'Revealed: the insidious creep of pseudo-public space in London', *The Guardian*, 24 July, Available from: www.theguardian.com/cities/2017/jul/24/revealed-pseudo-public-space-pops-london-investigation-map [Accessed 8 April 2021].

Shildrick, T. (2012) *Poverty and Insecurity: Life in Low-Pay, No-Pay Britain*, Bristol: Policy Press.

Shildrick, T. (2018) 'Lessons from Grenfell: poverty propaganda, stigma and class power', *The Sociological Review Monographs*, 66(4): 783–98.

Shildrick, T., MacDonald, R. and Furlong, A. (2016) 'No single spies but battalions: a critical sociological engagement with the idea of so-called troubled families', *The Sociological Review*, 64(4): 821–36.

Shiner, M. (2009) 'Theorizing criminal law reform', *Criminal Law and Philosophy*, 3(2): 167–86.

Shiner, M. (2013) 'British drug policy and the modern state: reconsidering the criminalisation thesis', *Journal of Social Policy*, 42(3): 623–43.

Shirani, F., Henwood, K. and Coltart, C. (2012) 'Meeting the challenges of intensive parenting culture: gender, risk management and the moral parent', *Sociology*, 46(1): 25–40.

Silver, D. and Crossley, S. (2020) '"We know it works": the troubled families programme and the pre-determined boundary judgements of decontextualised policy evaluation', *Critical Social Policy*, 40(4): 566–85.

Simon, J. (1993) *Poor Discipline: Parole and the Social Control of the Underclass 1890–1990*, Chicago and London: Chicago University Press.

Simon, J. (2007) *Governing Through Crime: How the War on Crime Transformed American Democracy and Created A Culture of Fear*, New York: Oxford University Press.

Singh Bhui, H. (2013) 'Introduction: humanizing migration control and detention', in K. F. Aas and M. Bosworth (eds) *The Borders of Punishment Migration, Citizenship, and Social Exclusion*, Oxford: Oxford University Press, pp 1–20.

Singh Cooner, T., Beddoe, L., Ferguson, H. and Joy, E. (2020) 'The use of Facebook in social work practice with children and families: exploring complexity in an emerging practice', *Journal of Technology in Human Services*, 38(2): 137–58.

Singleton, S. (2008) '"Not our borders": Indigenous people and the struggle to maintain shared cultures and polities in the post-9/11 United States', *Journal of Borderland Studies*, 23(3): 39–54.

Skeggs, B. (2004) *Class, Self, Culture*, London: Routledge.

Smart, C. (1976) *Women, Crime, and Criminology: A Feminist Critique*, London: Routledge & Kegan Paul.

Smith, N. (1996) *The New Urban Frontier Gentrification and the Revanchist City*, London and New York: Routledge.

Smith, P. S. (2012) 'A critical look at Scandinavian Exceptionalism: Welfare state theories, penal populism, and prison conditions in Denmark and Scandinavia', in T. Ugelvik and J. Dullum (eds) *Penal Exceptionalism? Nordic Prison Policy and Practice*, New York: Routledge, pp 38–57.

Smith, S. W., Cobbina, J. E., Bohmann, M. N., Kashy, D. A. and Morash, M. (2017) 'Women at the nexus of correctional and social policies: implications for recidivism risk', *The British Journal of Criminology*, 57(2): 441–62.

Smyth, C. and Craig, L. (2017) 'Conforming to intensive parenting ideals: willingness, reluctance and social context', *Families, Relationships and Societies*, 6(1): 107–24.

Smyth, S. and Anderson, G. (2014) 'Family nurse partnership: meeting the needs of teenage mothers', *British Journal of Midwifery*, 22(12): 870–5.

Social Justice Ireland (2020) *Poverty Focus 2020*, Dublin: SJI.

Social Welfare (Consolidation) Act (2005) Number 26 of 2005, Available at: http://www.irishstatutebook.ie/eli/2005/act/26/enacted/en/html [14 July 2021].

Society of Saint Vincent de Paul (2014) *"It's the Hardest Job in the World" An Exploratory Research Study With One-Parent Families Being Assisted by the Society of St. Vincent De Paul*, Dublin: OCS Consulting & SVP.

Society of Saint Vincent de Paul (2019) *Working, Parenting and Struggling? An Analysis of the Employment and Living Conditions of One-Parent Families in Ireland*, Dublin: SVP.

Soss, J., Fording, R. C. and Schram, S. F. (2011) *Disciplining the Poor Neoliberal Paternalism and the Persistent Power of Race*, Chicago: University of Chicago Press.

Soysal, Y. (1994) *Limits of Citizenship: Migrants and Postnational Membership in Europe*, Chicago: University of Chicago Press.

Spratt, T., Devaney, J. and Frederick, J. (2019) 'Adverse childhood experiences: beyond signs of safety; reimagining the organisation and practice of social work with children and families', *The British Journal of Social Work*, 49(8): 2042–58.

Spratt, T. and Kennedy, M. (2020) 'Adverse childhood experiences: developments in trauma and resilience aware services', *British Journal of Social Work*, 51(3): 999–1017.

Spicker, P. (2011) *How Social Security Works: An Introduction to Benefits in Britain*, Portland, OR: Policy Press.

Squires, P. (1990) *Anti-Social Policy, Welfare, Ideology and the Disciplinary State*, London: Harvester Wheatsheaf.

Squires, P. (2006) 'New labour and the politics of antisocial behaviour', *Critical Social Policy*, 26(1): 144–68.

Squires, P. (ed) (2008a) *ASBO Nation: The Criminalisation of Nuisance*, Bristol: Policy Press.

Squires, P. (2008b) 'The politics of anti-social behaviour', *British Politics*, 3(3):300–23.

Squires, P. and Lea, J. (2013) 'Introduction: reading Loïc Wacquant – opening questions and overview', in P. Squires and J. Lea (eds) *The Criminalisation of Advanced Marginality: Critically Exploring the Work of Loïc Wacquant*, Bristol: Policy Press, pp 1–18.

Staines, Z., Moore, C., Marston, G. and Humpage, L. (2020) 'Big data and poverty governance under Australia and Aotearoa / New Zealand's "social investment" policies', *Australian Journal of Social Issues*, 56(2): 157–72.

Standing, G. (2011) 'Workfare and the precariat', *Soundings*, 47: 35–43.

Standing, G. (2016) *The Corruption of Capitalism? Why Rentiers Thrive and Work Does Not Pay*, London: Biteback Publishing.

Starolis, H. (2020) 'Hostile architecture: the death of urban spaces', *Crit*, 86: 53–5, 57.

Staunton, C., Swanepoel, C. and Labuschaigne, M. (2020) 'Between a rock and a hard place: COVID-19 and South Africa's response', *Journal of Law and the Biosciences*, 7(1): lsaa052–lsaa052, doi:10.1093/jlb/lsaa052.

Stenson, K. (2013) 'The state, sovereignty and advanced marginality in the city', in P. Squires and J. Lea (eds) *Criminalisation and Advanced Marginality: Critically Exploring the Work of Loïc Wacquant*, Bristol: Policy Press, pp 41–60.

Stetter, E. (2018) 'The EU welfare state: past, present and future', in J. A. Ocampo and J.E. Stiglitz (eds) *The Welfare State Revisited*, New York: Columbia University Press, pp 191–212.

Stevenson, L. (2016) 'Councils setting numerical targets for adoption', *Community Care*, 18 November, Available from: https://www.communitycare.co.uk/2016/11/18/councils-setting-numerical-targets-adoption/ [Accessed 8 April 2021].

Stiglitz, J. E. (2013) *The Price of Inequality*, London: Penguin.

Stiglitz, J. E. (2018) 'The welfare state in the twenty-first century', in J. A. Ocampo and J. E. Stiglitz (eds) *The Welfare State Revisited*, New York: Columbia University Press, pp 3–37.

Streeck, W. and Thelen, K. (2005) (eds) *Beyond Continuity: Explorations in the Dynamics of Advanced Political Economies*, Oxford: Oxford University Press.

Stumpf, J. (2006) 'The crimmigration crisis: immigrants, crime, and sovereign power', *American University Law Review*, 56(2): Article 3.

Supreme Court of Ireland (2017) *Judgment of Mr. Justice John MacMenamin, P.C. and the Minister for Social Protection, Ireland and the Attorney General*, 27 July [Record No. 89/2016].

Svensson, K. (2003) 'Social work in the criminal justice system: an ambiguous exercise of caring power', *Journal of Scandinavian Studies in Criminology and Crime Prevention*, 4(1): 84–100.

Svensson, K. (2010) 'Performing caring power in the Scandinavian welfare state', *Revista de Asistenta Sociala*, 9(3): 49–58.

Swirak, K. (2018) 'Unmasking the "criminal justice voluntary sector" in the Republic of Ireland: towards a research agenda', *Irish Probation Journal*, 15: 24–46.

Swirak, K. and Forde, L. (2020) *Research Papers on Spent Convictions*, Dublin: Department of Justice and Equality.

Sykes, G. (1958) *The Society of Captives: A Study of a Maximum-Security Prison*, Princeton, NJ: Princeton University Press.

Taylor-Gooby, P. (2005) *New Risks, new Welfare: The Transformation of the European Welfare State*, Oxford: Oxford University Press.

Taylor-Gooby, P. (2016) 'The divisive welfare state', *Social Policy & Administration*, 50(6), 712–33.

Taylor-Gooby, P., Hvinden, B., Mau, S., Leruth, B., Schoyen, M. A. and Gyory, A. (2018) 'Moral economies of the welfare state: a qualitative comparative study', *Acta Sociologica*, 62(2): 119–34.

Taylor-Gooby, P., Leruth, B. and Chung, H. (2019) 'Identifying attitudes to welfare through deliberative forums: the emergence of reluctant individualism', *Party and Politics*, 47(1): 97–114.

Te Riele, K. (2010) 'Philosophy of hope: concepts and applications for working with marginalised youth', *Journal of Youth Studies*, 13(1): 35–46.

The Guardian (2021) 'Can a new Beveridge fix a broken welfare state?', 24 February, Available from: https://www.theguardian.com/politics/2021/feb/24/can-a-new-beveridge-fix-a-broken-welfare-state [Accessed 8 April 2021].

The Journal (2019) 'FactFind: How many homes is the Irish government actually building every year?', Available from: https://www.thejournal.ie/fact%20(find-irish-government-houses-built-4918423-Dec2019/ [Accessed 8 April 2021].

The Public Interest Litigation Project (2020) *Profiling and SyRI*, Available from: https://pilpnjcm.nl/en/dossiers/profiling-and-syri/ [Accessed 8 April 2021].

Tickle, L. (2016) 'How can it be right to have targets for breaking up families?', 13 December, *The Guardian*, Available from: https://www.theguardian.com/commentisfree/2016/dec/13/breaking-up-families-councils-child-adoptions [Accessed 14 July 2021].

Tonry, M. (2013) 'Evidence, Ideology, and Politics in the Making of American Criminal Justice Policy', 42 Crime & Justice, Minnesota Legal Studies Research Paper No. 13–52.

Tough, P. (2012) *How Children Succeed, Grit, Curiosity and the Hidden Power of Character*, Boston: Houghton Mifflin Harcourt.

Turnbull, S. and Hasselberg, I. (2017) 'From prison to detention: the carceral trajectories of foreign national prisoners in the United Kingdom', *Punishment & Society*, 19(2): 135–54.

Turner, J. (2017) 'Domesticating the "troubled family": racialised sexuality and the postcolonial governance of family life in the UK', *Environment and Planning D: Society and Space*, 35(5): 933–50.

Turrini, A., Koltay, J., Peirini, F., Goffard, C. and Kiss, A. (2015) 'A Decade of labour market reforms in the EU insights from the LABREF database', *IZA Journal of Labour Policy*, 4(1): 1–33.

Tyler, I. (2013) *Revolting Subjects: Social Abjection and Resistance in Neoliberal Britain*, London: Zed Press.

Tyler, I. (2020) *Stigma: The Machinery of Inequality*, London: Zed Books.

Ugelvik, T. (2013) 'Seeing like a welfare state: immigration control, statecraft, and a prison with double vision', in K. F. Aas and M. Bosworth (eds) *The Borders of Punishment: Migration, Citizenship, and Social Exclusion*, Oxford: Oxford University Press, pp 183–200.

Ugelvik, T. (2016) 'Prisons as welfare institutions? Punishment and the Nordic model', in J. Bennett, Y. Jewkes and B. Crewe (eds) *Handbook on Prisons*, London: Routledge, Available from: https://papers.ssrn.com/sol3/papers.cfm?abstract_id=2767985 [Accessed 7 April 2021].

Ugelvik, T. (2017) 'The limits of the welfare state? Foreign national prisoners in the Norwegian crimmigration prison', in Peter Scharff Smith and Thomas Ugelvik (eds) *Scandinavian Penal History, Culture and Prison Practice: Embraced by the Welfare State?*, Basingstoke: Palgrave Macmillan, pp 405–23.

Ugelvik, T. and Scharff Smith, P. (2017) *Scandinavian Penal History, Culture and Prison Practice: Embraced by the Welfare State?* Basingstoke: Palgrave Macmillan.

Uggen, C. (2000) 'Work as a turning point in the life course of criminals: a duration model of age, employment, and recidivism', *American Sociological Review*, 65(4): 529–46.

Ugwudike, P., Raynor, P. and Annison, J. (eds) (2018) *Evidence-Based Skills in Criminal Justice*, Bristol: Policy Press, pp 99–126.

UK Home Office (2015) 'Statutory guidance: prevent duty guidance for England, Scotland and Wales', Available from: https://www.gov.uk/government/publications/prevent-duty-guidance [Accessed 8 April 2021]

UK Supreme Court (2019) 'Judgment given on 30 January 2019 In the matter of an application by Lorraine Gallagher for Judicial Review (Northern Ireland) R (on the application of P, G and W) (Respondents) v Secretary of State for the Home Department and another (Appellants) R (on the application of P) (Appellant) v Secretary of State for the Home Department and others (Respondents)', Available from: https://www.supremecourt.uk/cases/docs/uksc-2016-0195-judgment.pdf [Accessed 8 April 2021].

UN CRC (2019) General comment No. 24 on children's rights in the child justice system, Available from: https://digitallibrary.un.org/record/3899429 [Accessed 9 April 2021].

Underwood, E. (2020) 'California has begun screening for early childhood trauma but critics urge caution', 29 January, Available from: https://www.sciencemag.org/news/2020/01/california-has-begun-screening-early-childhood-trauma-critics-urge-caution [Accessed 8 April 2021]

UN General Assembly (1985) United Nations Standard Minimum Rules for the Administration of Juvenile Justice ('The Beijing Rules'), A/RES/40/33.

UN General Assembly (1989) United Nations Convention on the Rights of the Child, A/RES/44/25.

UN General Assembly (1990) United Nations Standard Minimum Rules for Non-custodial Measures (The Tokyo Rules), A/Res/45/110.

UN General Assembly (2010) United Nations Rules for the Treatment of Women Prisoners and Non-custodial Measures for Women Offenders (the Bangkok Rules), A/RES/65/229.

UN General Assembly (2016) United Nations Standard Minimum Rules for the Treatment of Prisoners (the Nelson Mandela Rules): resolution / adopted by the General Assembly 8 January 16, A/RES/70/175 preliminary observation one and rule 4.

United Kingdom (2014) Anti-social Behaviour, Crime and Policing Act.

Urban Institute Justice Policy Centre (2003) A Portrait of Prisoner Re-entry in New Jersey, Washington.

US Department of Homeland Security (2018) 'Office of the inspector general ICE's inspections and monitoring of detention facilities do not lead to sustained compliance or systemic improvements', 26 June, OIG-18–67, Available from: https://www.oig.dhs.gov/sites/default/files/assets/2018-06/OIG-18-67-Jun18.pdf [Accessed 7 January 2021].

Valverde M. (2011) 'Questions of security: a framework for research', *Theoretical Criminology*, 15(1):3–22.

Van Der Waal, J., De Koster, W. and Van Oorschot, W. (2013) 'Three worlds of welfare chauvinism?', *Journal of Comparative Policy Analysis: Research and Practice*, 15(2): 1–18.

Van der Woude, M. A. H., van der Leun, J. P. and Nijland, J. A. (2014) 'Crimmigration in the Netherlands', *Law and Social Inquiry*, 39(3): 560–79.

Van Oorschot, W. (2006) 'Making the difference in social Europe: deservingness perceptions among citizens of European welfare states', *Journal of European Social Policy*, 16(1): 23–42.

Van Parijs, P. (2013) 'The universal basic income: why utopian thinking matters, and how sociologists can contribute to it', *Politics & Society*, 41(2): 171–82.

Van Swaaningen, R. (1999) 'Reclaiming critical criminology:social justice and the European tradition', *Theoretical Criminology*, 3(1): 5–28.

Vanstone, M. (2021) 'Give them money: an illustrative history of forms of reimagined rehabilitation in probation practice in England and Wales', *Howard Journal of Crime and Justice*, 60 (2): 157–84.

Vanwesenbeeck, I. (2017) 'Sex work criminalization is barking up the wrong tree', *Archives of Sexual Behavior*, 46(6): 1631–40.

Van Wel, F. (1992) 'A century of families under supervision in the Netherlands', *British Journal of Social Work*, 22: 147–66.

Van Zoonen, L. (2020) 'Data governance and citizen participation in the digital welfare state', *Data & Policy*, doi: 10.1017/dap.2020.10.

Varadkar, L. (2016) Social Welfare Bill 2016: Committee Stage, 17 November. Parliamentary Debate, Available from: https://www.oireachtas.ie/en/debates/debate/select_committee_on_social_protection/2016-11-17/ [Accessed 8 April 2021].

Vaughan, B. (2015) 'Neoliberalism, crime and punishment', in D. Healy, C. Hamilton, Y. Daly and M. Butler (eds), *The Routledge Handbook of Irish Criminology*, Abingdon: Routledge, pp 486–99.

Vercellone, C. (2015) 'From the crisis to the "welfare of the common" as a new mode of production', *Theory, Culture & Society*, 32(7–8): 85–99.

Vitale, A. S. (2017) *The End of Policing*, London: Verso Books.

Vitale, S. (2010) 'The safer cities initiative and the removal of the homeless: reducing crime or promoting gentrification on Los Angeles' Skid Row', *Criminology and Public Policy*, 9(4): 867–73.

Wacquant, L. J. D. (1993) 'Urban outcasts: stigma and division in the black American ghetto and the French urban periphery', *International Journal of Urban and Regional Research*, 17(3): 366–83.

Wacquant, L. (2001) 'The penalisation of poverty and the rise of neoliberalism', *European Journal on Criminal Policy and Research*, 9(4): 401–12.

Wacquant, L. (2007) 'Territorial stigmatization in the age of advanced marginality', *Thesis Eleven*, 91(1): 66–77.

Wacquant, L. (2008) *Urban Outcasts: A Comparative Sociology of Advanced Marginality*, Cambridge and Malden: Polity Press.

Wacquant, L. (2009a) *Punishing the Poor: The Neoliberal Government of Social Insecurity*, Durham, NC and London: Duke University Press.

Wacquant, L. (2009b) *Prisons of Poverty*, Minneapolis, MN: University of Minnesota Press.

Wacquant, L. (2010) 'Prisoner reentry as myth and ceremony', *Dialectical Anthropology*, 34: 605–20.

Wacquant, L. (2013) 'The wedding of workfare and prisonfare in the 21st century: responses to critics and commentators', in P. Squires and J. Lea (eds) *Criminalisation and Advanced Marginality: Critically Exploring the Work of Loïc Wacquant*, Bristol: Policy Press, pp 243–58.

Wacquant, L. (2014) 'Marginality, ethnicity and penality in the neo-liberal city: an analytic cartography', *Ethnic and Racial Studies*, 37(10): 1687–1711.

Wadia, K. (2015) 'Regimes of insecurity: women and immigration detention in France and Britain', in G. Lazaridis and K. Wadia (eds) *The Securitisation of Migration in the EU: Debates since 9/11*, London: Palgrave Macmillan, pp 91–118.

Walby, S. (2018) 'Policies for inclusive economic growth', *Soundings*, 69: 32–49.

Wall, G. (2010) 'Mothers' experiences with intensive parenting and brain development discourse', *Women's Studies International Forum*, 33: 253–63.

Walsh, D., McCartney, G., Smith, M. and Armour, G. (2019) 'Relationship between childhood socioeconomic position and adverse childhood experiences (ACEs): a systematic review', *Journal of Epidemiological Community Health*, 73: 1087–93.

Walsh, J. P. (2019) 'Education or enforcement? Enrolling universities in the surveillance and policing of migration', *Crime, Law and Social Change*, 71: 325–44.

Ward, T. and Langlands, R. (2009) 'Repairing the rupture: restorative justice and rehabilitation of offenders', *Aggression and Violent Behavior*, 14(3): 205–14.

Warr, J. (2016) 'The deprivation of certitude, legitimacy and hope: foreign national prisoners and the pains of imprisonment', *Criminology and Criminal Justice*, 16(3): 301–18.

Wastell, D. and White, S. (2017) *Blinded by Science: The Social Implications of Epigenetics and Neuroscience*, Bristol: Policy Press.

Watts, B. and Fitzpatrick, S. (2018) *Welfare Conditionality*, London: Routledge.

Watts, B., Fitzpatrick, S. and Johnsen, S. (2017) 'Controlling homeless people? Power, interventionism and legitimacy', *Journal of Social Policy*, 47(2):235–52.

Weaver, B. (2011) 'Co-producing community justice: the transformative potential of personalisation for penal sanctions', *The British Journal of Social Work*, 41(6): 1038–57.

Webber, F. (2018) in Fekete, L. 'Migrants, borders and the criminalisation of solidarity in the EU', *Race & Class, Institute of Race Relations*, 59(4): 65–83.

Welshman, J. (2017) 'Troubles and the family: changes and continuities since 1943', *Social Policy and Society*, 16(1): 109–17.

Wei Wei, A. (2018) 'The refugee crisis isn't about refugees. It's about us', Available from: https://www.theguardian.com/commentisfree/2018/feb/02/refugee-crisis-human-flow-ai-weiwei-china?CMP=share_btn_fb [Accessed 8 April 2021].

Weishaupt, J. T. (2011) *From the Manpower Revolution to the Activation Paradigm: Explaining Institutional Continuity and Change in an Integrating Europe*, Amsterdam: Amsterdam University Press.

Welch, M. (2000) *Flag Burning: Moral Panic and the Criminalization of Protest*, New York: Aldine de Gruyter.

WelCond Project Team (2018) Welfare Conditionality Project 2013–2018. Final findings report, University of York, Available from: http://www.welfareconditionality.ac.uk/wp-content/uploads/2018/06/40475_Welfare-Conditionality_Report_complete-v3.pdf [Accessed 8 April 2021].

West, D. J. and Farrington, D. P. (1973) *Who Becomes Delinquent? Second Report of the Cambridge Study in Delinquent Development*, London: Heinemann.

Whelan, A. (2020) '"Ask for more time": Big data chronopolitics in the Australian welfare bureaucracy', *Critical Sociology*, 46(6): 867–80.

Whelan, J. (2020a) 'Work and thrive or claim and skive: experiencing the "toxic symbiosis" of worklessness and welfare recipiency in Ireland', *Irish Journal of Sociology*, Available from: https://doi.org/10.1177/0791603520957203 [Accessed 8 April 2021].

Whelan, J. (2021) 'We have our dignity, yeah? Scrutiny under suspicion: experiences of welfare conditionality in the Irish social protection system', *Social Policy & Administration*, 55: 43–50.

White, K., Yeager, V. A., Menanchemi, N. and Scarinci, I. C. (2014) 'Impact of Alabama's immigration law on access to health care among Latina immigrants and children: implications for national reform', *American Journal of Public Health*, 104: 397–405.

White, S. (2017) 'The rise and rise of prevention science in UK family welfare: surveillance gets under the skin', *Families Relationships and Societies*, 6(3): 427–45.

White, S., Edwards, R., Gillies, V. and Wastell, D. (2019) 'All the ACEs: a chaotic concept for family policy and decision-making?' *Social Policy & Society*, 18(3): 457–66.

Whitt-Woosley, A. and Sprang, G. (2014) 'When rights collide: a critique of the adoption and safe families act from a justice perspective', *Child Welfare*, 93(3): 111–34.

Widding, U. (2018) 'Parental determinism in the Swedish strategy for parenting support', *Social Policy and Society*, 17(3): 481–90.

Wiggan, J. (2015) 'Reading active labour market policy politically an autonomist analysis of Britain's work programme and mandatory work activity', *Critical Social Policy*, 35(3): 369–92.

Wiggan, J. (2017) 'Contesting the austerity and "welfare reform" narrative of the UK government: forging a social democratic imaginary in Scotland', *International Forum of Sociology and Social Policy*, 37(11–12): 639–54.

Wildeman, C., Edwards, F. R., and Wakefield, S. (2020) The Cumulative Prevalence of Termination of Parental Rights for US Children 2000–2016', *Child Maltreatment*, 25(1): 32–42.

Wiles, P. and Pease, K. (2000) 'Distributive justice and crime', in R. Matthews and J. Pitts (eds) *Crime, Disorder and Community Safety*, London: Routledge, pp 219–40.

Wilkinson, R. and Pickett, K. (2010) *The Spirit Level: Why Equality Is Better for Everyone*, London: Penguin.

Wilkinson, R. G. and Pickett, K. (2019) *The inner level: how more equal societies reduce stress, restore sanity and improve everyone's well-being.* Penguin Books.

Williams, E. (2021) 'Unemployment sanctions and mental health: the relationship between benefit sanctions and anti-depressant prescribing', *Journal of Social Policy*, 50(1): 1–20.

Williams, F. (2016) 'Critical thinking in social policy: the challenges of past, present and future', *Social Policy and Administration*, 50(6): 628–47.

Wilson, J.Q. and Kelling, G. L. (1982) 'Broken windows: the police and neighborhood safety', *The Atlantic*, March, Available from: https://www.theatlantic.com/magazine/archive/1982/03/broken-windows/304465/ [Accessed 8 April 2021].

Wilson, S. (2020) 'Pandemic leadership: lessons from New Zealand's approach to COVID-19', *Leadership*, 16(3): 279–93.

Wilson Gilmore, R. (2007) *Golden Gulag: Prisons, Crisis and Opposition in Globalizing California*, Berkeley: University of California Press.

Wincup, E. (2013) *Understanding Crime and Social Policy*, Bristol: Policy Press.

Wincup, E. and Monaghan, L. (2016) 'Scrounger narratives and dependent drug users: welfare, workfare and warfare', *The Journal of Poverty and Social Justice*, 24(3): 261–75.

Wonders, N. A. (2017) 'Sitting on the fence – Spain's delicate balance: bordering, multiscalar challenges, and crimmigration', *European Journal of Criminology*, 14(1): 7–26.

Wong, K., Fox, C. and Albertson, K. (2014) 'Justice reinvestment in an "age of austerity": developments in the United Kingdom', *Victims & Offenders*, 9(1): 76–99.

Wright, E. O. (2013) 'Transforming capitalism through real utopias', *American Sociological Review*, 78(1): 1–25.

Wright, S., Fletcher, D. R. and Stewart, A. B. R. (2020) 'Punitive benefit sanctions, welfare conditionality, and the social abuse of unemployed people in Britain: transforming claimants into offenders?', *Social Policy & Administration*, 54(2): 278–94.

Wright, S. and Patrick, R. (2019) 'Welfare conditionality in lived experience: aggregating qualitative longitudinal research', *Social Policy and Society*, 18(4): 597–613.

Wright, S., Stewart, A. B. R. and Dwyer, P. (2018) 'Final findings: social security in Scotland', Available from: http://www.welfareconditionality.ac.uk/wp-content/uploads/2018/09/40677-Scottish-final2.pdf [Accessed 8 April 2021].

Y-Foundation (2017) 'A home of your own: housing first and ending homelessness in Finland', Available from: https://www.feantsaresearch.org/download/a_home_of_your_own_lowres_spreads60696618169577904.pdf [Accessed 8 April 2021].

Ye, D. and Reyes-Salvail, F. (2014) 'Adverse childhood experiences among Hawai'i adults: findings from the 2010 behavioral risk factor survey', *Hawai'i Journal of Medicine and Public Health*, 73(6): 181–90.

Youngballymun (2021) Available from: https://youngballymun.org/practitioner-resources/adverse-childhood- experiences/ [Accessed 8 April 2021].

Young, I. M. (1988) 'Five faces of oppression', *Philos Forum*, 19(4): 270–90.

Young, J. (2011) *The Criminological Imagination*, Cambridge: Polity Press.

Young, T. R. (1996) 'Beyond crime and punishment: part 2 – democratic proposals for social justice", *Critical Criminology*, 7(2): 92–107.

Yuval-Davis, N., Wemyss, G. and Cassidy, K. (2018) 'Everyday bordering, belonging and the reorientation of British immigration legislation', *Sociology*, 52(2): 228–44.

Yuval-Davis, N., Wemyss, G. and Cassidy, K. (2019) *Bordering*, Cambridge: Polity Press.

Zappone, K. (2016) *Civic Forum on Lone Parents*, Dublin: Seanad Éireann.

Zarnowiecki, D., Nguyen, H., Hampton, C., Boffa, J. and Segal, L. (2018) 'The Australian nurse family partnership program for aboriginal mothers and babies: describing client complexity and implications for programme delivery', *Midwifery*, 65: 72–81.

Zedner, L. (2013) 'Is the criminal law only for citizens? A problem at the borders of punishment', in K. F. Aas and M. Bosworth (eds) *The Borders of Punishment Migration, Citizenship, and Social Exclusion*, Oxford: Oxford University Press, pp 40–57.

Zigon, J. (2018) *Disappointment: Toward a Critical Hermeneutics of Worldbuilding*, New York: Fordham University Press.

Index